DISSENT
IN THE
HEARTLAND

DISSENT IN THE HEARTLAND

The Sixties at Indiana University

Revised and Expanded Edition

Mary Ann Wynkoop

Indiana University Press

This book is a publication of

Indiana University Press
Office of Scholarly Publishing
Herman B Wells Library 350
1320 East 10th Street
Bloomington, Indiana 47405 USA

iupress.indiana.edu

The paper used in this publication meets the minimum requirements
of the American National Standard for Information Sciences—
Permanence of Paper for Printed Library Materials, ANSI Z39.48-1992.

Manufactured in the United States of America

The Library of Congress has cataloged the earlier edition as follows:

Wynkoop, Mary Ann.
Dissent in the heartland : the sixties at Indiana
University / Mary Ann Wynkoop.
p. cm. — (Midwestern history and culture)
Includes bibliographical references (p.) and index.
ISBN 0-253-34118-3 (cloth : alk. paper)
1. Indiana University—History—20th century. 2. Indiana
University—Students—Political activity—History—20th
century. 3. Student movements—Indiana—Bloomington—
History—20th century. I. Title. II. Series.
LD2518.8 .W96 2002   378.772'255—dc21
2001007662

ISBN 978-0-253-02668-2 (paperback)
ISBN 978-0-253-02674-3 (ebook)

1 2 3 4 5   22 21 20 19 18 17

In memory of
JEFF SHARLET AND CLARENCE "ROLLO" TURNER

Contents

LIST OF ILLUSTRATIONS   viii

ACKNOWLEDGMENTS   ix

INTRODUCTION TO THE NEW EDITION   xi

INTRODUCTION   xiii

Prologue   1

Chapter 1. The Dawn of Dissent   9

Chapter 2. The Awakening of Activism   22

Chapter 3. The Antiwar Movement   49

Chapter 4. A Precarious Peace   89

Chapter 5. Student Rights/Civil Rights: African Americans
and the Struggle for Racial Justice   115

Chapter 6. The Women's Movement: An Idea Whose Time Had Come   135

Chapter 7. Bloomington and the Counterculture in Southern Indiana   153

Epilogue: The End of an Era at Indiana University   172

Epilogue to the New Edition   185

Conclusion   190

NOTES   195

BIBLIOGRAPHY   209

INDEX   213

Illustrations

1. March to the courthouse   15
2. Guy Loftman speaking to students   39
3. Secretary of State Dean Rusk   58
4. Protestors holding up peace armbands   58
5. Spring 1969 student gathering in Dunn Meadow   84
6. Former University of California chancellor Clark Kerr   95
7. James Retherford in devil costume   96
8. WITCH demonstration   107
9. First Earth Day celebration   107
10. IU students march after Kent State incident   110
11. Clarence "Rollo" Turner   125
12. Students gathered at the Black Market   129
13. The Black Market after the Klan bombing   131
14. Martha Vicinus   149
15. *Spectator* "Headitorial"   159
16. *Spectator* cover art   160
17. *Spectator* reader   161
18. Keith Parker   177

Acknowledgments

To David P. Thelen, my advisor: I offer thanks for your enthusiasm, your irrepressible sense of humor, and your support for this project. It's been a long, winding road from Columbia, Missouri, to Bloomington, Indiana, but I couldn't have asked for a better guide or a better friend. Muchas gracias.

To James Madison: the fact that these words are being printed is tribute to your faith and determination and sound advice. Thank you.

To Terry H. Anderson: your suggestions about revising this manuscript were invaluable.

To Gregory D. Black: you provided much-needed support and words of wisdom about how to survive academic life that have been immensely helpful.

Thanks also to Susan Armeny, Casey Blake, Richard Blackett, Susan Curtis, Jim O'Brien, and Tom Poe, who have all provided valuable counsel at critical times.

Brad Cook at the Indiana University Archives gave much-needed help with lost citations and photographs. Indiana University and the Indiana State Historical Society offered essential financial support. Rosalie Donavan and Bonita Lewis helped with organizing the revisions of my revisions.

When you're a slow runner, you have lots of time to talk—thanks to Suzanne Crews for the proper perspective on life in general and to Molly Jessup for early morning walks. My brother, Allen Brauninger, has been generous and good-humored even when I have not. I owe him more than I can say. Finally, I want to acknowledge two people who died before I had a chance to thank them: Clarence "Rollo" Turner and Richard McKenzie.

This book is dedicated to the memories of my father and mother, Clarence and Edna Brauninger, whose love, patience, and compassion were a constant source of strength, and last, but certainly not least, to Thomas the tomcat, who at the age of twenty-five decided that he had done all that he could. I loved them all very much.

Introduction to the New Edition

Since *Dissent in the Heartland* was first published in 2002, America has changed in ways that few of the activists at Indiana University (IU) in the 1960s could have imagined. Many of the causes they fought for and the policies they struggled to make possible have become more or less real. Others remain on the horizon for future generations to grapple with. The war in Vietnam did end, only to be followed by a series of conflicts never named as wars. The civil rights movement achieved its most dramatic goal when Americans elected the first African American president, but segregated schools and communities remain very much a part of our landscape. Presently, the women's movement can claim one of its own as the Democratic nominee for the highest office, yet women continue to earn less than their male counterparts and dominate the poorest populations along with their children. *Roe v. Wade* (1973) made abortion legal, but continuing conservative attacks have left large numbers of women without accessible providers. Marriage equality for same-sex and transgendered citizens is legal at the same time that homophobia rears its ugly head in acts of violence and hatred.

Since 2002, I spent several years teaching American history and culture, including a course on the 1960s that usually drew a respectable number of students. I was encouraged by the continued interest in a period of history that I had studied and written about, though at the same time I was sometimes troubled by the misconceptions that popular culture had presented to many students about that decade. Like a wet blanket at a beach party, I tried to describe the very dark periods that many Americans lived through while simultaneously injecting the sense of humor and creativity that kept activists sane and productive. Contrary to television shows and films, many

Americans supported the war in Vietnam, although by the early seventies a majority of citizens had turned against it. Only small groups of women embraced feminist ideals in the sixties, but twenty years later, the movement was successful enough to promote a backlash against it. While many African Americans and their white allies exhibited enormous courage in the civil rights movement, there were also substantial numbers who feared racial integration and either actively fought against it or retreated to restricted enclaves. The riot at Stonewall was an early milestone in the struggle for gay/lesbian rights, but it took decades of patient organizing and hard work for the recent judicial and legislative victories. And, yes, there were sex, drugs, and rock and roll, but it wasn't always the good time that we think of today. It was often hard to counteract the nostalgia students felt for a part of history they hadn't experienced directly.

Still, I will continue to argue that the experiences of 1960s activists, including those at Indiana University, provide valuable lessons for today's students. The fact that IU students were from mostly average backgrounds in the middle of the country makes the point that the entire country underwent significant challenges during those years, ones that we continue to face in one way or another today. In the end, they left the university a more open and egalitarian institution than it was before they came, but there will always be new causes, different roadblocks, and higher goals for future generations. The point they made, I think, is to keep trying, keep organizing, and keep on believing that you can make a difference.

In the end, while I tried to present the sixties as realistically as I could, I also concluded that it remains a significant period in my own experience as well as our larger national history. It was a time that was visionary in ways that continue to provide hope to those who share ideals of a more peaceful and humane society. I was only marginally a part of it, but I'm very glad that I wrote about it, and I will be forever grateful to the people who shared that part of their lives with me, many of whom have pointed out errors and significant omissions in the text. I wish I could have corrected all of them, but I nevertheless dedicate this new edition to activists at IU in the 1960s (and 1970s), some of whom are gone but many of whom are still very much alive. This book would not exist without your generosity of spirit and willingness to tell your stories.

Introduction

This book is about students at Indiana University in Bloomington, Indiana, during the 1960s. They came of age during a decade that stands as a turning point in American history. Many Americans who were young adults in the 1960s realized that their lives were inevitably changed by the war in Vietnam, the civil rights movement, the women's liberation movement, or the counterculture. Many will disagree about whether these events and movements were successful, and will offer either praise or criticisms based on their own experiences. Few, however, would contest the idea that the Sixties were a decade filled with dramatic and significant events that changed American culture.

Student activists who were part of the movement have written their own accounts of the events of that tumultuous decade. They have expressed pride in the ways in which they feel they changed this country for the better, and some have written of their disappointment in their failure to establish more permanent networks for reform.

For those historians and critics born during or after the 1960s, the significance of the Sixties is much more ambiguous. Viewing the Sixties in the light of the growth of the conservative right, cultural narcissism, and consumer capitalism during the 1970s, 1980s, and 1990s, they are much more likely to see the period in terms that reflect their own attitudes about the baby-boom generation that has cast such a long shadow over their own cultural, historical, and, given the number of Sixties activists who became educators, intellectual development. The debate is, to a certain extent, generational and lends a special poignancy to the old Sixties adage "Don't trust anyone over thirty." Some aging Boomers are now more likely to mutter under their breath, "Don't trust anyone under thirty." So it goes.

Certainly all of the former IU students I spoke with who took part in the movement in Bloomington agreed that their experiences in the Sixties made a profound difference in their lives. Most have gone on to become teachers, lawyers, artists, musicians, public servants, and community organizers. They have not followed the clichéd path of "hippie to yuppie" that writers for the popular magazines are so fond of discussing in superficial references to a few former activists. And there are very good reasons why so many folks from the Sixties retain the values and ideals that they struggled for as college and university students.

The confluence of the civil rights movement and the war in Vietnam created an environment in which most young Americans were forced to take a stand on these two important political and moral issues. This highly charged atmosphere provoked students to examine their hearts, their spiritual values, and their ideas about what kind of a country America really was and what it meant to be a human being in this place, at that time. Is the color of someone's skin the essence of their existence? Should we ask young men to kill other young men in a conflict that has not been clearly or adequately explained to the American people? These were—and are—questions that cannot be answered without a good deal of soul-searching. They were—and are—hard questions to waffle on. The answers to those questions could change, or cost, your life. Depending on your perspective, students in the Sixties were either cursed or blessed to be living at a time when such choices had to be made.

The intellectual world that students entered in the Sixties was different from the one that students encounter today. Because of a robust postwar economy, most young Americans who were able to go to college could look forward to a job that would provide a certain level of physical comfort and security. Their parents, products of the Great Depression and World War II, had worked hard—some had sacrificed their lives—to ensure that their children would never have to face the difficulties that they had endured. But for their children, the prospect of taking their place in the ranks of white-collar management or professional personnel provoked feelings of anxiety and questions about the meaning of such an existence. This was a generation that benefited from the safety nets provided by increased federal government spending, either in New Deal programs or through Cold War military policies. Most did not face the threat of poverty or homelessness. Instead, they asked themselves, "What makes life worth living?" And many—to the consternation of their parents—had a difficult time answering.

When the first members of this baby-boom generation arrived on college campuses in the middle of the 1960s, they enrolled in philosophy courses in subjects such as existentialism that challenged them to discuss the meaning of human action, or in literature classes that focused on Beat writers like Jack Kerouac or Allen Ginsburg, who questioned the basic nature of American culture. J. D. Salinger's *Catcher in the Rye,* an attack on upper-middle-class pretension, remained popular. At Columbia University, professors like sociologist C. Wright Mills developed an almost cult-like following among students who read his pathbreaking book *The Power Elite,* a critical examination of the economic, political, and military structure that dominated American society. Thousands of students read Paul Goodman's *Growing Up Absurd,* a book that indicted American schools for their emphasis on competition and superficial goals.

At the same time, America was in the midst of the Cold War with the Soviet Union and young Americans were the targets of politicians who urged them to excel in academic disciplines considered crucial for military and political success. In 1957, after the spectacular Russian launch of the satellite *Sputnik,* Congress passed the National Defense Education Act, which made millions of dollars available for students pursuing degrees deemed vital to national security interests. Yet many young Americans began to question the need for this increasingly dangerous competition with the Soviet Union and wondered out loud whether there might not be peaceful ways in which all nations could exist together on this earth.

Part of the problem for members of the baby-boom generation was that they actually believed what they had been taught about traditional religious values and democratic traditions. If "thou shalt not kill" was a religious commandment, then when did killing in war become a patriotic duty? If God created all members of the human race, then why did skin color matter? The Jewish community in particular had an established tradition of working with antidiscrimination groups and civil rights organizations that struggled to make America a more equitable society.

Aside from these religious and spiritual roots, some students came from families with leftist political backgrounds. Known as "red diaper babies," these young Americans had grown up in families where socialist ideas were a part of dinner-table conversations, and many had spent summers at socialist camps. They were well aware of the bitter arguments that often broke out among various factions of the Communist and Socialist parties and were determined not to let their own political vision fall prey to narrow, strident infighting. Concerned that socialist ideas were still branded "foreign" and "alien," they argued that students should "speak American" when they talked about their plans for political action. Differentiating themselves from their Old Left parents, they called themselves members of the New Left.

The vast majority of young Americans responded to the call of one of the youngest American presidents, John F. Kennedy, elected in 1960, who called on them to ask not what their country could do for them, but what they could do for their country. Students began their campaign for a more participatory democracy by challenging university officials to allow more student involvement in decision-making processes. However, the real challenge to authority came when students who had witnessed the power of collective action in the civil rights movement returned to their respective campuses. African Americans in the South took up the cause in the 1950s and early 1960s. Working first with established organizations like the National Association for the Advancement of Colored People (NAACP), the Congress of Racial Equality (CORE), and the Southern Christian Leadership Conference (SCLC), students soon realized they needed their own vehicle for the fight against racism. With the help of SCLC executive director Ella Baker, black and white students joined forces by forming the Student Nonviolent Coordinating Committee (SNCC), which became the most significant student group of the decade. It was based on principles of civil disobedience and passive resistance, and its members saw that racial discrimination was not just a southern problem but a national one, and that it demanded immediate attention and action.

As the war in Vietnam continued to escalate, students questioned the military role of the United States in Southeast Asia and began the largest antiwar protest movement in American history. In questioning conventional attitudes about patriotism and duty, young Americans found themselves in bitter debates with older citizens whose ideas about national service were formed before and during World War II, and with members of their own generation who agreed with their elders. The inter- and intra-generational divisions that formed in the 1960s left wounds that, in many instances, have still not healed. When Americans elected Bill Clinton to the presidency in 1992 and 1996, those who voted against him usually cited his antiwar protest during the 1960s as their main objection to his candidacy.

Students who believed in racial justice and peace worked together in various organizations: SNCC, Students for a Democratic Society (SDS), the Committee to End the War in Vietnam (CEWV), and the Young Socialist Alliance (YSA), among others. While these groups varied in goals and membership, they had one thing in common: during the 1960s, women rarely held leadership positions in them. SNCC provided a more supportive environment for African-American women than did the others, though it was also the birthplace of the women's liberation movement— one of the most significant reforms of the decade—which was initially made up mostly of white women. In 1964 Casey Hayden and Mary King, both members of SNCC, wrote a memorandum to the membership asking them to consider the fact that women were often confined to menial tasks like mimeographing flyers or making coffee. That one memo sent shockwaves through the New Left that resulted in women organizing to make gender equity a reality within these organizations. Their efforts influenced other women throughout American society, and the result has been the creation of a whole new way of looking at women's roles in both their public and private lives.

This was a generation that embraced change, experimented with new ways of looking at old problems, and welcomed the idea that even though this was a great country, it could be even better. Sometimes their ideas about creating a more perfect world were a little disconcerting to their parents—especially when they involved experimenting with drugs or challenging traditional conceptions of gender roles and lifestyles. They also asked important, and often uncomfortable, questions about human impact on nature and the environment. Yet all of these exuberant expressions of youthful reform grew out of the idea that America was still a place where dreams could become reality and where humanity could move to higher levels of existence.

The questions raised by students in the Sixties were traditional and revolutionary at the same time. They looked back to the roots of American democracy and asked, Are all Americans equal? Do we really live in a country that protects every citizen's right to life, liberty, and the pursuit of happiness? Have we in fact created a society that comes close to that earlier Puritan vision of a city on a hill? The possibility of such a society remains a focus for American culture and an essential part of the American dream. And it continues to provide a challenge for Americans in the new millennium.

DISSENT
IN THE
HEARTLAND

Prologue

  While I was interviewing people for this project, I was struck by the way that nearly all of them spoke about their time in Bloomington with a kind of loving remembrance. Of course, many graduates of other universities are nostalgic about their university community—it is not uncommon to hear people reminiscing about the special qualities of Madison or Berkeley. Bloomingtonians, however, are protective of the place, and they convey the sense that recording its history in the 1960s needs special care. When they talked about the richness of Bloomington's music and art scene, the quiet joys of the surrounding hills and forests, or the friendly neighborliness of most of the community, I began to understand that what makes Bloomington such an unusual place is its differences from other towns and cities in the state.

  Indiana's largest city and capital, Indianapolis, is undergoing its own refurbishing, but a city whose main claim to fame is an automobile race has a long way to go in the eyes of many urban enthusiasts. The middle part of the state, raked flat by glaciers eons ago, is dotted with small farming towns. In towns located in the heavily industrialized region near Chicago, residents encounter most of the problems and not many of the benefits of urban sprawl. Bloomington is a long way from any other large cultural center. Chicago is the closest city with a nationally recognized symphony, theater, or opera, with renowned restaurants and universities, or, for that matter, with an international airport and traffic jams. The protectiveness that many people feel for Bloomington may come from its unique characteristics, its separateness from the rest of the state. Yet it is a part of Indiana and it both reflects and contradicts state and regional traditions.

When the wave of political and social activism swept through Indiana University and Bloomington, it met both a welcoming shore and hostile reefs. Some of the reasons for this complicated response can be found in the way that Bloomington and the university grew up together in southern Indiana. Part southern, part Midwestern, this region is a blend of two cultures. The university is a community in and of itself, with its own set of traditions and mores. Its existence is tied to the town in ways that can be both benevolent and threatening to the goals of an institution of higher education. It is, therefore, impossible to write about this decade without at least acknowledging the history of the community and the institution, a history that provided a set of memories and traditions that contributed to the sometimes volatile reactions to the people and events of this story.

The township that President James Madison chose as the site for the public university of the new state of Indiana was heavily wooded and dotted with natural springs of clear, clean water flowing from a limestone base—a propitious place for students and teachers to gather. Formerly home to the Miami tribe, the area was mostly uninhabited when Madison signed the act that created the state of Indiana in 1816. Soon afterward, however, settlers from south of the Ohio River, mainly Kentucky and western Tennessee, moved in, attracted by the prospect of living near a state school. These early Hoosiers founded the town of Bloomington (some say it was named for the flowering trees in the area) next to Seminary Township, the school's site, and made it the Monroe County seat. The first citizens of Bloomington were southern farmers, for the most part. The hilly forested land of southern Indiana was similar to the land they came from and they continued to raise corn and hogs. They built mills along the streams and rivers, using the abundant water power to grind corn and other grains into flour. They used corn to make whiskey as well—and merchants in the new town dispensed it freely to customers. An early historian notes that "one of the most noteworthy features of the town then was the liquor traffic."[1]

Hoosiers were tied to southern markets by the river trade and to southern culture by family connections. While few owned slaves, they were generally hostile to blacks. Neither wealthy nor poor, most were hard-working, self-reliant, practical people for whom the necessity of making a living made learning a luxury. For these people, settling near the site of Indiana University was more a matter of good business than a move toward higher culture.

Although its early years were filled with several rancorous disputes and somewhat shaky finances, Indiana Seminary, as the school was first named, made steady progress. The state constitution provided that Hoosiers would have a "general system of education ascending in a regular gradation from township schools to a State University, wherein tuition shall be gratis, and equally open to all." One professor and ten boys walked through the doors of its single building, constructed "on the plan of Princeton College, in New Jersey—the historic Nassau Hall," in 1824.[2]

The school was renamed "Indiana College" in 1828, and the trustees added another building to accommodate a total of thirty-five students. The following year, they appointed Andrew Wylie, formerly head of Washington College in Pennsylvania, as its first president, and in 1838 the state legislature officially created Indiana University in Bloomington. The students came mostly from Indiana, but some came from nearby Kentucky and Illinois, and a few had followed Wylie from Pennsylvania. The curriculum consisted of Greek, Latin, mathematics, philosophy, and theology. A college of law was added in 1842.

When the United States Congress passed the Morrill Act in 1862, providing for agricultural education in all the states, Indiana University lost its bid for federal funds to promoters in West Lafayette who founded Purdue University on land donated by John Purdue. Enrollment at IU declined during the Civil War. Bloomington residents supported the Union cause and raised regiments with enthusiasm. However, as the war went on far longer than most people had anticipated, older sympathies reappeared. The citizens of Bloomington were more enthusiastic about preserving the Union than about freeing slaves. Prejudice against blacks was strong throughout the area both before and after the war.[3]

Shortly after the Civil War, the state legislature made its first appropriation of funds ($8,000) for the university. Until then most people in the state had thought that higher education should be privately financed.[4] Despite meager resources, periodic fires, and political imbroglios, the university grew, adding sciences, modern languages, literature, and history to the curriculum in the postwar years. IU was a pioneer in coeducation, admitting the first woman undergraduate in 1867. A disastrous fire consumed all the buildings constructed on the original Seminary Township site in 1883, and rather than rebuild there, the trustees voted to use the insurance money to buy twenty acres east of the town square, on land known as Dunn's Woods. Construction of the new campus began in 1884.

From its earliest years, the university attracted scholars, public figures, and cultural leaders to Bloomington. Students heard Theodore Roosevelt, Henry George, Bronson Alcott, Susan B. Anthony, and Frederick Douglass as guest lecturers. Richard Owen, whose father had founded the utopian community at New Harmony, Indiana, taught geology. Sociologist Edward A. Ross spent one year at Indiana University before moving on to the University of Wisconsin. David Starr Jordan, president of Indiana University from 1879 to 1891, went on to become president of Stanford University and played a major role in establishing that school's reputation. In a state that spent very little on public education, Indiana University managed to give Bloomington "a literary and social caste . . . possessed by no other town in the State."[5]

During the first half of the twentieth century, Indiana University and Bloomington lived together in relative harmony. William Lowe Bryan was president of IU from 1902 to 1937. Under Bryan's presidency, the university expanded physically and intellectually. The campus grew from 20 to 135 acres. In addition, Bryan developed new graduate schools and founded professional schools of education, business administration, and dentistry, as well as a new school of music.

For this story, Herman B Wells, president of Indiana University from 1938 to 1962, is a singularly important figure. A native Hoosier, IU alumnus, and faculty member, Wells combined a real love for the university and the Bloomington community with savvy political skills that helped transform Indiana University into a center for higher education both within the state and throughout the nation and the world. His vision of the university changed it from a member in good standing among the ranks of Midwestern state universities to a real competitor for international leadership in the sciences, languages, music, and the arts. When he changed the university, Wells set in motion reactions both within it and in Bloomington that established the background for much of what happened in the 1960s.

When Wells became acting president in 1937, he faced an aging faculty, many of whom planned to retire soon. With characteristic energy, he traveled across the country on a series of hiring campaigns, trying to convince scholars to come to Bloomington. He continued this effort throughout his life, and his results were impressive. Wells brought the following academic stars to the Bloomington campus: Hermann J. Muller, professor of genetics, a pioneer in the use of the X-ray, and winner of the 1946 Nobel prize; Vaclav Glavaty, professor of mathematics and an internationally recognized scholar for his work with Einstein's equations; and Charles F. Voegelin and Erminie Wheeler Voegelin, professors of linguistics and anthropology, who coauthored an award-winning study of North American Indians and Eskimos. Wells gave enthusiastic support to Wilfred C. Bain, dean of the school of music, in his efforts to promote professional training for performers, especially his programs for young opera singers. He encouraged Eli Lilly, a wealthy pharmaceutical manufacturer from Indianapolis, to donate his rare book collection (with over 100,000 volumes and 1,500,000 manuscripts) to the university. Later, Upton Sinclair's donation of his papers enhanced the Lilly collection. A dedicated traveler himself, Wells opened Indiana University to foreign students, leading the way to bringing young scholars from Asia, Africa, Eastern Europe, and the Soviet Union. Wells helped to establish IU as one of the United States Department of Education's centers for training teachers from abroad. He worked especially hard at establishing international studies on the Bloomington campus, and Indiana University remains a leader in Russian studies, Slavic studies, and Uralic and Asian languages.

Despite all these accomplishments, Wells may have won more fame for his defense of Alfred C. Kinsey, whose research on human sexual behavior was so "socially explosive and intimately personal" that some saw it as an "adventure into an unexplored cavern of many unpredictable labyrinths—the most threatening of which was loss of institutional prestige and vital financial support."[6] In many ways, Wells's role in the resolution of the Kinsey controversy was typical of his subsequent administrative successes. Never a flamboyant crusader and certainly aware of the potentially explosive nature of the matter, Wells worked quietly behind the scenes, making public gestures only when necessary and then in the most understated manner.

Kinsey began his research as part of a course on marriage that he taught at IU in the 1930s. A dedicated scientist and researcher internationally respected for his work with gall wasps, Kinsey focused his attention on his human subjects with the same rigorous care and detachment that he had used with insects. He collected case histories of students who planned to take his course, interviewing them privately before allowing them to attend lectures. When word of the nature of the discussions and classes reached parental ears, there was sufficient criticism to cause President Wells to force Kinsey to choose between teaching his course or conducting research.

Kinsey chose research and founded the Institute for Sex Research in 1941. He received grants from the Rockefeller Foundation and used offices at the university. Kinsey was continually the target of outraged alumni, "concerned" citizens, and conservative members of the Catholic Church. Wells often interceded on his behalf, writing soothing letters and calming angry callers. Wells engaged the best lawyers in the country when Indiana University was forced to sue the United States government for its refusal to allow Kinsey to receive a collection of erotica from Europe. The case, begun in 1950, was finally settled in 1957, a year after

Kinsey's death. The university's legal victory was a landmark for freedom of scientific research, and Wells's steadfast defense of Kinsey's right to conduct that research remains one of his most significant achievements as president of Indiana University.

Wells defended IU faculty against attacks during Senator Joseph McCarthy's investigations in the 1950s. He also fended off threats from members of the American Legion who demanded an investigation of the presence of members of the Communist Party within faculty ranks. However, he was less supportive of students who made fun of the McCarthy hearings by blanketing the campus with green feathers—a symbolic reference to Robin Hood and his merry men, books about which were banned by public librarians because they felt the stories promoted communism. The American Association of University Professors (AAUP) supported the students, who were all members of the Baptist Youth Foundation. The students argued that the act of spreading green feathers all over campus mocked the book ban and thus promoted the cause of academic freedom. Wells replied, "The University should not take a position pro or con on controversial issues."[7]

The contrast between Wells's attitude toward the green feathers incident and his quiet but effective defense of academic research by Kinsey and other faculty members demonstrates how he perceived his role as a university president. As IU's leader and principal public defender, he felt he could and should protect those members of the university community whose activities provoked attacks that brought into question the principle of academic freedom. He did not see his role as defender of those who criticized political adversaries from within the walls of the university itself. He summarized his attitude about student demonstrations in a speech on Founders Day, May 3, 1961:

> In our institution, therefore, it is a little surprising that students would elect to substitute demonstration for discussion and debate. The articulate intellectual frequently criticizes the noisy demonstrations of a political campaign as an appeal to mass emotions. Perhaps this is necessary in an era of mass communication. Nevertheless, it hardly seems compatible with the campus atmosphere.[8]

Herman Wells had worked with Indiana politicians and educators long enough to know the limits of their tolerance for behavior that strayed too far from the mainstream of Hoosier traditions. A bachelor all his life, Wells focused all his considerable energy on the university. Bloomington was his community, and Hoosiers, especially those who were state politicians, were his main source of support. He devoted most of his time to trying to maintain mutual respect and appreciation among all three points of the triangle of university, town, and state. He understood the potential that the university held, not just for itself, but for all the citizens of Indiana. He also understood its vulnerability if it lost popular support. Wells talked to everyone: students, faculty, staff, administrators, politicians, and voters. He listened as well.[9]

In 1960, Wells announced his decision to retire in two years, when he would have completed his twenty-fifth year as university president. While nearly everyone on campus regretted his departure, no one could argue that Herman Wells had not devoted his entire adult life to making Indiana University an internationally known institution of higher learning. His keen understanding of Indiana's students, faculty, administrators, and, above all, state politicians made him an extraordinarily difficult person to replace. However, all agreed that he certainly deserved a rest after a lifetime of achievements at IU.

CHAPTER 1

The Dawn of Dissent: 1960–65

Herman B Wells announced his decision to retire in 1960. Although the actual event was two years away, university officials immediately began to consider the problem of choosing his successor. After an extensive national search, the board of trustees selected Elvis J. Stahr to be IU's next president.

Stahr was secretary of the army under President John F. Kennedy and had been president of the University of West Virginia. In addition, he was a lawyer, and his understanding of the working of corporate boardrooms and government bureaucracies was among the many assets that he brought to Indiana University. What Stahr represented was a new breed of corporate scholar, who brought a perspective to the office very different from Wells's intimate understanding of Hoosier students, faculty, and politics.

Stahr was forty-six years old when he arrived in Bloomington. Born in Hickman, Kentucky, he went to the state university in Lexington, graduated with the highest scholastic record in the university's history, went to Oxford University as a Rhodes scholar, and earned a law degree. When he returned to the United States, his academic career took a bit of a twist—he went to Yale University for a diploma in Chinese languages. Then he joined a prestigious New York City law firm. During World War II he served as an infantry officer in China, Burma, and India. After the war, he went back to Kentucky to teach law and was appointed dean of the University of Kentucky's School of Law in 1948. During the Korean conflict, he served as an advisor to the assistant secretary of the army, and then became vice chancellor for the professional schools at the University of Pittsburgh. He left Pittsburgh to become president of the University of West Virginia and was then selected by President Kennedy to be his secretary of the army.

Stahr had not gotten on well with Secretary of Defense Robert Mc-Namara, one of the generation's "best and brightest," and was eager to leave the Kennedy administration. Yet as a former Kennedy appointee, Stahr came to Bloomington with the glamour of the New Frontier still surrounding him. Like the president he had served, Stahr had an active young family. His wife, Dorothy, was attractive and supportive, reporting that she expected her role to be "raising children and pouring tea."[1]

Stahr had traveled all over the world, had served at high levels of government, and was at ease with corporate and political leaders. His academic achievements allowed him to command faculty respect. Most observers probably would have predicted that he would continue to build on the substantial legacy of Herman Wells for the next decade. Few would have guessed that this highly touted new president would leave Indiana in six years, exhausted by a job for which he seemed, in the beginning, such a good match.

The wheels of change that began spinning the year that Elvis Stahr was hired as president of Indiana University were multiplied and enlarged across the nation. Everywhere, it seemed, "the times they were a-changing."

On February 1, 1960, four students from North Carolina A&T College, an all-black school, walked into the local Woolworth's in Greensboro and asked a white waitress for a cup of coffee at a lunch counter that operated under state laws enforcing racial segregation. That simple act touched off one of the greatest social movements of our time. Drawing on the ideas of Mahatma Gandhi, Reinhold Niebuhr, and Jesus Christ, among others, these African-American students began to teach America how to live up to the principles of its Constitution. Their call to the citizens of this country to end the hypocrisy of racial discrimination marked the beginning of a new era of student activism that made the coming decade unique in American history. Inspired by their mentor Ella Baker, executive director of the Southern Christian Leadership Council (SCLC), they formed the Student Nonviolent Coordinating Committee (SNCC), an organization that influenced nearly every student group during the 1960s. Based on the idea of grass-roots support, leadership "from the bottom up," and a sense of spiritual camaraderie that came to be known as "beloved community," SNCC transformed students' self-images, leading them to see themselves as agents of social change.[2]

White students from the North were inspired to join in the struggle, and as they did they were impressed with the courage of their black brothers and sisters in the South. Swept up in their spiritual commitment to the civil rights movement, many went back to their college and university campuses and began initiating reform movements of their own. One such was Tom Hayden. After a summer in the South, Hayden returned to the University of Michigan, contacted other political progressives among the student body, and spearheaded a meeting on the shores of Lake Huron that led to the creation of The Port Huron Statement, a seminal document of the student movement of the 1960s. With its call to "people of this generation, bred in at least modest comfort, housed now in universities, looking uncomfortably to the world we inherit," Hayden and other New Leftists challenged their peers to make America a truly democratic and decent society. Disavowing the sectarian rancor of the Old Left, these young idealists saw themselves as agents of a new source of energy that could transform the nation, a human response to President John F. Kennedy's call in his inaugural address in January 1961 to "ask not what your country can do for you, but what you can do for your country."

The Port Huron Statement concluded that "as students for a democratic society," they were committed to stimulating a new social movement on campuses and within communities across the country. Their organization, Students for a Democratic Society (SDS), focused on issues of economic equity and the ideal of engaging an active citizenry in "participatory democracy." At the same time, SDS members honored SNCC workers' demand to take the struggle against racism into the North and into white suburbs. This multi-pronged attack on American hypocrisy and complacency reverberated in the hearts and minds of students across the country—including those attending Indiana University in Bloomington, Indiana.[3]

However, the students that most Americans heard about were those attending the University of California, Berkeley. They, along with others on campuses across the country, had protested the vicious campaigns to hunt out communists in every aspect of American life initiated by Wisconsin's Senator Joseph McCarthy in the 1950s and carried out by the House UnAmerican Activities Committee (HUAC) into the next decade. These government-sponsored inquisitions grilled citizens about their political affiliations and resulted in public humiliation, loss of jobs, and even suicide. Opponents to these witch hunts, including college students, responded by forming progressive political groups, publishing journals, and demonstrating for a variety of causes: civil rights, free speech, and a ban on nuclear weapons.

During the spring of 1960, HUAC began an investigation of communist activities in the Bay Area. Berkeley students responded by organizing peaceful demonstrations in San Francisco's city hall. On the second day of the demonstrations (later known as Black Friday), police arrived with billy clubs and fire hoses and proceeded to drag students, drenched and bleeding, off to jail. For many participants and observers, this was the beginning of the Sixties and student protest.

In the fall of 1964, four thousand protestors gathered on Sproul Plaza on the Berkeley campus to challenge university restrictions on free speech, specifically those that banned the dissemination of political literature. The Free Speech Movement (FSM) was organized by activists who had been involved in the civil rights movement in the South and who were trained in techniques of nonviolent civil disobedience. They were also firmly committed to the idea of the university as a place where ideas should be exchanged, debated, and confronted. In December, graduate student Mario Savio inspired hundreds of students to take part in a sit-in at the administration building in a speech that described the university as a machine and urged students to "put your bodies upon the gears and upon the wheels, upon the levers, upon all the apparatus and you've got to make it stop." The sit-in at Sproul Hall led to the largest mass arrest in California history.

With faculty support, students were finally able to declare victory when university president Clark Kerr and administrators at the Berkeley campus bowed to a vote by the faculty senate that supported the students. The FSM received attention from national media and raised new issues on campuses across the country. Students of the 1960s no longer behaved like subordinates toward faculty and administrators. They challenged authority and began asserting their rights as citizens and students to control the rules that governed their lives on campus. Rights such as free speech might be taken for granted by many Americans, but young activists, who had seen First Amendment freedoms trampled by anticommunists and segregationists in the South, were more likely to defend those freedoms within their own communities. They were especially sensitive to their right to discuss political issues on campus, where, they believed, all points of view must be heard in order to pursue true intellectual honesty. Berkeley became synonymous with the new spirit of student activism in the 1960s—a symbol of hope for some, a nightmare for others.

Students at Indiana University launched their own campaign for free speech, which actually preceded the one at Berkeley. However, the IU movement was neither as broad based nor as well known as the Free Speech Movement.

In the early 1960s, Indiana University was, in the opinion of one eastern university president, "an educational bargain."[4] Tuition was relatively low for both Indiana residents and nonresidents. The university's national reputation was on the rise, due in large part to the progress made during Wells's administration in spite of the rather meager resources allocated for the university's development by the state legislature. While many Hoosiers were quick to support IU's athletic accomplishments, they were less eager to raise taxes to promote corresponding academic achievements. In the context of a pioneer tradition of distrust of government involvement and reluctance to support public education, the university's growing strengths in international programs, human sexual research, physical and natural sciences, music and art, linguistics, folklore, and social sciences were a source as much of suspicion as of pride for some of the state's citizens.[5]

As the 1960s began, there were about sixteen thousand students enrolled at Indiana University. The housing crush of the postwar years was over, and undergraduates and graduates lived comfortably in recently constructed dormitories and fraternity and sorority houses. The grounds were well kept, with large trees and neat flower beds. On quiet, warm days, students sat and studied on the banks of Jordan River, a stream of clear water that cut through the campus. IU students were, for the most part, sons and daughters of the middle class. Their political views reflected their upbringing, conservative and respectful of authority. Still, the spirit of the Green Feathers movement had not disappeared.

The first indication that President Stahr was not in for a smooth ride occurred on October 4, 1962, shortly before his inauguration and during the Cuban missile crisis. Members of the Ad Hoc Committee to Oppose U.S. Aggression in Cuba organized a demonstration on the steps of the Indiana University Auditorium. James Bingham, son of a prominent Indianapolis attorney and a member of the Young Socialist Alliance (YSA) and the Fair Play for Cuba Committee, was one of the leaders of the group of about thirty protestors. They carried signs that denounced President Kennedy's naval blockade of Cuba as an act of hostile aggression.

This small group of protestors was challenged by a counter-rally by the conservative Young Americans for Freedom (YAF), led by Tom Charles Huston at the Phi Kappa Psi fraternity house. If the University of Michigan can be called the birthplace of SDS because its founding members included Michigan students like Tom Hayden, who became a prominent antiwar protestor and progressive politician, then Indiana University might rightly be called the birthplace of YAF, because of students like Tom Charles Huston. After graduating from IU, Huston became national chairman of YAF and served as a member of President Richard Nixon's administration. He became famous for proposing the "Huston Plan," which urged the president to coordinate domestic intelligence with other government agencies in order to spy on Nixon's "enemies." The president approved the plan, but FBI director J. Edgar Hoover opposed it, and it was never put into action.[6]

A crowd of about two thousand students watched as the Ad Hoc Committee members, led by two young women, Polly Smith and Paulann Groninger, began to march from the auditorium toward Bloomington's courthouse square. Twenty city policemen with three police dogs and twenty campus policemen followed behind the marchers. FBI investigators were on hand as well as policemen in plain clothes. The marchers were taunted and heckled as they walked down Kirkwood Avenue toward the city square. As they passed the Swing Inn Pizzeria, Fred Rice, one of its employees, grabbed a sign from marcher Polly Smith. The sign said, "A nuclear cloud would be devastating to my flowers." Smith was a representative of the Indianapolis Mothers' Club and the Parent-Teachers Association. As Rice grabbed for Smith's sign, he hit Ralph Levitt, an IU graduate student standing next to Smith. Fellow protestor Jim Bingham later observed, "Hitler would have been proud of such mob hysteria." Fistfights broke out and the marchers retreated up Kirkwood Avenue to seek shelter in the main library building at the head of the street. Students stood outside, jeering the protestors and singing the national anthem. President Stahr urged students to remain calm, and after the attack on the protestors he defended their right to express views with which he and a majority of the students disagreed. The hostility that the protestors aroused among both students and townspeople was an early indication that the free expression of dissent, by even so small a group, was an emotional issue that threatened to disrupt both campus and community.[7]

The incident might have been considered closed with Rice's arrest. But Thomas Hoadley, recently elected prosecuting attorney for Monroe County, decided to call a grand jury to investigate the activities of YSA, a small campus political group whose leaders had been involved in the Cuban protests. Hoadley, a member of an old Bloomington family whose wealth came from limestone quarries, had graduated from Indiana University's law school and was active in the Republican Party. Claiming that he merely wanted to "fight the internal community threat," Hoadley focused his attention on YSA because it described itself as "an independent socialist league which is against Stalinism and capitalism. It endorses the Marxist-Leninist theory of socialism." Bingham and Levitt, history graduate students, along with Thomas Morgan, an undergraduate in the government department, were indicted under the Indiana

Supporters of the Ad Hoc Committee to Oppose U.S. Aggression in Cuba carry signs as they march to the courthouse. © Dave Repp.

Anti-Subversive Act (1951), which made the assembly of two or more people for the purpose of advocating the overthrow of the state government a felony. This same law banned the teaching of communism.[8]

Hoadley based his indictment of the YSA members on the grounds that during a campus meeting guest speaker Leroy McRae, national secretary of YSA, had argued that American blacks had to obtain their legal and political rights. He said, "Those who have the power are those who have denied us our rights. We will achieve that necessary power . . . one way or another." According to Hoadley, McRae's speech was a call for revolutionary overthrow of the state government.[9]

Behind all this was Hoadley's dispute with the university's Committee for Student Activities. The committee had recognized YSA as a legitimate campus organization and allowed the group to use university facilities for its functions. Hoadley wanted the university to withdraw recognition of YSA, because he thought that the group advocated international revolution. He based his judgment on a statement that he quoted from *The Young Socialist*, YSA's official journal: "The YSA declares its political solidarity with revolutionary youth in all countries." Hoadley commented, "My basic interest is not particularly to put these students in jail, but to remove it [YSA] from the campus facilities. It would have been cleared up months ago if the university had simply decided to remove it."

However, Indiana University vice president Samuel Braden checked with the state attorney general's office and found that YSA was not on the state's list of subversive organizations. Braden said, "We view his [Hoadley's] demand upon the University to withdraw our recognition as a violation of the independence and integrity of the academic community."[10]

The faculty was angered by Hoadley's blatant attempt to interfere with campus activities. A committee of 136 professors took out a full-page advertisement in the *Bloomington Herald-Telephone* to make the following statement, "A Message to the Students and All the Citizens of Our Community":

> We find it particularly objectionable that the members of a campus organization should be indicted for remarks made by a guest speaker. . . . This principle . . . could paralyze the intellectual life of the community by discouraging the appearance of any challenging or stimulating . . . speakers.[11]

Some students in IU's folklore department found the episode ridiculous and satirized Hoadley's efforts in a song that aired on the university's radio station, WFIU. Titled "Hoadley, Poadley, Piddley, Poo," it included these lines:

> There's a lawyer in town with just one aim,
> To bring publicity to his name
> Chorus: Hoadley, Poadley, Piddley, Poo
>   Hoadley, Poadley, full of (deleted)
> Prattling verbally, none of it true
> Just wants a place to call his own,
> All over the Herald-Telephone.
>
> (Repeat chorus)
>
> There's just one office he thinks he's worth
> Attorney-General of the Earth!
> So all you Birchers, perish not,
> McCarthy's dead, but still you've got
> (Repeat chorus)[12]

The administration worried about the effect of national publicity concerning the case on state legislators' enthusiasm for university funding. Local newspaper editors were annoyed at what they perceived as the prosecuting attorney's attempts to "make a name for himself."[13]

Hoadley's charges kept the "Bloomington 3" (Bingham, Levitt, and Morgan) involved in legal entanglements for four years. Friends and supporters formed the Committee to Aid the Bloomington Students, raised money to organize national speaking tours and pay the costs of their defense, and distributed literature about the case. The national office of YSA sent the Bloomington 3 to speak at campuses across the country. Morgan, Levitt, and Bingham were clean-cut, articulate, and persuasive young men. They described the repressive tactics that local officials had used in their prosecution and their speeches generally elicited sympathetic responses.

The families of the Bloomington 3 had mixed opinions of their sons' political activities. Jim Bingham's father, an attorney in Indianapolis, felt that his son was innocent and hired local lawyer James Cottner to defend the three. But he remarked to reporters, "I'm not saying I agree with what he believes, though." Ralph Levitt's father blamed the university for corrupting his son, a Ph.D. candidate in Eastern European history. The elder Levitt said, "Now I ask you, what group of people do you come in contact with in Eastern Europe? That's the whole trouble. The university should restrict courses like that. . . . This group of fifteen or so kids is a bunch of idiots. They are just making martyrs out of them with all this publicity." John Morgan, Tom's father, owned a tavern on the south side of Terre Haute, Indiana. He was "tight-lipped" and refused to comment on his son's legal battles, although he was considered to be sympathetic to his cause. His son, Tom, was an excellent student at IU and had put himself through school. He had recently returned from a hitchhiking tour of Europe and Russia.[14]

Stories about the Bloomington 3 and their cause appeared in newspapers throughout the country as the three students traveled to speak in their own defense on college campuses. The *New York Times* reported that the prosecuting attorney was splitting the Bloomington community. Other newspapers investigated the case as an attack on academic freedom. The editor of the *Bloomington Star Courier* wrote that while it was interesting to read about Bloomington in newspapers from New York City, Minneapolis, Milwaukee, and Detroit, the stories all had a "condescending" attitude, as though they were about some small town in Mississippi. Bloomington was the center of a lot of journalistic attention, but "it wasn't like being famous. It was more like being at the wrong end of a microscope."[15]

In the end, the charges against the Bloomington 3 were dismissed. New York civil liberties lawyer Leonard Boudin led a defense team made up of lawyers from Louisville, Kentucky. With Boudin's expertise and experience in defending clients on First Amendment issues, the team made short work of the prosecution's case, and the decision to dismiss all charges demonstrated that the case had been based on politics, not law. However, the incident had important implications for the university's future political embroilments.

The Bloomington 3 were among the first of a growing number of IU students who did not conform to conventional behavior and ideas during the early 1960s. These students were unusual in the way they looked and dressed, in what they thought, in how they acted, and, most important, in how they saw themselves. They were called "greenbaggers" because of the green book bags they usually carried. They could usually be found hanging out in one of Bloomington's coffee houses or visiting friends in off-campus apartments, arguing politics or debating literature or philosophy. Many of them attended the weekly meetings of the Folk Music Club. Greenbaggers wore their hair a little longer than normal and favored jeans over coats and ties or matching skirts and sweaters. They took ideas seriously and talked with each other long into the night. They were aware of a larger world beyond IU's campus and were sensitive to, if not always active in, the challenges presented by the civil rights movement and United States foreign policies in Latin America and Southeast Asia. While a few came from radical or politically active families, most were the sons and daughters of moderate Republicans or New Deal Democrats. These students did not want to be part of the sorority and fraternity scene. They were a conscious minority with their own priorities and culture. On a campus that congratulated conformity, greenbaggers celebrated individualism.

In 1964, greenbaggers and other activists successfully challenged the university's requirement that all male undergraduates participate in the Reserve Officers Training Corps (ROTC). Previously, administrators had tried to brush off questions about ROTC by saying that the university had to require the courses under the terms of the Morrill Act of 1862, which did, in fact, require military training as part of the federal land grant. However, as students correctly pointed out, only Purdue University was established in Indiana under that law. IU was not a land-grant institution, since it was created by the state's first constitution in 1816. Going from dormitory to dormitory, anti-ROTC activists inspired their peers to successfully challenge the ROTC requirement. Administrators had to admit they could not legally force men to take the course, and the next fall, enrollment in ROTC dropped 60% among entering freshmen. While the point about ROTC was important, greenbaggers argued that it was also important for students to realize that administrators did not always tell the truth. The lesson here was clear: "challenge authority."[16]

It was from the ranks of the greenbaggers that the first Indiana chapter of SDS was formed in the fall of 1965, and it was with the emergence of this group that the full force of the 1960s student movement began to arrive on the Bloomington campus. With the ROTC victory behind them, students were eager to organize for other reforms, and SDS was the most accessible and attractive national organization available. SDS vigorously promoted the ideas that were most appealing to campus reformers. The Port Huron Statement, SDS's initial declaration written by Tom Hayden and others in 1962, eloquently summarized the principles of participatory democracy that many Bloomington activists had already been discussing among themselves. It was time, they felt, to gain more control over the university rules that governed their lives, especially arbitrary restrictions like those that forced women to return to their residences at specific hours on weeknights and weekends.

The political activism and idealism of SDS leaders like Hayden provided positive models for local action against the exercise of arbitrary authority, racism, and national policies of foreign imperialism and domestic repression. Moreover, SDS assimilated students with varying interests and ideas because it was, by self-definition, opposed to a rigid ideological program or hierarchical administrative structure. Finally, SDS was an incredibly easy organization to join. It had been founded by students who were suspicious of centralized authority in general, and its national office was not interested in administrative details, so getting together a local chapter did not involve much effort. Dues were minimal and not always necessary for affiliation even though they were appreciated when contributed.

Early records of IU's SDS group are sketchy, but the first contact with the national organization appears to have been made by Rick Ross, a graduate of Wabash College (a small, private, all-male liberal arts institution in Crawfordsville, Indiana), who was doing graduate work at IU and wrote to SDS to ask about the possibility of starting an SDS chapter. Ross had failed in previous efforts to establish a liberal group at Wabash and was warned that while radical groups like YSA did exist in Bloomington, any SDS chapter was likely to be a "persecuted minority" because of the strength and conservatism of the fraternities on campus.[17] Other early organizers, such as Karl North, John Grove, Joseph Fuhrman, Peter Montague, Robin Hunter, Jim Wallihan, and David and Bernella Satterfield, were, for the most part, older students who had been politically active before they came to IU and were interested in forming some kind of organization at IU.

Members of SDS and other student groups across the country began criticizing the war in Vietnam, and on Easter 1965 twenty thousand protestors marched on the Washington monument. Folksingers Joan Baez, Phil Ochs, and the Freedom Singers led the crowd in singing "We Shall Overcome." The demonstrators presented Congress with a petition to end the war. In Bloomington, SDS members spent that summer distributing leaflets against the war, holding a folksong benefit for a local branch of the Journeymen Stonecutters Association of North America, and marching to commemorate Hiroshima Day. By the beginning of the fall semester they had agreed on a written constitution, which they sent to the national SDS office in Chicago, along with a letter stating that there were about thirty founding members. John Grove wrote to Chicago staffer Robert Pardun, who was supposed to sign the membership cards, and received the following advice, typical of SDS's free-flowing style: "[Carl] Oglesby is supposed to sign the cards but he never will since we will either forge his name or use a stamp. You might as well forge them as us, so go ahead." With that casual start, SDS members began to make their presence known at Indiana University.[18]

By the end of the mid-1960s, activists at Indiana University had compiled an impressive, if little noticed, record. Well before the Free Speech Movement at the University of California, Berkeley, the Bloomington 3 made a significant contribution to the promotion of First Amendment freedom on university campuses. By making speeches on college and university campuses across the country, these three IU students were at the forefront of a student movement aimed at protecting students' constitutional rights against repressive local politicians. While they did not inspire hundreds of IU students to engage in acts of civil disobedience, as occurred in Berkeley's free speech movement, and thus were largely ignored by the national newspapers and television networks, their legal struggle for students' right to express their political views on campus prefigured later events at Berkeley.

Just as significant was the campaign to end compulsory ROTC training on the Bloomington campus. One of the students involved in that effort, Mike Kelsey, remembered how transformative the moment was when he understood that the mere fact that an administrator said ROTC was required did not mean the requirement was legal. The experience of challenging those in authority with the truth and succeeding in that challenge liberated and empowered those who took part in the campaign. That understanding of the power of information created a whole new way of dealing with university administrators and faculty. Their saying something was so did not automatically make it so. And for those who had chafed at compulsory ROTC training, liberation from that requirement was reward enough for the effort involved in convincing administrators that they were right. Ending required ROTC was more than just a bureaucratic victory; it marked a new sense of commitment on the part of students who saw Indiana University as *their* university. No longer content with being told what to do, these activists wanted to be part of the system, a part of what made IU a major part of their lives, of who they were as students, as citizens, and, most of all, as human beings.

Even before the full force of the protests against the war in Vietnam and support for the civil rights movement appeared on the IU campus, a small but vocal group expressed its dissent from mainstream opinions through nonviolent action. Reactions to this dissenting voice tended to be hostile, even violent, especially from some townspeople. Moreover, community concern over campus events, particularly those involving leftist political groups or support for civil rights issues, was often expressed in emotional and combative ways. These issues touched sensitive roots within the town that reached back into its history as a crossroads between east and west, north and south. Many southern Hoosiers distrusted people who supported unfamiliar or radical ideas and who promoted racial integration.

The student movement of the 1960s washed over the country during the rest of the decade. Like a series of waves, it changed people and places in many ways, depending on the obstacles or openings it encountered along its course. Some welcomed the fresh, exhilarating energy. Others feared and fought the personal and social rearrangements it forced on those in its path. Indiana University and Bloomington, Indiana, are part of the history of that movement and of its effects on universities and their communities.

CHAPTER 2

The Awakening of Activism: 1965–67

Among students today, there is a common misconception that students in the 1960s were all long-haired radicals who spent most of their days engaged in protesting the war in Vietnam, smoking dope, and making love. In fact, the reality was much less colorful. First, for most students, alcohol was the most popular drug in the early and mid-1960s. Second, most young women (and their parents) viewed pregnancy out of wedlock as a fate slightly worse than death or injury, so most sexual activity tended to be fairly tame by today's standards. And third, the majority of students at Indiana University and most other campuses could not have located Vietnam on a world map, much less have been concerned about what was going on in that country. The path toward student activism, especially in the Midwest, was gradual and somewhat winding.

At Indiana University, most students in the 1960s were like students today—concerned about getting an education, graduating, and getting a job. However, a small group of students were thinking about larger issues, including American military involvement in Vietnam. In their determination to arouse others to the dangers of that involvement, these young activists began by working on causes closer to the hearts and minds of their peers. They used the university's rules governing student conduct, primarily the ones that determined when women had to return to their rooms at night, as a way of engaging student interest in politics.

From that initial campaign, activists built a larger constituency promoting free speech on campus and criticizing American policy in Southeast Asia. Political organizing is hard work, not always popular, often frustrating, and extraordinarily time-consuming. Yet these young men and women were committed to their cause—to change their university, their country, and, yes, even the world.

In the fall of 1965, a scouting crew for the television program *Candid Camera* selected Indiana University as the setting for one of its episodes because it was, in their eyes, a "typical Midwestern college campus." With its ivy-covered stone buildings, neatly trimmed grounds, and tree-lined walks, IU was a postcard vision of a typical American state university. And it reflected national trends as well. The post–World War II baby-boom generation was arriving on campus in ever increasing numbers. Enrollment had gone from 20,900 in 1964 to slightly over 23,000 in 1966, to 26,000 in 1967. IU was the eleventh largest university in the country in 1966, and according to the American Council of Education, it was consistently ranked among the top twenty-five schools in the country.[1]

Campus social and political life was dominated by fraternities and sororities, whose members were white, relatively affluent, and eager to get along to get ahead. Clark Kerr, president of the University of California, said in 1959, "Employers will love this generation. . . . They are going to be easy to handle," but his description fit IU students better than they did his own.[2]

In fact, in the early 1960s administrators at Indiana University predicted that the current student body would be easy to handle as well. Most students went along with all the rules laid out in the student handbook. Acting *in loco parentis* ("in place of the parents"), university deans told students how to dress, where to live, and, for women, when to be back in their rooms at night. These rules were meant to assure parents who sent a child to Indiana University—or to any other institution of higher learning, for that matter—that in their absence, university administrators would make sure their child was safe, secure, well dressed, and well behaved. More to the point, parents believed that sending their sons and daughters off to college did not mean sending them off to indulge in unacceptable behavior, i.e., excessive drinking and sexual activity. Like students at other colleges and universities, young men and women at Indiana University could not wear jeans at mealtimes, faced disciplinary action if they were found drinking or using drugs on campus, and were not allowed to move off campus unless they were over twenty-one and lived in university-approved housing.

Yet even the most law-abiding student sometimes found these rules irritating, and the most chafing ones were the parietals, which restricted women's hours. Women at IU had to be in their dormitories or sorority houses by 11:00 P.M. every weeknight and by 1:00 A.M. on weekends, and similar curfews were maintained on most campuses. Men, on the other hand, were free to come and go as they pleased; the idea was that if women were in their dorms, then presumably men would return home as well. This policy was demeaning to both women and men. On the one hand, it assumed that women couldn't be trusted to know when to end their evenings out, and on the other, it strongly suggested that men were so lacking in either imagination or direction that, without women around, they would go back to their rooms for lack of anything better to do.

During the late 1950s and early 1960s, student politicians had raised the issue of eliminating women's hours during student body elections, but they had never managed to create enough interest on the part of either students or administrators to effect any change. In 1965, administrators decided on their own to give senior women freedom to set their own hours, because most were twenty-one years old, but that was as far as they were prepared to go, fearing negative reactions from parents and alumni if they gave the same privilege to freshmen, sophomores, or juniors.

During the 1960s, the majority of IU students were generally apathetic about political issues both on and off campus. Brought up during the 1950s, when "Father knows best" was more than just the title of a television comedy, most accepted parietal rules without much discussion. However, there was a small group on campus for whom the university's parental role was more than just a minor irritation. About fifteen or twenty members of SDS decided to make university regulations the major target of their campaign to raise students' political consciousness. They realized that trying to organize IU students to act on any national or international issues would be futile if more students could not see the connection between unchallenged authority on campus and unquestioned policies in Washington, D.C. And so they began a concerted effort to provoke interest in campus politics by making the personal political, especially with reference to women's hours.

Early in the fall semester of 1965, the IU chapter of SDS held elections. Most of the newly elected committee were graduate students (Bernella Satterfield took charge of foreign affairs; David Satterfield, of countercultural events; John Grove, of internal education). However, the new chairman was a junior economics major, Guy Loftman, a recent convert to the politics of the New Left. Loftman was intense and highly energetic, and he embraced this new cause with an exuberant enthusiasm. The son of a DuPont Chemical Corporation executive, Loftman came from a family of conservative political views. His older brother had graduated from

IU's medical school in Indianapolis and Guy's choice of IU had been based on his family's favorable impressions and their friends' recommendations. Once he arrived in Bloomington, he joined a fraternity but then slowly began changing his mind about politics and lifestyle. A trip to Europe opened up new intellectual vistas, and voracious reading in politics, economics, and literature convinced him that the fraternity life of parties and political networking was not what he wanted.[3]

Loftman read the Port Huron Statement soon after it was published by SDS in 1962, and it had a profound effect on his own political philosophy. He realized that the idea of participatory democracy as it was articulated in that document made sense to him in terms of his own views about the value of political activism. More than anything, Loftman wanted to create a new kind of community on the Bloomington campus. He envisioned a community where students could not only find ways to gain more control over their own lives, but could also influence the ways in which the university exerted its influence both internally and beyond campus boundaries. He passed along copies of the Port Huron Statement to friends to read and began discussing how to make its ideals real at IU.

Having been a member of a fraternity, Loftman was all too aware of the role that campus politics had traditionally played. Young men and a few women typically used student government offices as items on their résumés to improve their chances for admission to professional graduate schools or for management positions. Loftman wanted to make student politics meaningful by moving student elections out of the realm of play or "sandbox" politics, focusing instead on issues that really affected individual lives and on substantive challenges to university policies. He gained notoriety for his first campaign, in 1964, against the requirement that all IU male students take ROTC.

In 1965, Loftman and other SDS members decided to form a new organization devoted to purely campus issues, the Organization for University Reform (OUR). They circulated a petition with the following proposals: abolish women's hours; eliminate dress regulations; eliminate restrictions on cars off campus; allow students who were over twenty-one to live where they wanted; and establish student and faculty participation in setting policies that affected the university community. The petition won the support of a wide variety of students: student senate president Dave Frick called the university's rules "trivial," and the national chairman of the conservative Young Americans for Freedom, Tom Huston, complained of "creeping deanism." At an OUR rally, a young folksinger accompanied herself on the guitar while singing,

IU's administration is liberal to a degree;
Wants freedom for the Russians but not for you and me;
We try to protest about it, and ask for more than we got;
But they say jeans at dinner
Is part of a communist plot.[4]

At the rally, students spoke about frustrations they experienced at IU. Classes were large, dormitories and dining halls were impersonal and run by a staff they rarely saw—even the "make-out" rooms were big public lounges. All of these were standard complaints of students at large state universities in the 1960s. IU was part of the growing number of "multiversities," a term used to describe postwar universities that served multiple constituencies, from thousands of students who came to campus to earn degrees to government administrators who doled out grants to faculty for research programs. University administrators from Harvard to Michigan to Berkeley responded to growing enrollments and increased demand for faculty research grants by increasing class sizes, using teaching assistants as instructors, and relying on televised lectures. At the University of Minnesota, for example, students in Sociology 101 watched a professor lecture on television and never knew whether the man was dead or alive for the entire semester because they never saw him in person. Papers were often returned with a letter grade but no comments, as if they had been graded by machine. Students increasingly saw themselves as nothing more than numbers on a computer card that they were taught not to fold, spindle, or mutilate.[5]

At the same time, university administrators continued to treat students as children, enforcing hundreds of irritating and confusing rules concerning details of dress and behavior. At the University of Illinois, men and women who were sitting together on sofas in dormitory lounges had to keep three of their four feet on the ground at all times. Dormitories were segregated by sex but men and women were allowed visitation hours. At Earlham College, the doors to dorm rooms had to be kept open the width of a book—but students interpreted that to mean a book of matches.[6]

Robin Hunter, a graduate student in political science from Canada and one of the founders of IU's SDS, expressed his belief that the "university should live up to democratic standards. I am arguing that in a free society the university should be a sort of 'pilot study' for expanding the limits of community self-government and democratic aspirations. And that, sadly, is far from the case today. . . . I.U. is a buttress of the status quo, the ideological apologist for the me-too-ism of our time."[7] Later, Jim Wallihan, vice chairman of OUR and a political science graduate student from the University of California, Davis, commented, "Let's face it—dress regulations are no big deal. The I.U. administration makes them a big deal, and forces students to launch a major campaign to prevent them from getting on to more significant issues."[8]

OUR got over three thousand students to sign its petition. University administrators began to make some changes in dress regulations, leaving the decisions on these regulations to democratic procedures within each residence hall, and allowed students who were twenty-one years old to live off campus. Since hours had been eliminated for senior women in the spring of 1965, students pressed for an extension of this freedom to juniors and sophomores too. A petition for the extension was circulated and won widespread support. The OUR coalition had made its point. Students from many different political perspectives agreed that changes needed to be made at IU.

Loftman and Hunter, both active in SDS, saw new opportunities to build a campus political organization that could seriously challenge the fraternity-dominated groups and the administration as well. Their idea was to make everyone at IU take student politics seriously—no more sandbox games. OUR had given them a taste for what campus politics could be, if they succeeded in winning the attention and respect of moderates as well as of those committed to more radical views. During the spring term of 1966, they gathered a group of activists and formed the Progressive Reform Party (PRP) as the vehicle for their next drive for participatory democracy.[9]

Launching a direct assault on "sterile, irresponsible campus political parties," the PRP platform called upon students to "re-integrate the academic community with the 'outside world.'" Party spokeswoman Lynn Everroad told students that they had to take an active role in changing IU, "which hands us 'knowledge' in mass classes, which covers us with a morass of rules and regulations, and which tries to force our character development along predetermined lines." PRP proposed that all women's hours be eliminated, that students and faculty should reexamine the quality and content of academic courses, and that the student senate should have ultimate authority over all nonacademic policies on student life. In their initial position paper, PRP founders said that they wanted to "help in building at I.U. a dynamic community profoundly committed to maximum educational opportunity for every student." They intended to promote their ideas by seeking "open confrontation" with the administration. Specifically, PRP candidates said that the library should be open twenty-four hours a day, that IU should provide a free bus service for all students, that the student newspaper should be independently operated, and that the student union should serve liquor.

The PRP platform accomplished its goal of introducing controversy into student politics. *Indiana Daily Student* commentator Joel McNally wrote, tongue in cheek, "A perusal of the PRP position paper will reveal to any right-thinking student that it intends to bring political views into politics. My God, it would undercut the entire system." Chuck Ott, an undergraduate from Southport, Indiana, and former president of the Young Democrats (part of the national Democratic Party), was PRP's unsuccessful candidate for student body president. Loftman and Hunter won their bids for senate seats.[10]

The student activists' campaigns of 1965 were beginning to have some effect. At the beginning of the fall term in 1966, Dean of Students Robert Shaffer announced that university administrators had decided to extend the elimination of hours to juniors as well. He explained that after seniors had been given this freedom the year before, "parental objections were more moderate than expected." Freshmen and sophomores were not included, but, as the *Indiana Daily Student* announced, "The I.U. Chastity Belt [Was] Withering."[11]

In the spring of 1967, the Progressive Reform Party made the elections for student body officers into a campaign for increased student power. About fifty PRP delegates met in a classroom in the business building in the middle of March to pick their candidates. Chairman Dave Hunter presided over two hours of "factionally disturbed and often chaotic discussion," an evening "almost hopelessly entangled in motions and amendments," while he sprawled or sat cross-legged on top of a desk. By the end of the meeting, Guy Loftman and Barry Wheeler had won the nomination with the charge to "make this institution into a real university." After referring to opposition parties Action and Tryus as Tweedledum and Tweedledee, PRP called its platform "Student Power Now" and promised to "end sandbox government and establish student self government."[12]

The main themes were similar to those Loftman and Hunter had run on in the student senate elections the previous year. PRP had a more extensive program for increased student power than either of the other two parties: its platform called for an end to university control over dormitories, bookstores, food service, and off-campus housing, as well as the elimination of registration requirements for student groups and restrictions on students' visitation rights in dorm rooms. It wanted to keep the library and music practice rooms open twenty-four hours a day, allow alcohol on campus, organize a teaching assistants' union, initiate a pass/fail grading system, and form student research committees to investigate university policy. Hitting themes that he had honed throughout the year, Loftman charged that IU did not really educate students. Instead it processed them. "This is a factory, we are all raw material, and the product is the skillful manipulation of facts and people. . . . An independent student government with some guts could stand up for student interests. The administration will tell us 'Don't rock the boat' and will tie us up in red tape for ever, if we let them. But the boat desperately needs rocking, . . . after all, it's our boat." Despite PRP's weak showing in previous student campaigns, Loftman vowed, "I'm running to win."[13]

In the middle of the campaign, university service and maintenance employees went on strike for recognition of their union (AFSCME, the American Federation of State, County and Municipal Employees, Local 832). They also demanded that the university drop its recently enacted parking system, which required employees to purchase expensive parking permits or face having their cars towed. At a meeting at the Owl, a local coffee house, union leaders explained their demands to about fifty students, mainly members of PRP, who voted to support the strike. Since the union had been enjoined from blocking deliveries of food to the dormitories, students organized to keep supplies from getting into the buildings. Their lines held for four hours on the first morning of the strike, Saturday, April 8, 1967, until police warned them that they would be arrested for helping the strikers. They returned to the Owl and set up a soup kitchen for strikers and their families and for any students who did not want to eat in the dormitories, which were temporarily staffed with nonunion workers. The strike was settled on Monday, April 10, when university officials agreed to recognize the employee union and to reduce parking fees.[14]

Reinforcing PRP demands for the elimination of women's hours, the Association of Women Students (AWS), whose members were elected to establish guidelines for women students' conduct, demanded the right to legislate rules for women and announced that it was abolishing hours for freshmen and sophomores with parental consent. Dean Shaffer told AWS members that the matter could not be decided until the next meeting of the board of trustees. Members of the Progressive Reform Party had backed both AWS and the strikers. Loftman and Wheeler had consistently supported the right of women to eliminate parietals. During the strike, they organized students to work on the picket lines and in the soup kitchen. The other parties made no comment on AWS; they issued statements of support for the strikers but took no direct action. The union's quick victory and the AWS statement exhilarated PRP campaigners, who passed out over twenty-five thousand leaflets explaining their positions on student power, women's hours, and the recent strike. Their opposition put up expensive posters. In a surprise move and over objections by journalism faculty, the *Indiana Daily Student* endorsed Loftman and Wheeler as the best representatives of IU students, "with more experience, more intelligent ideas, and more potential for progress in student government than all other proposed candidates in both parties." Editor Jerry Harris praised Loftman's senate record and Wheeler's work on student evaluations of faculty and courses.[15]

More students turned out for that election than ever before in IU history. Over ten thousand votes were cast, with a winning plurality of slightly more than four thousand for Loftman and Wheeler. Since the other two presidential candidates were both members of fraternities, PRP's victory was, in part, a result of a split in the Greek vote, but it was also a show of strength by students living off campus and in dormitories. And it was a tribute to the low-budget, grass-roots organizing that Loftman's campaign manager and wife, Connie Kiesling Loftman, had done with such skill. A Hoosier whose conservative upbringing had undergone considerable revision at IU, Connie, initially a music major, had dropped out of school during the fall semester because of the university's "rigid, conservative system of controlling education and students' personal lives." Working tirelessly on the telephone to get students out to vote, bringing musicians to campaign events to entice larger crowds, and making sure that campaigners picked up leaflets and signs after events so as not to litter the campus, Connie Loftman proved to be the best political manager at IU in the spring of 1967. "Toward the end of the campaign we had persons making and hanging signs that we didn't even know about. Everyone pitched in. That was when I knew we had won," Guy Loftman commented.[16]

The PRP victory signaled the arrival of a new breed of student politicians on the Bloomington campus. Connie Loftman, Guy Loftman, Barry Wheeler, Robin Hunter, and others like them were dedicated to opening up communication among students, faculty, and staff. They had enormous energy, quick minds, and high ideals. Challenging professors and administrators was part of their plan for promoting students to positions of influence in the university. Loftman and Wheeler did not want student government to be "sandbox politics," a training ground for ambitious young fraternity members to learn the finer points of fawning over senior bureaucrats. Participatory democracy was not just an idealistic phase; it was a demanding way of life as well. Students had to be prepared to know as much about university policy as administrators did in order to ask the right questions, challenge policies, and initiate reforms. Administrators could no longer expect easy acquiescence from student leaders.

Soon after the student government elections, Loftman and other activists pressed President Stahr for an open meeting to discuss students' roles in the university power structure. About five hundred students gathered in the auditorium to listen to him. While seemingly sympathetic to increased student power in nonacademic matters, Stahr defended university regulations on student conduct because it was necessary for the public to perceive the campus as a safe place for their daughters and sons. Yet when asked specifically why women students had hours regulations, he conceded, "I sometimes wonder myself." In a somewhat rambling analysis of the role of the board of trustees, the administration, and the faculty, Stahr said he did not make university policy; he worked for the university like the rest of the administration. "I am only a channel for policy recommendations to others. . . . I inherited more than a desk and chair, I inherited a whole tapestry of ideas and policies which were in effect and which I could not change." The faculty were an "assembly of professional partners, not employees." The board of trustees, acting for the citizens of the state, made policy and delegated responsibilities for carrying out those policies to the faculty or to the administrative staff, Stahr told his audience. Finally Ken Abraham, vice president of the student body, got up and said, "I don't know who has the power to change women's hours, if it's you or Dean Robert Shaffer or the Board of Trustees. But I do know this. Students aren't the ones who have the power and we want it." To which Stahr replied, "I can't change the law and neither can the students." Saying that he thought the evening had been a lot of fun, Stahr left. In a startling contrast of styles, Vice President and Dean of the Faculties Joseph Sutton informed his audience, "If anyone thinks the Dean of Faculties has no power, let him be hereby disillusioned."[17]

The issue of women's hours would not be resolved for another year. However, it had served the purpose of arousing student interest in university policies and politics.

The Progressive Reform Party's success in transforming student politics from fraternity games to engagement with substantive issues was helped by some heavy-handed suppression of free speech on the part of university administrators. During the Free Speech Movement at the University of California, Berkeley, Jackie Goldberg observed that just when momentum seemed to be slowing down, the administration would commit another "atrocity" and students would once again be aroused. In fact, Goldberg asserted, the administration's suppression of free speech brought groups together who might never have even spoken to each other under normal circumstances.[18] So, too, at IU, activists were sometimes unwittingly aided by an administration whose actions spurred students to form coalitions they might not otherwise have considered. And, as at Berkeley, the issue was free speech.

Earlier in the 1960s, a small group of students had gathered together to form a chapter of the W. E. B. Du Bois Club. The national Du Bois Club was known to be a front for the Communist Party, and it was under investigation by U.S. Attorney General Nicholas Katzenbach. In 1966, the chairman of the IU Du Bois Club was a graduate student in chemistry, Gaylord "Skip" King. King had received a prestigious National Science Foundation (NSF) grant to finance his studies at IU. He defended the group's advocacy of socialism as part of its work for social justice, civil rights, and civil liberties. While he admitted that some members were also members of the Communist Party and that he had once been part of a Marxist student group at Portland State University, King insisted that the Bloomington chapter was open to anyone who wanted to join. Some townspeople called for the administration to ban the Du Bois Club from campus, and Republican state representative Richard Roudebush began efforts to get the federal government to withdraw King's NSF grant because of his affiliation with the group. Roudebush received support from Republican state chairman Charles D. Hendricks, who called King "target No. 1" for denial of federal funds.

SDS co-chairs Jim Wallihan and Bernella Satterfield supported the Du Bois Club's presence on campus despite the club's differences from SDS in ideology and organization. They issued a statement attacking the 1950 McCarran Act, which had established the Subversive Activities Control Board, as a "misguided violation of freedom of association."[19] King did lose his NSF grant (and soon dropped out of school), but not, as university president Elvis Stahr tried unconvincingly to assure students, because of his membership in the Du Bois Club, but rather because he "did not survive the competition" in IU's chemistry department.[20] Not surprisingly, few students believed this. King had obviously lost his grant because of his political views and his leadership in the Du Bois Club.

Despite its notoriety, the Du Bois Club was one of the smallest of the many organizations on the IU campus that were open to all students who wanted to participate. Part of the annual fall scene at IU was the Activities Fair, held in the Alumni Room and the solarium of the Union Building. The fair gave campus organizations an opportunity to explain their purposes to students and to recruit new members. Representatives set up tables with signs, gave out literature, and answered questions. On a large campus like IU, the Activities Fair was one of the few chances students had to see the wide variety of extracurricular activities open to them.

All student organizations had to be registered with the office of the dean of students. The only group for which this was a problem was the W. E. B. Du Bois Club. Since the spring of 1965, when the U.S. attorney general's office had begun to investigate their national offices, the club's status on campus had been in doubt. Even though it had been officially registered, members of the board of trustees were uneasy about the charges of communist influence that surrounded the national organization. During the trustees' regular June meeting in 1966 they declared that the group's registration was "deferred" until a university policy could be set on the rights of groups whose national organizations were under investigation by the Subversive Activities Control Board to exist on campus. In the meantime, the trustees decided that the Du Bois Club could not use university facilities.[21]

The decision by the trustees was unclear (how could registration, once granted, be deferred?), and since the fair was ostensibly open to all students, two Du Bois Club members, Bruce Klein and Allen D. Gurevitz, went into the solarium, set up a booth, and began passing out literature. Klein, formerly president of the student body at IU's Northwest campus in Gary, Indiana, was about to begin his first year of graduate study in the history and philosophy of science. Gurevitz, who grew up in Gary, had been a student on the Bloomington campus and was then working as a model in the fine arts department. No longer enrolled in the university, Gurevitz had been reclassified as eligible for service by his local draft board and was worried about being called into the army. He realized that being affiliated with a group like the W. E. B. Du Bois Club might serve several purposes at once. Not only could he make a political statement, but his affiliation with a suspicious organization like the Du Bois Club might also persuade his draft board that he was unacceptable for military service.[22]

On the afternoon of September 14, 1966, union board members and Dean of Students Robert H. Shaffer, acting on the intent of the trustees' (dubiously legal) decision, told Klein and Gurevitz to leave and took away their table. As the dean stepped away, the two students found another card table behind the Young People's Socialist League booth and set up shop again. By this time, a curious crowd had gathered and Dean Shaffer's patience was beginning to wear thin. As he left the room, Shaffer warned Klein and Gurevitz that they faced disciplinary action if they did not stop what they were doing and get out of the Union Building. Undeterred, the two young men continued to stand by their table for the rest of the afternoon.

They were still there when Dean Shaffer returned that evening with Dean Thomas C. Schreck, union board members, and other staff from the office of student personnel. Shaffer told Klein and Gurevitz that they would be suspended and recommended for dismissal, respectively, if they did not leave in five minutes. When neither made a move, Shaffer suspended Klein for refusing to obey a university official's request and told Gurevitz he would recommend his dismissal from his job for the same reason. He also warned them that they would be arrested on charges of trespassing if they tried to return to the Union Building. Shaffer then left for the day, although telephone calls from Klein and other concerned students kept him up until midnight.[23]

Student leaders had extensive discussions with Klein and Gurevitz and decided that there were important free speech issues involved in their banishment from the Union Building. The next day at the Activities Fair, Robin Hunter, a PRP senator, read a statement from Klein and Gurevitz that proclaimed their right to enter the building and the fair as individuals, and to set up a table as members of the Du Bois Club. The two then entered the building, whereupon they were arrested by Captain William Spannuth of the University Safety Division and taken to the Monroe County jail. They refused to post the $500 bond and announced that they were going on a hunger strike. Four days later, a judge waived the bond requirement and they were released on their own recognizance.[24]

Despite the fact that the Du Bois Club never had more than about thirty dues-paying members, reactions to the arrest of the two students showed with unusual clarity the divisions between the students, the administration, and local townspeople. Editorials in Bloomington newspapers congratulated university administrators on enforcing rules: "We find it wholly proper for quick, positive action to have been taken to enforce the order of an Indiana University administrator. It shows the university is still in command of its campus, and this is as it should be." Concerns about the radical nature of the Du Bois Club continued to surface, and local readers were told that it was "a communist-front organization, created, dominated and controlled by the Communist Party and primarily operated for the purpose of giving aid and support to the Communist Party." More to the point, a Bloomington editor warned Indiana taxpayers about the use of "public funds to support an organization that they regard as a threat to freedom itself."[25]

In contrast, nearly every organization on campus endorsed the club's right to exist, even if only to support the right to free speech and an open exchange of ideas at IU. After the trustees had banned club members from using university facilities in June, the faculty council had passed a resolution urging the trustees to reconsider. The IU chapter of the American Association of University Professors (AAUP) sent a letter to the same effect. The student senate passed a resolution, drafted by Guy Loftman, urging the trustees to continue to support freedom of expression at IU and not to restrict the registration of campus organizations. Student activists' reaction to the arrest of Klein and Gurevitz was one of outrage. At first, a group of about fifty picketed Bryan Hall, the administration building, carrying signs saying "Free General Stahr's Political Prisoners" and "The Free Interchange of Ideas, Does It Exist at I.U.?" The prisoners received visits from Arthur Lloyd, minister at the nearby Trinity Episcopal Church, and William R. Webster, minister at First Baptist Church. The Bloomington chapter of the American Civil Liberties Union (ACLU) charged that arresting Klein and Gurevitz was a violation of their First Amendment rights. After the two were released from jail, five hundred protesters gathered in front of Bryan Hall. Guy Loftman charged that the trustees had been pressured into acting against the Du Bois Club by conservatives in Bloomington, many of whom were members of local fraternal and veterans' organizations, and said, "This university must be run by students and faculty—not the American Legion."[26]

Even moderate and conservative students and faculty expressed their dismay at the way the administration handled the Du Bois Club. Bob Turner of the IU Conservative League declared that even though he thought the club might be a communist front, students should be allowed to listen and decide for themselves. The president of the Young Democrats, Jim King, urged that the Du Bois Club be reinstated. The *Indiana Daily Student* followed up with an editorial criticizing the trustees for banning the club. The IU chapter of the Committee to End the War in Vietnam (CEWV) sent an open letter to the trustees pleading for the right of unpopular causes to be peacefully advanced. The AAUP passed a resolution calling the administration's arrest of the Du Bois Club members "indicative of how an institution's first moves toward curbing basic freedoms lead it step by step down a path of suppression."[27] At a concert held on October 22 to raise money for the Klein-Gurevitz Legal Aid Fund, the Subversion Singers, a group of student musicians and activists, sang an original composition called "Big Boy Bob" that began with the following verses:

> Folks was standin' in the Union
> Up in the Activities Fair
> When all of a sudden up pulled a Batmobile
> And out stepped a Dean with grey hair.
> Kiwanis rings on every finger
> And a 1939 suit
> He had a bottle of aspirin and a cigarette
> And some tranquilizer pills to boot.

He charged on up to the Solarium
Mad as-a he could be
He pulled out his pencil and turned around
He said, "I'm Big Boy Bob, the Dean." [28]

Later in the month, Shaffer announced that Bruce Klein had been reinstated but placed on disciplinary probation for the rest of the year. However, by this time Klein had decided to withdraw from graduate school. Allen Gurevitz was not rehired by the fine arts department, but his arrest made him ineligible for the draft and his board reclassified him as unacceptable for military service, a not unwelcome outcome as far as Gurevitz was concerned. All charges against Klein and Gurevitz were dropped the following spring. In the midst of local fears about the threat of radical disruptions of campus order, IU students, with support from liberal faculty members and a few local organizations, had made a strong stand in defense of the principle of free speech on the Bloomington campus. [29]

The ease with which a student had been arrested and sent to jail during the Du Bois Club controversy made it clear to even the most conservative students that their rights needed strong protection. In November 1966, David Cahill, attorney general of the student senate, presented to the student senate a draft of a student bill of rights that he had been working on for several months. After months of discussion, the bill was passed by the senate and approved by the dean of students in February 1967. The bill put into more precise language policies that were already in place, especially those involving freedom of speech, publication, and distribution of information. It also introduced some new rights for students involved in judicial proceedings. The new bill gave students the right to have an advisor, either a student or faculty member, present at any hearing and the right to confront witnesses testifying against them. PRP senator Robin Hunter commented that the student rights bill was better than nothing but argued that it "stops short in too many ways." Students, he said, need "the unqualified right to authoritative participation in the decisions which affect the individual's life." [30]

Activists kept up pressure on the administration to resolve the status of the Du Bois Club throughout the spring semester. SDS president Jeff Sharlet and Bob Grove, a former officer of the Du Bois Club, helped to organize about 150 students for a student power rally in front of the president's house, a large, attractive residence located in the middle of the campus. They held the rally during a meeting of the board of trustees on the afternoon of March 10, 1967, and although the president was not there at the time, several trustees were. After listening to student demands for the president to talk about the Du Bois Club's deferred registration, trustee Robert Mencke stepped outside and explained that the problem with the club was its association with communism. Since IU received its funding from the state legislature, whose members were politically conservative, the club's presence posed problems for the administration when it asked for state funds to be spent on the Bloomington campus, he said. Then, in a conciliatory gesture, Mencke remarked, "I'm not against you people. . . . The good thing that has come out of this is that academic freedom has opened up."[31]

Mencke's optimism about academic freedom would be tested in the coming years as thousands of young men sought refuge on campuses as a way of avoiding military service and the war in Vietnam. Every young American male in the 1960s had to register for the draft when he turned eighteen and would be considered available for duty in the armed forces until he was twenty-six. With the build-up of American forces in Vietnam, the January 1965 draft calls were the largest since the early 1950s, during the Korean conflict: 45,224 inductees were needed, 10,000 more than at the last draft call.[32]

Local draft boards, usually composed of community leaders or at least those considered "solid citizens" (i.e., white and middle class), gave deferments to college students for five years as long as they were attending school full time and were in good standing academically. In the mid-1960s, graduate students could usually count on receiving deferments for at least two years and sometimes longer. From 1963 to 1966, married men were given special draft treatment, and many couples decided to have children right away in order to avoid the husband's being called up. Men who went to work for industries considered to be in the national interest would also be deferred for service, especially if they were employed by companies with Department of Defense contracts, such as Dow Chemical Corporation or General Electric. Moreover, men could avoid the draft by enlisting in the National Guard if they could find a unit with openings, by joining the Peace Corps, or by proving themselves to be conscientious objectors.[33]

While these options were available in 1965, they became less dependable as the decade wore on and as draft quotas increased. In 1967, under pressure to respond to the army's needs, many draft boards denied deferments to graduate students, Peace Corps volunteers, conscientious objectors, and married fathers. One sure way to avoid the draft was to leave the country, but that was an option that many young men either could not afford or could not come to terms with, for a variety of reasons.[34]

In the mid-1960s, most students at IU, like those at other universities in the Midwest, either supported the war in Vietnam or were apathetic about it. At the same time, a growing number of students and faculty around the country criticized the war and sought to organize opposition to it. In March 1965, several members of the University of Michigan faculty met with concerned students and decided to organize an all-night teach-in to discuss the war. The reason for a teach-in was that so little was known about the history and political structure of Vietnam and the nature of American policies in Southeast Asia in general that students and faculty had to do research and teach themselves. The teach-ins gained added impetus when President Johnson ordered U.S. Air Force planes to drop bombs on North Vietnam. This extension of the war concerned critics, who argued that bombing North Vietnam would only intensify and expand American military commitments.

Those who concluded that the war was wrong believed, rather naively, that if the facts of our involvement in Vietnam were made clear, even those who had previously supported the war would turn against it. Over three thousand people took part in the teach-in at the University of Michigan. Reasoned but passionate exchanges between faculty and students broke down traditional hierarchical relationships. As sociologist Tom Wells concluded, "The campus was now alive with debate on Vietnam. It was impossible to avoid the controversy whether one wanted to or not."[35]

At Indiana University, members of SDS took part in the teach-in through a telephone hook-up in Ballantine Hall, the central classroom building, that allowed them to listen to and take part in the discussions on the Michigan campus. Even before the teach-in, SDS had sponsored discussions about the war on Friday afternoons in Dunn Meadow, a large grassy area in front of the student union. While the debates were often lively, they did not attract large numbers of students.

Unlike students who attended colleges and universities on the East Coast, especially elite institutions like Harvard University and Columbia University, most IU students, like others in the Midwest, were largely indifferent to foreign policy issues. In fact, the main obstacle that many Midwestern antiwar activists faced was not opposition but student apathy. When Richard Nixon arrived on the Bloomington campus in October 1965, only about two hundred protesters marched around Showalter Fountain in front of the auditorium where Nixon praised U.S. intervention in Vietnam. The protesters were members of SDS along with representatives from YSA, the Young People's Socialist League (YPSL), and Americans for Democratic Action (ADA). One demonstrator who joined the group as he was passing by was history professor Leonard Lundin, who had once been a member of YPSL and who decided on the spur of the moment to take part in the protest.[36]

New Left activist Guy Loftman speaks to students in Dunn Meadow. *Arbutus,* 1966.

IU students took part in national protests as well. On a cold, grey day in November 1965, a small group of about twenty-five IU students joined thirty thousand other war protesters in Washington, D.C. The Committee for a Sane Nuclear Policy (SANE), in conjunction with SDS, was trying to bring together liberal Americans who were against the war but who were not members of organizations affiliated with the Old Left. In a direct response to SANE's middle-of-the-road position, SDS president Carl Oglesby issued a blistering attack on liberalism and its alliance with imperialist policies. The crowd listened and applauded enthusiastically.

In response to the demonstration, one member of the IU group wrote in the Bloomington SDS newsletter, "We are convinced that the only way to stop this and future wars is to organize a domestic social movement which challenges the very legitimacy of our foreign policy; this movement must also fight to end racism, to end the paternalism of our welfare system, to guarantee decent incomes for all, and to supplant the authoritarian control of our universities with a community of scholars."[37]

Despite the strength of these antiwar protesters' convictions, they knew that the majority of IU students were either apathetic about foreign policy or actively supported the war in Vietnam. Many young Americans in the mid-1960s accepted the idea that they should support their country's foreign policy, especially when American troops were fighting overseas. When, for example, the Red Cross announced a blood drive on IU's campus during the fall term of 1965, the fraternity-dominated student senate initiated an all-campus "bleed-in" as a way of supporting American troops in Vietnam. Students contributed 1,276 pints of blood during the three-day campaign.

In an informal poll, most donors said they would have given blood no matter where it was sent and, in fact, the Red Cross denied that it had any control over their contribution's destination. Yet the senate president claimed that the bleed-in proved IU students' patriotism and said the school had received "unbelievable publicity" from it. The senate also sponsored "Operation Cheer-Up" to send Christmas presents, mainly baked goods and letters from undergraduate women, to American soldiers in Vietnam. Dwight Worker, a member of SDS, wrote an ironic letter to the *Indiana Daily Student,* the main campus newspaper, suggesting that students could donate little white dolls to Vietnamese children. Worker suggested that if there were any Vietnamese children left alive, the dolls might cheer them up.[38]

Antiwar activists, who were at that time primarily SDS members, were only too well aware of the challenges they faced in trying to win support among IU students. In their efforts to meet those challenges, they looked to advice from the SDS national office and studied techniques that others were using in community organizing efforts like the Economic Research Action Project (ERAP), whose members lived among the poor in urban ghettos in order to raise residents' political consciousness. As Karl North wrote in the November 1965 SDS newsletter, "we must tackle the only ghetto we know and live in the university." Considering that ghetto, North described most IU students as "*worse* than apathetic." Most had no experience in politics and few understood the importance of reform within the university. Demonstrations had so far involved only a small group of those who were already initiated into political action and often alienated students who stood apart as spectators. Even speeches, debates, and passing out leaflets were too passive, North wrote. "They fail to involve the mass of students and faculty in convincing political experiences."[39]

In order to encourage more students to identify with SDS, members were urged to visit dormitories and to start discussion groups without specifically proposing any reforms, but to solicit ideas. In this slow, methodical way, SDS hoped to involve more students in activities that could lead to changes within the university.[40]

When the national office sent a referendum to local chapters proposing that SDS distribute guides to becoming a conscientious objector, IU members voted against it. Bernella Satterfield's letter to national officers stated that it would not help local efforts at all, "rather it could perhaps destroy much of the work that we have attempted to do. We here in Bloomington are in an extremely isolated position on the Viet Nam issue . . . so far we have had little success in reaching the 'typical' student; in fact, we will never . . . if we cannot dispel some of his misconceptions about what SDS is and does." They did, however, support promoting alternative service as an option to military service. Satterfield continued, "SDS must stress positive, imaginative programs . . . rather than simply negative ones; too often we have been asked in exasperation, 'Well, what in the hell are you guys *for*?'"[41]

The fact was that most IU students either did not know or did not care about American policy in Southeast Asia or about SDS. The military buildup that began in 1965 had not yet begun to affect large numbers of young men and their families. On the Bloomington campus, as on others in the Midwest, antiwar protestors were in the minority and were often viewed as weird, troublesome, and slightly crazy. In other words, antiwar activists were not in any danger of winning popularity contests.

The disappointing turnout for rallies against the war in Vietnam made it clear to SDS members they were not reaching the majority of IU students. The rallies attracted those already converted to the cause. Because they believed in the idea of participatory democracy, SDS activists wanted to involve as many students in the political process as possible. If U.S. involvement in Vietnam did not elicit interest, they sought other ways to gain student support. Their aim was not just to radicalize a sympathetic segment of the student body, but to engage those moderate or apathetic students who had never been interested in campus or national affairs.

During the mid-1960s, the national antiwar movement was made up of a loose coalition of students, religious activists, Old and New Leftists, and long-time peace advocates. For the most part, politicians in Washington, D.C., remained unmoved by protests in the streets and on campuses.

A few members of Congress, however, did join the ranks of those who opposed the Vietnam war. Among them were senators Wayne Morse of Oregon and Ernest Gruening of Alaska, the lone holdouts against the Gulf of Tonkin Resolution of 1964, which gave President Johnson a blank check for funding military action in Vietnam. Another was Senator Vance Hartke, from Evansville, Indiana. Hartke had captured national attention in 1958 when he won the seat formerly held by conservative Republican William E. Jenner, who had been a strong supporter of Senator Joseph McCarthy's anticommunist witch-hunts during the 1950s. It was Jenner who accused General George Marshall of being a "front man for traitors" and "a living lie."[42]

Hartke was a liberal Democrat and expressed his opposition to the Vietnam war long before it became politically popular to do so. Students at Indiana University decided to show their support for Hartke in a demonstration in March 1966 that was organized by CEWV to coincide with a campus appearance by General Maxwell Taylor. Demonstration leaders Steve Cagan (a founder of the Du Bois Club), Jim Wallahan, Jeff Sharlet, Prof. James Dinsmoor, and Rev. Gil Sirotti urged demonstrators to "appear neat, clean and orderly," with women in skirts and men in coats and ties, and to ignore any heckling from bystanders. Finally, they reminded students that the demonstration was not to be perceived as "*AGAINST* General Taylor as a person. We are demonstrating instead our *positive* support for Hartke and those other Senators who have had the courage to question the 'no-compromise' escalation policy represented by Taylor and the veterans' organization."[43]

At the same time, there were signs that the war was becoming an issue in local campaigns. In 1966 Robert Scheer, editor of *Ramparts* magazine and a member of the California antiwar movement, announced that he would run in a primary election in Oakland for Congress as a peace candidate against a Democratic incumbent, Jeffrey Cohelan. Although he lost by a narrow margin, Scheer's campaign showed that there was considerable support for antiwar policies and eventually pushed Cohelan to oppose the war.[44]

A similar campaign took place in Bloomington that spring. James Dinsmoor, a professor of psychology, ran for the Democratic Party's nomination for Congress from the seventh district as a peace candidate. Dinsmoor, a former national secretary of YPSL, argued with students, especially SDS members, who questioned his decision to take part in mainstream Democratic party politics. He told them that "you can best present people with new, minority, or unconventional ideas by clothing them in conventional dress." Dinsmoor said that he hoped to inject antiwar issues into "normal, local politics" and that although he did not expect to win, he would have "encouraged people to think of the issue as a legitimate one."[45]

In the end, Dinsmoor did indeed lose the election, but he carried Monroe County, thanks to the efforts of students and faculty who campaigned for him in and around Bloomington. Even Dinsmoor's supporters were surprised at his strong showing, given the generally pro-war sympathies of most local Democrats.[46]

While the majority of students on the Bloomington campus were apathetic about the war in Vietnam in the mid-1960s, there were those who supported it as well as those who opposed it. In this sense, Indiana University was like other Midwestern campuses at that time. In 1965, war supporters had harassed antiwar demonstrators at Kent State University while police looked on passively. A year later, students at IU who supported the war cheered Lt. Gen. Lewis B. Hershey, director of the Selective Service, who came to talk to students about the military necessity for the draft. A native Hoosier himself, Hershey was a popular figure with many students and townspeople. However, he had recently announced that draft boards could take students in the bottom ranks of their classes. Draft boards were told to look at students' grades and their performance on an aptitude test that would be given in May. Students at IU and elsewhere were stunned to realize that they could be drafted and sent to Vietnam. Antiwar activists, organized by CEWV, felt that Hershey's appearance demanded a demonstration.

Members of CEWV distributed flyers to students announcing their plans to demonstrate against General Hershey on May 2. They reported that one of the University of Michigan students whose draft status had recently been changed as a result of antidraft activities would be there, and promised to peacefully picket Hershey in front of the auditorium where he would speak. Another flyer challenged students to ask, "Just Whom Are We Defending in Viet-Nam?" and charged that U.S. troops were protecting "anti-democratic and tyrannical regimes in Saigon."[47]

The 350 marchers who showed up with signs criticizing the draft and the Vietnam war at Showalter Fountain were soon confronted with a crowd of about 1,500 to 2,000 supporters of the war in Vietnam, who called themselves University Students for America. They stood around the fountain, waving flags donated by the American Legion. Flag waving turned to heckling, then egg throwing. Many of the egg throwers wore Greek-lettered sweatshirts, and they taunted the antiwar protesters with challenges to their patriotism.

One protester who received a direct hit was Jeffrey Sharlet, an army veteran who had served a tour of duty in Vietnam before returning to IU to finish his undergraduate degree. Sharlet's opposition to the war was based on first-hand observations of the problems that U.S. military personnel were creating in Vietnam and not on any lack of zeal for American ideals of freedom and democracy.[48]

On the day after Hershey's speech, IU students were given the opportunity to hear Herbert Aptheker, thanks to the combined efforts of the Du Bois Club and YPSL. Aptheker, director of the American Institute for Marxist Studies in New York City and a member of the Communist Party, talked to a packed crowd of about 450 in Whittenberger Auditorium about his recent trip to North Vietnam, reporting that U.S. policy there was "standing in quicksand." Dr. Aptheker was escorted by detectives from the Bloomington Police Department to Whittenberger Auditorium, and university security officers checked everyone who attended the speech for identification, rejecting anyone who was not connected to IU. These precautions were necessary, as Bloomington chief of police James R. East explained, because of "the high feeling in the community concerning his visit." Some of that feeling was exhibited when a hundred members of Students for an Orderly Society, a conservative organization, hung an effigy of Aptheker in front of the north entrance to the Indiana Memorial Union. Detectives escorted Dr. Aptheker back to his room at the Union following his speech, where he stayed quietly until his departure the next morning.[49]

Local businessmen criticized President Stahr for allowing Aptheker to speak on campus. Stahr defended his policy of free speech on campus, arguing that banning Aptheker "could have wrecked IU." Frank E. McKinney, president of IU's board of trustees, supported Stahr. Banning Aptheker, he said, would have made him a martyr.[50]

Antiwar protestors did not take a vacation during the summer. About a hundred people from Bloomington, members of the Bloomington Peace Forum and the IU chapter of CEWV, joined other Indiana antiwar demonstrators in Indianapolis on July 23, 1966, to protest a speech by President Lyndon B. Johnson. The Indianapolis police had been alerted to plans for the demonstration and had contacted the Secret Service about them. State troopers had notified Indianapolis officers of the license plate numbers of cars leaving from Showalter Fountain that morning. Despite being told by state officials that the protestors were within their rights to demonstrate peacefully, the police began arresting them as they arrived in Monument Circle in Indianapolis, the center of the downtown area.[51]

One group was arrested on a church lawn on the Circle even though they had been given permission to stand there by the church minister. A man who identified himself as a federal agent ordered the arrests over a walkie-talkie, telling the police that the demonstrators refused to move. In all, around twenty-eight people were arrested and taken to the Indianapolis jail, where they were held until ACLU lawyers could get them released. Among those arrested were IU student and Vietnam veteran Jeffrey Sharlet and psychology professor James Dinsmoor.

The IU-CEWV began raising money to pay the legal fees and bonds of those arrested. Talking to supporters over lunch at the Athletic Club, President Johnson had remarked that "We will abide civil protest." Demonstrators worried about possible jail terms were not so sure.[52]

On August 6, Hiroshima Day, about two hundred students, described by the conservative *Indianapolis Star* as "mop-haired and bearded," marched peacefully around the Bloomington square carrying signs of protest against the war. Later that day, Professor Dinsmoor addressed a crowd of around five hundred IU students, mostly members of CEWV, and urged them to form a splinter group within the Democratic Party and support Senator Robert F. Kennedy for President in 1968.[53]

Indiana University remained a relatively peaceful place in the mid-1960s. But President Elvis Stahr was apprehensive. While he presented an air of confidence, allowing well-known political critics like Herbert Aptheker to speak on campus, Stahr worried about the growth of the antiwar movement, not only in Bloomington, but across the country.

By the 1966–67 academic year, Stahr was well aware of his colleague Clark Kerr's recent experience with the Free Speech Movement at the University of California, Berkeley and the impact of the antiwar teach-ins at the University of Michigan. Despite the fact that students at IU had been relatively restrained in their political activities, Stahr was worried about potential disruptions and the effect that they would have on state legislators as they considered university appropriations, and this worry was evident in his annual "State of the University" speech to the faculty council in December 1966.

Stahr disparaged the New Left as a threat to academic freedom and drew an analogy to the challenges German universities before World War II faced from the Hitler Youth. As an administrator, he warned professors that New Leftists were trying to "drive a wedge between us" and that they would also try to "alienate the students from either or both of us." More to the point, however, he predicted, "If those determined either to disrupt or control us [i.e., the New Left] can alienate our public support from us, they will joyously do so, I can assure you."[54] His implications were fairly clear: if the legislature cuts the university's budget, the fault is with New Leftist activists.

In fact, Stahr was right to be concerned. Early in 1967, the Indiana state legislature cut the university's budget by $32 million in what the president and others read as a rebuff to IU's budding student movement. Activists were outraged at Stahr's remarks to the faculty. Robin Hunter, president of the student senate, wrote to Stahr, accusing him of "irresponsible and unethical behavior" in characterizing the New Left as a disruptive force, since "the facts surrounding student political organizations on this campus do not support your charges." Hunter then introduced a resolution in the senate requesting that Stahr furnish evidence to support his charges against the New Left or withdraw them. The bill failed to pass and Hunter, who had set out to take student politics out of the sandbox and into the university political arena, resigned. He called the senate's failure to pass the resolution "gutless . . . particularly when such an act implied taking a public stand against the sort of political intolerance and stifling of a free academic atmosphere which Stahr's speech, intentionally or not, contributed to." He told the senators, "You don't represent students—you represent people who want to get ahead in a system." Hunter's reaction was supported by SDS president and Vietnam veteran Jeffrey Sharlet, who described the New Left as "the outrage of Americans confronted with disparities between the real and the ideal. The role of the left is to make possible the visible confrontation of ideas on this campus." That state of the students, he said, showed the state of the campus better than President Stahr's address. In an editorial, the *Indiana Daily Student* called Hunter "one of the brightest members of an otherwise lackluster student senate," whose "ideas had forced the senate to think." Faced with administrative refusals to give students more control over their own lives, "the Robin Hunters throw up their hands in despair. We need their ideas. The administration is to blame."[55]

At the end of the 1966–67 academic year, IU's fledgling New Left had learned some lessons about organizing on a largely apolitical campus. The core of SDS remained true to its original cause of educating students to become concerned about and involved in the policies of their university as they connected with the injustices of the war in Vietnam, racial discrimination, and economic poverty in America. These early SDS members, such as Jim Wallihan, Bernella Satterfield, and David Satterfield, continued to believe that working with small groups of students in the dormitories, holding free university classes, and supporting other groups whose views were close to their own were the only way to achieve their long-term goal of bringing participatory democracy to the Bloomington campus. It was a slow process and one that did not bring immediate victories, but, as political organizers, they held on to these strategies.

Others, like Guy Loftman and Robin Hunter, argued that the best way to bring the message of the Port Huron Statement to more students at IU was to work with them on issues that directly affected their daily lives. Those students who joined the Progressive Reform Party saw student government as the most immediate vehicle for transforming an apathetic student body into one that could make dramatic changes in the way the university community functioned. Their style was confrontational, but they were willing to work within the existing student government framework in order to exert more student control. Loftman and Hunter felt that it made more sense to put international and national issues aside until a majority of students had become part of the decision-making process through personal involvement in more immediate matters, such as university parietal policies.

Finally, there were small groups, like YSA, YPSL, and the Du Bois Club, who felt their purpose was to serve as connections to national organizations with more radical ideologies. Their struggle at IU was not to win elections or to change policies but rather to give voice to larger issues of political dissent and, mainly, to survive.

Mirroring the movement on campuses across the country, student activists at IU in 1965–67 included a wide range of people, political ideas, organizations, and purposes. The smaller, more radical groups made no pretense of trying to build a large following among the student body. They held on to their own ideological positions without compromise, either with each other or with the majority. SDS wanted to change the way students thought about politics and social change at IU, in America, and around the world, and decided that success in achieving a radical transformation of Bloomington students demanded patient organizing. The founders of PRP, many of whom were still part of SDS, took a different approach. They wanted, in effect, to turn the system into an agent of change by trying to persuade students who had never been involved in politics before or those who had grown dissatisfied with earlier political action to join them in an aggressive campaign to gain control of student life. The people in SDS who disagreed with this approach were, for the most part, graduate students who did not see much of value in undergraduate political activities, mainly because they thought the administration had too much control over undergraduate affairs. Moreover, they were suspicious of playing to large crowds ("grandstanding") and worried that the rhetoric of student rights could get in the way of a more thoughtful and wide-ranging approach to radicalizing IU's student body.[56]

Student activists at IU tended to try to work together and support each other. When the Du Bois Club was threatened by university officials, SDS offered support, even though their political programs were quite different. When Loftman decided to form the Progressive Reform Party and run for student government office, not everyone in SDS went along with his ideas, but they generally voted for him and helped out when necessary. Loftman observed later that at one point, in the early days of PRP, he got together with other people in SDS and "we agreed to disagree."[57] At the same time, the opposition that New Leftists faced forced a certain amount of harmony within their ranks. When pro-war administrators tried to block their efforts to organize, SDS, CEWV, YSA, YPSL, and PRP might have had different initials but their general cause was much the same: to open the gates of the campus to a new wave of political and social consciousness that promised to do nothing less than change everyone's lives and change the world.

In the spring of 1967, Indiana University was a series of contradictions. With its picturesque grounds and almost completely white student population, IU appeared, on one level at least, to be a haven of traditional education at its Midwestern best: Hoosier parents' dreams come true. Yet Guy Loftman's success in the recent student elections ruffled the calm surface and brought an ominous hint of stormy student protests. Nightmares of Berkeley appeared in the minds of administrators, some faculty, and state legislators. Within the coming year, everyone in Bloomington would witness the storm's breaking.

CHAPTER **3**

The Antiwar Movement

From 1967 to 1969, student activists focused on the war in Vietnam. The antiwar movement increased in numbers and effectiveness and began to turn the nation against American policy in Southeast Asia. Beginning with the March on the Pentagon in October 1967, when thousands of young people gathered in the nation's capital to protest the war, more and more students—and their families—began to agree with critics of the war in Vietnam. When policymakers came to university and college campuses to make the government's case for the war, students asked questions that they could not or would not answer satisfactorily. Recruiters from large corporations faced protestors who criticized their companies' involvement in the war effort. Young men confronted national leaders directly when they defied the law and burned their draft cards, found ways of avoiding the draft, or, once in the army, began organizing resistance within their units.

Throughout this period, President Lyndon Baines Johnson, his military leaders, especially General William Westmoreland, and the press insisted that the war was going well. Americans received consistently positive reports about military progress in Vietnam and were promised "light at the end of the tunnel." But in February 1968, the Viet Cong launched an offensive against American bases during the Tet holiday, the Buddhist celebration of the lunar new year, usually a time when fighting ceased. The incredible fury of the guerrillas' attack, which included a brief assault on the American embassy in Saigon, left Americans stunned. Despite the fact that military leaders insisted that the Tet Offensive was a terrible defeat for the enemy because of the thousands who were killed in its aftermath, the Viet Cong won a psychological victory that was impossible to deny. After showing film of the Tet Offensive, veteran news analyst Walter Cronkite's reaction was, "What the hell is going on? I thought we were winning the war!" And if one of the most trusted newscasters in the nation was concerned, then lots of other Americans must have been as well.[1]

If the Tet Offensive left Americans stunned, then the assassinations of Dr. Martin Luther King, Jr., and Senator Robert F. Kennedy in April and June that same year left them numb. Two men who preached peace and brotherhood were gunned down within months of each other. These killings, in the wake of President John F. Kennedy's assassination in 1963, made it seem to many young people that their best and their brightest were victims of violence. Young blacks erupted in cities across the nation. Antiwar activists expressed their fury by demonstrating at the Democratic National Convention in Chicago. The Chicago police reacted with brutality that everyone could see on their television sets during the evening news. Protestors looked up at the cameras and chanted, "The whole world is watching"—and it was.

The result was that the Republican candidate, Richard M. Nixon, was elected president in November 1968. He hinted that he wanted peace in Vietnam and that he had a plan to end the war. He promised Americans that he would bring peace with honor and began implementing a policy—later known as "Vietnamization"—which involved placing heavier responsibility for fighting the ground war on Vietnamese troops while gradually withdrawing American forces. By the end of the decade, the antiwar movement, despite its successes, was fractured, discouraged, and, in some instances, a little crazy.

By 1969, America seemed to be splitting apart. And yet it was the antiwar movement that brought groups of all ages and all races together in opposition to the war that threatened our nation's soul. But as the war ground on, it was difficult for those inside the movement to see that any real progress had been made.

When IU students leave for summer vacation, Bloomington becomes a small town. The local residents are the "summer people," the regulars, the permanent citizens. As well as the students, many members of the faculty leave to pursue research projects or go to summer homes in places like Martha's Vineyard or the woods of Maine. There is, of course, a summer session at the university, but the number of students and faculty is not even half the number of the regular year. Parking places abound; shoppers cross once-busy streets with ease; there are no lines at the bank or at checkout stands in local markets. Business slows down and there is time for an extra cup of coffee at Ladyman's, a small restaurant on the town square that has daily lunch specials featuring solid fare like biscuits and gravy or meatloaf and mashed potatoes. When it gets hot, kids who grew up in town know the best quarry swimming holes. In short, Bloomington in the summer is an ordinary, pretty Midwestern town.

The summer of 1967 did not seem so blissful to some Bloomingtonians. For one thing, while most of the students followed their normal patterns of departure, many of the New Leftists, some of them graduate students with jobs or research grants, stayed on. Their presence guaranteed that quiet would not return peacefully in June. In fact, the summer began with a protest by about two hundred university and high school students against merchants on Kirkwood Avenue, the main street that connects the campus with the town square, lined with restaurants and small shops. Late one evening, students crowded outside restaurants where managers had ordered students with long hair to leave. The owner of the Pizzaria, one of the places that students frequented, said he asked them to leave because they sat in booths and did not order anything. The protestors claimed that their rights were being denied because of the way they looked. They gathered together on the sidewalk. Store owners, fearing violence, called the police and seven university students were arrested. Most were active in SDS, CEWV, or the Du Bois Club. Among those taken by the police were SDS members Jeffrey Sharlet and Jim Wallihan, and Joseph Fuhrman and Allen Gurevitz of the Du Bois Club. The arrests in and of themselves were not marked by any violence and the students were released shortly afterward. But the arrests indicated a new sense of confrontation between student activists and the local community.[2]

Members of the First Methodist Church began to complain about sponsoring projects that met at the Wesley Foundation's coffee house, the Owl, the place where students had met to support striking IU employees that spring. Not surprisingly, the president of Bloomington's American Legion rejected CEWV's float for a Fourth of July parade with a theme of "Let's Support Our Boys in Vietnam by Bringing Them Back."[3]

In August, SDS sponsored a "love-in" along the banks of the Jordan River in Dunn Meadow to commemorate Hiroshima Day. About three hundred people listened to songs and poems of protest against the war in Vietnam. Robert Johnson, president of the IU chapter of the NAACP, talked about race riots breaking out in U.S. cities.

Guy Loftman and Barry Wheeler, leaders of the Progressive Reform Party (PRP), had been successful in getting five thousand copies of the new faculty evaluations ready for distribution to new and returning students. Based on answers to 17,600 questionnaires, the 350-page document was designed to help students select courses more knowledgeably than ever before. Loftman also wanted to help students learn how the university operated, especially how the budget was set. However, when Loftman tried to get answers to questions of his own from the university treasurer's office, he found that the administration had quietly changed its policy on giving out information to inquiring students. All questions had to go through the dean of students instead of directly to the department involved. Making the dean the middleman in handling the increased number of student questions was done, according to one of the president's assistants, to help "speed things up."[4]

Events at IU were indeed speeding up. In his opening speech to students that fall, President Stahr noted that enrollment had more than doubled since he first came to Indiana in 1962, with more than 22,000 people now registered for classes. More construction was planned for the Bloomington campus: a new sports arena and assembly hall at the north side of the campus. This was one of the projects that Loftman and other students had been trying to find out about, particularly how the university was going to finance building these large facilities. Upon learning that student fees were to cover part of the costs, Loftman circulated petitions among over five thousand students, half of whom were opposed to building new sports facilities, and asked that the contracts be delayed. Stahr ignored Loftman and the petitions, and construction on the buildings began later that year.[5]

The war in Vietnam was speeding up as well, along with opposition to it. SDS began organizing buses to take students to Washington, D.C., for the October march against the war. As draft calls increased, individual IU students had protested at the Indianapolis induction center by passing out leaflets, turning in their draft cards, or refusing induction. The *Bloomington Tribune* reported that Guy Loftman had painted peace symbols on his body when he went for a preinduction physical examination in July, a story that Loftman refused to comment on and that a friend denied.[6] Another IU student protested the draft somewhat less dramatically by passing out antiwar leaflets at the Indianapolis army induction center and was promptly arrested by FBI agents.[7] In order to coordinate antidraft protests, about thirty representatives from SDS, CEWV, and the Du Bois club formed the Anti-Draft Union in October 1967. CEWV organizer Mark Oring brought student musicians together with traditional folk artists Roger Salloom and Peter Aceves for "Folk Movement," a musical benefit for the union. Some IU faculty members formed a group called Negotiation Now and sponsored a series of full-page advertisements against U.S. policy in Vietnam. Members of Negotiation Now joined with yet another local group, Hoosiers for Peace in Vietnam, to send petitions against the war to Indiana's representative in Washington, D.C.

While the petitions went to Washington in the mail, CEWV leader Mark Ritchey put together a caravan of buses and cars to take about two hundred IU students to march in Washington, D.C., on October 21, 1967. They joined a large contingent of Midwesterners from other colleges and universities. FBI sources counted a hundred students from Notre Dame and St. Mary's in South Bend, Indiana; another hundred from Earlham College in Richmond, Indiana; 150 from Southern Illinois University in Carbondale; and 150 from the University of Illinois at Urbana-Champaign. In all, over 100,000 protestors gathered in the nation's capital for a massive, peaceful demonstration against the war.[8]

The National Mobilization Committee to End the War in Vietnam (nicknamed "the Mobe") had organized a Stop the Draft Week from October 14 to 21, 1967. The point of this campaign was to confront Washington policymakers with the fact that thousands of young Americans—straights and hippies, blacks and whites, working class and middle class—were opposed to the war in Vietnam. The week ended on October 21 with the March on the Pentagon. Protestors gathered at the Lincoln Memorial, where they listened to music by Peter, Paul, and Mary and Phil Ochs and speeches by David Dellinger and Dr. Benjamin Spock.

Then the crowd marched across the Arlington Bridge toward the Pentagon, where they were met by military police. The protestors sang songs, talked to the troops, and joined together in a sense of community. Allen Ginsberg and Abbie Hoffman chanted "om" as they and others tried to levitate the Pentagon. However, by midnight the police were replaced by the 82nd Division and the scene turned ugly. Paratroopers cleared the area by beating peaceful protestors, who faced their attackers singing the national anthem. By the next morning, only a few hundred were left. The protest was over.

One IU student reported that she cried as she watched a young military policeman standing on guard with his rifle, his own cheeks washed with tears as he watched the demonstrations. Many of the IU students echoed Guy Loftman's description of the bus ride back to Bloomington as "one of the intellectually engaging times of my life." Organizer Mark Ritchey remembered sitting in the dark of the bus, reviewing the things he had seen and the speeches he had heard, and considered that the trip had transformed his view of America. From that time on, he saw himself as part of a movement that was larger than his own life. Those students from IU who had gone to the Stop the Draft Week in Washington realized that their resistance to the war was no longer a private, individual act. They were now part of a community that reached across the country and nothing would ever be the same for them again.[9]

The issue of the war in Vietnam simply could not be avoided in the fall of 1967. Student protests were escalating, not just in Washington, D.C., but on nearly every campus in the country. At the University of Wisconsin–Madison, three hundred protestors picketed outside the Commerce Building on October 18, protesting the presence of recruiters from Dow Chemical Company, manufacturers of napalm and chemical defoliants used by U.S. forces in Vietnam. Dow was a special target for those who opposed the war because its products most often hurt or killed noncombatants caught in villages under the flight paths of the American planes that sprayed the Vietnamese countryside from the air. During the Madison protest, local police used tear gas to break up the picketers, who fought back; in the confrontation fifty students and twenty policemen were injured. The university community was shocked at the outbreak of violence and faculty voted to condemn the use of Madison police on the campus. Three days after the Dow incident, two thousand students marched from the university to the state capitol building to protest the war in Vietnam, the presence of Dow recruiters on campus, and the use of force by police against demonstrators.

The rapid escalation of the Dow protest at Wisconsin might have served as a warning to university administrators that calling in local police could be counterproductive. Unfortunately, Indiana University officials drew somewhat different conclusions from the incident.[10] When Prof. J. Douglas Snider, director of the placement office at IU's business school, heard about the Dow protests and realized that the company would be recruiting on the Bloomington campus on Oct. 30, he called Capt. William G. Spannuth, IU's safety director, and warned him almost a week in advance. Spannuth went over to the business school to look over the recruiting offices and began planning the best way to remove any protestors from the area. He ordered four safety officers to patrol the building near the interview room. As an extra precaution, the sheriff of Monroe County deputized all the safety division officers, so that they could arrest students if they had to. Spannuth made sure that a campus bus would be available if he needed to take students to the county jail. Spannuth said that he did not inform President Stahr of these plans, nor did he talk with any students.[11]

Antiwar activists were indeed planning a demonstration, but not against Dow. Secretary of State Dean Rusk had announced that he would give a speech at Indiana University on October 31. In the eyes of most of the activists, his presence on campus was much more important than that of a couple of recruiters from Dow. Throughout the weekend, a co-alition of members of CEWV, SDS, and PRP made signs and leaflets to hand out before Rusk's speech. They had long strategy sessions, trying to decide the most effective way to express their opposition to the war at his speech, which they knew would bring national television and press cov-erage as well as a packed audience in the university's four-thousand-seat auditorium. They knew that Rusk was coming to the Midwest in search of a friendly reception for the administration's war policies. They were committed to denying him that pleasure. While they believed in the principle of nonviolent protest, they also felt that marching with signs was no longer enough. They decided that they would make sure that Rusk heard their dissent by heckling him throughout his speech.

Interspersing themselves throughout the hall, the two hundred or so demonstrators, wearing black armbands symbolizing their opposition to the war, would sit quietly, but at appropriate points in Rusk's speech would stand up and yell "murderer," "liar," or whatever other comment occurred to them. The idea of just being rude to Rusk appealed to them: it was nonviolent but a little dramatic, and, they hoped, it would disrupt Rusk's effort to persuade the country that Midwestern Americans sup-ported the war. As one antiwar activist explained,

> [Rusk] intrudes into all of our lives; he makes us all willing and unwilling accomplices in the destruction of Vietnam. . . . In the light of such political realities a breach of good manners seems of rather little consequence. . . . What possible good can a display of bad manners accomplish? After all, a man's mind is rarely changed by insults. It is not the administration's mind which must be changed, but its policy. One way that this can be done is by breaking the conventions of good manners by making it clear to Mr. Rusk and other policy makers that there is a vociferous group in the electorate which will not tolerate being filibustered or lied to and is not afraid to use social nastiness to combat the nastiness of war.[12]

On the morning of October 30, the day that Dow recruiters were in-terviewing job applicants at the business school and the day before Rusk's speech, CEWV members Mark Ritchey and Russell Block decided that the Dow visit could not go unnoticed by students opposed to the war. None of the students were aware that campus police had been preparing for a demonstration against Dow recruiters. However, students did under-stand that whenever they protested on campus against the war, they were subject to disciplinary action and, perhaps, arrest. They talked with others who were involved in the Rusk protest. Some agreed to join with them to demonstrate against Dow; others, including Guy Loftman, de-clined. Loftman reasoned that demonstrating against the secretary of state was much more important than protesting the policies of Dow Chemical. Moreover, he pointed out, if the Dow protests resulted in any arrests, someone had to be free to get everyone else out of jail.[13]

At 1:00 P.M. Block and Ritchey spoke to about thirty students in the plaza by Ballantine Hall, the main arts and sciences classroom building. When faculty members complained that they were disturbing classes, they marched over to the business school. Walking at the head of the small group, Block turned to Ritchey and asked ironically, "Is this what it feels like to lead a revolution?"[14]

When they arrived at the business school's placement office, they asked to see the Dow representative in order to ask him about the company's production of napalm for use in Vietnam. A secretary told them that only those who had already submitted résumés and signed up for appointments could come into the office. They sat on the floor in the hallway and began tearing out pages from their notebooks, scrawling signs saying, "Check your appearance. Are you responsible enough to be interviewed by the makers of jellied death?" A small group of curious business school students looked on, and some engaged in a little heckling, but the demonstrators sat next to the wall, leaving space to walk along the hall, and handed out leaflets to those walking through the building. Dean Herbert Smith, from the office of the dean of students, joined Captain Dillon, the head of the campus police, in telling the demonstrators they would be arrested if they tried to get into the interview room. After talking quietly among themselves, the protestors decided that they should try to get into the interview room in a peaceful way to demonstrate their commitment to opposing the war. Captain Dillon stood in the doorway as the students linked arms and began to push against him. They succeeded in breaking his grip, walked through the door, settled down on the floor of the interview office's reception area, and waited to meet with the Dow recruiters. Dillon called the Bloomington police department, and officers soon arrived. The police were followed by deputies from the county sheriff's office, who immediately informed the students they were under arrest and ordered them to leave quietly. About half of them got up and were led outside to a campus bus for the ride to the county jail. The police then began dragging out those who remained in the business school, and in the process they began hitting students with newly issued riot sticks. One girl yelled out, "police brutality." A policeman ordered, "get the colored boy" (Robert Johnson was the only African American in the group) and the scene deteriorated quickly into violence. Several students were hit in the head and upper body, leaving them with bruises and contusions. George Walker, Russell Block's roommate and a graduate student in English, was dragged into the bus with blood streaming from his ear, the result of a perforated eardrum.

The thirty-five demonstrators who were arrested on the afternoon of October 30 were taken to the county jail and charged with disorderly conduct. Guy Loftman met them at the jail and began contacting history professors Leonard Lundin and Irene Neu and local businessman Larry Canada to help post bond. Walker and fellow protestor Dwight Worker were taken to the Bloomington hospital with head injuries. What had begun as a spontaneous gesture against Dow Chemical Company became the most violent confrontation on the Bloomington campus.[15]

The next day the protest against Rusk went exactly as scheduled. After a march around Showalter Fountain, about two hundred protestors sat in various places in the auditorium, which was, as expected, filled to capacity with cheering supporters. They carried out their plan to heckle Rusk, who refused to acknowledge their taunts and continued his speech. There was one small scuffle when an enraged elderly woman in the audience hit a protestor over the head with her umbrella. Rusk finished his remarks and left campus with a police escort.[16]

While the Rusk protest had gone as planned, antiwar activists had not anticipated the extraordinarily negative reaction their demonstration created. It seemed that nearly everyone—students, faculty, and townspeople—was angry at their treatment of the secretary of state. Activists' faith in nonviolence may have led them to underestimate Bloomington's and Indiana University's regard for politeness. Bad manners left a bad taste.

About fourteen thousand students signed apologies to Rusk for the protestors' actions, and an anonymous donor paid for two students to fly to Washington, D.C., to present them to Rusk at a televised press conference. The antiwar faculty group Negotiation Now joined in the denunciation of the Rusk hecklers. History professor Leonard Lundin offered a lone voice in their defense in a letter to the *Indiana Daily Student*. Arguing that Rusk threatened students' lives much more than those of the faculty or the administration by forcing them to fight in a war that they considered immoral, he wrote,

> It is an ugly thing to call a man a murderer. It is an uglier thing to force a man to be a murderer; and that is precisely what many young men think Mr. Rusk and his associates are trying to do to them. Is it really such a terrible, unforgivable thing, then, when anger—in my opinion a rationally-based anger—at this state of things explodes into epithets—not, it seems clear to me, against a speaker as such but against a shaper and implementer of policy?[17]

Secretary of State Dean Rusk waves as he enters the auditorium. *Arbutus*, 1968.

As pro-war students cheer Rusk, protestors hold up peace armbands and heckle the secretary of state during his speech. *Arbutus*, 1968.

In the midst of the outrage over the protest against Rusk, the Dow demonstrators, out on bail, faced university disciplinary charges as well. Most of them had been involved in the Rusk protest, with the exception of George Walker and Dwight Worker, who were injured during the Dow protest. Campus reaction to the Dow demonstration was different— mainly because students and faculty resented the use of Bloomington police on campus and the excessive force they displayed during the arrests. On November 1, over one hundred students went into the president's office to protest the police action and to argue that allowing Dow to use university facilities to recruit employees constituted implicit support of the company's part in the Vietnam war.

While the board of trustees and the faculty council congratulated the administration on its actions against the Dow demonstrators, the student senate charged Dean of Students Robert Shaffer with violating the student bill of rights, violation of due process, and a general lack of fairness. The accused students, the senators noted, faced double jeopardy: they were being tried by both civil and university authorities. About sixty-five members of the faculty met in December to criticize the university's handling of the Dow incident. The final faculty committee report, written by professors Albert Klassen (sociology), Frederick Stare (psychology), Priscilla Zirker (English), and Charles Eckert (English), was highly critical of the administration, charging that the university safety division's advance planning and inflexible policy contributed to the violence of the incident. They also condemned the calling in of the city police and county sheriff's office.[18]

About forty faculty members who opposed the war organized the Faculty Committee for Peace in Vietnam. Historian Fritz Ringer noted that many committee members were unhappy with the conservative views expressed by the faculty council and the "overly cautious" local chapter of the AAUP.[19]

Early in October, as soon as antiwar activists in CEWV and SDS knew that the secretary of state was going to speak about national war policy at IU, they had joined with the faculty committee to invite historian Howard Zinn, an outspoken civil rights activist and critic of the Vietnam war, to lead a Vietnam teach-in on the theme "The Logic of Withdrawal." IU faculty, a local Unitarian minister, and Willie Meyers, who had resigned in protest from the International Voluntary Service after serving in Vietnam, also participated in the daylong event early in December. Speaking to an audience of over 2,500, Zinn attacked President Lyndon Johnson and the war and urged students to address themselves to fundamental issues that contributed to promoting life, not ending it.

Zinn's appearance was followed the next week in December by an un-scheduled visit by Carl Davidson, national secretary of SDS and author of a widely read article, "Toward Student Syndicalism," who rallied New Leftists to continue in their struggle to gain control over their lives, break down the myths and rhetoric of power, and decentralize authority. "A participatory democracy is not a political system," he told other members of SDS (along with two deans in the audience), "but a set of values."[20] Davidson's visit preceded a national meeting of SDS in Bloomington at the end of the year. While the New Left gathered in Indiana, Hoosier football fans celebrated their first trip to the Rose Bowl in the university's history.

Indiana University SDS members who stayed for the national meeting talked with national SDS officers and other members about the war, racism and poverty in America, and what their roles should be in trying to resolve these issues. Was SDS a university organization or did its members belong out in the community?

SDS members debated the effectiveness of demonstrations like the Dow protests at Bloomington, Madison, and other university campuses. While some agreed that these events attracted new people to SDS, others argued that they used up scarce financial resources in legal defenses. Members also discussed the value of large national protests like the recent demonstration at the Pentagon. Previously, SDS had stood apart from single-issue, antiwar activity. However, most now agreed that this type of action was valuable, even though it would not broaden the base of the movement. They agreed to participate in ten days of protest in April 1968, in Washington, D.C. FBI observers noted that a few members of YSA had set up an information table at the conference and sold $180 worth of publications. One of the best sellers was a pamphlet by Malcolm X.[21]

For IU SDS members the new year brought the consequences of their antiwar activities. A local judge found six of the Dow protestors guilty of disorderly conduct, fined them from $25 to $100, and sentenced them to ten days in jail. Robert Johnson was singled out for a more severe punishment. Although his lawyer argued that the confusion in the business school office made the prosecution's case difficult if not impossible to prove, he was found guilty of assault and battery against a police officer, sentenced to sixty days in jail, and fined $130. Another protestor, George Walker, recovered from his injuries only to learn that he had lost his position as a student teacher in the Unionville school district because of his participation in the Dow incident. The ACLU began an investigation and Walker, a former member of the Marine Corps, defended his position: "Signing up to work for Dow isn't like signing up with everyone else. I don't like what napalm does to kids in Vietnam."

Walker eventually completed his student teaching at the Bloomington University School, operated by the university's school of education, but his case was a clear signal that antiwar activists who dared to question the morality of the war and those who participated in it were not welcome in southern Indiana communities.[22]

CEWV organizers Mark Ritchey and Russell Block began planning a demonstration against representatives of the CIA, who were scheduled to visit IU in February 1968. Taking a lesson from the Dow protest, they urged antiwar activists to sign up for interviews in order to ask recruiters questions about CIA policies and programs. After learning about the signups, the CIA canceled its visit to IU, explaining that the agency did not want to disrupt normal academic life.

Dow Chemical Company was not as easily discouraged as the CIA, and Dow recruiters again appeared on the IU campus in March. They refused to meet with CEWV members to discuss their role in the war. About 250 students marched to the business school, where they were met by the Victory in Vietnam Committee (students who supported the war) holding signs saying "Welcome Dow Chemical." Having worked out arrangements with administrators before the demonstration, CEWV members burned a plastic doll to symbolize the children burned by Dow's napalm in Vietnam while Dean Shaffer mingled with the crowd. Dow executives did agree to send a representative to debate Dow's war role with a student. When students listened to David Coslett, Dow's news and information manager, and Robin Hunter, IU graduate student and antiwar organizer, they voted 361 to 176 against Dow's position that it manufactured napalm for use in Vietnam as part of its national duty.[23]

Student elections were held that spring. The 1968 campaign offered IU students a clear choice of candidates for student body president. Impact, one of the student political parties, was led by Ted Najam, son of an IU faculty member who had served as dean. Ted was an active fraternity member, clean-cut, and on good terms with many administrators, especially Herman B Wells. He argued that IU students would be better served by a student body president who looked respectable to the state legislature and who could argue for student rights in a conciliatory style.

PRP members had been shocked when they learned that, after receiving his draft notice, Guy Loftman had resigned as president of the student body, dropped out of graduate school, and moved to a friend's farm in nearby Brown County. After examining his beliefs and seriously discussing them with his wife, Connie, Guy chose to declare himself a conscientious objector on religious grounds. Under the terms of the draft law, conscientious objectors were required to perform two years of alternative service, and Guy chose to work as an orderly in the Bloomington Hospital.[24]

Dean Robert Shaffer announced his resignation as dean of students at about the same time. Shaffer said he wanted to rest before returning to IU to resume teaching in the school of education.[25]

Mark Oring, a New Yorker who had been active in New Left politics in the East, stepped in to run as PRP's candidate. Oring continued to advocate Loftman's principles of participatory democracy and student power over their own lives. This time, unlike in the 1967 election, the fraternity vote was solidly united behind a single candidate and PRP election management was not in Connie Loftman's capable hands. Najam won by over a thousand votes. New Leftists were cynical about the defeat: "Indiana University students have a monomania for self-destruction; no other group of college students in the world could possibly sign away self-determination in order to keep up appearances."[26]

The Young Americans for Freedom (YAF) were delighted at PRP's defeat. R. Emmett Tyrell, Jr., a graduate student in history and conservative activist, concluded that the New Left "is burning itself out" and that Indiana University was "the first university to toss out the New Left." Tyrell was especially hostile to New Leftists, describing them as "an expanding crowd of bug-eyed messiahs heralding a New Age." With financial support from the Lilly Foundation, he founded a conservative student publication, *The Alternative: An American Spectator,* and focused his attention on condemning New Leftists on campus.[27]

Despite setbacks in campus politics, CEWV and YSA members planned a three-day series of events at the end of April as part of a national protest against the war. On April 25, *Time* magazine sponsored a poll called Choice 68, a mock presidential election, on campuses across the country, so that students could express their support for or opposition to the war. The next day saw a peace fair in Dunn Meadow and a student strike, part of the National Student Mobilization Committee's International Student Strike against War, Racial Oppression, and the Draft. About one-fourth of the student body and sixty faculty members honored the strike. On April 27, CEWV members joined with the IU Faculty Committee for Peace in Vietnam and the Committee of Returned Volunteers in Indianapolis to march with other Hoosiers from Purdue University, Notre Dame, Indiana State University, Indiana Central University, and Ball State University who were against the war. They walked from the War Memorial, a large monument in the city center, to the state house, where they asked the governor, Democrat Roger D. Branigin, to refuse to support President Johnson's war policy.[28]

Governor Branigin had been President Johnson's stand-in candidate in the Indiana Democratic primary election. President Johnson announced his decision not to run for reelection on March 31, and Robert F. Kennedy won the primary on May 7, 1968. He defeated both Johnson and Senator Eugene McCarthy of Minnesota, who had come out against the war first and had nearly defeated Johnson in the earlier New Hampshire primary. Kennedy's campaign in Indiana had reached out to Hoosier students even though most radical activists despaired of both "peace" candidates, seeing both men as inextricably part of the liberal establishment that was the cause of American racism at home and involvement in Vietnam. However, some IU students had campaigned for McCarthy in Wisconsin and Indiana and remained loyal to him because of his political courage in being the first candidate to oppose a sitting president and his war policy, even though many were uncomfortable with his unwillingness to discuss racial issues.

Kennedy made the most eloquent speech of the campaign in Indianapolis, on April 4, 1968, the day Dr. Martin Luther King, Jr., was assassinated. Speaking in a sad voice from the back of a flat-bed truck to a crowd of African Americans, Kennedy said,

> I ask you tonight to return home, to say a prayer for the family of Martin Luther King, that's true, but more importantly for our own country. . . . Let us dedicate ourselves to what the Greeks wrote so many years ago; to tame the savageness of man and make gentle the life of this world.
> Let us dedicate ourselves to that, and say a prayer for our country and ourselves.[29]

On April 24, 1968, over four thousand IU students and faculty listened to Kennedy give a major foreign policy speech in Bloomington. Thousands of Purdue students and faculty applauded when he spoke there about poverty in America. And, in Indianapolis, Kennedy confronted hostile conservative IU medical students in a question-and-answer session about racism, poverty, and the war. Many activists regarded Kennedy as an opportunist and a ruthless politician, but he did address the important issues of that year—the divisions produced by class and race at home and the war in Vietnam.[30]

Finally, in a year filled with unexpected twists and turns, Elvis J. Stahr announced his resignation. Citing "presidential fatigue," Stahr made his statement to a surprised group of trustees at their meeting in June. Chancellor Herman B Wells had agreed to serve as interim president until a successor could be hired, and in the meantime Stahr would stay on in Bloomington until he decided what his next move would be.

Within a few months he accepted the presidency of the National Audubon Society and moved to Washington, D.C.[31]

By June 1968, many of IU's administrators and activists were exhausted. Yet a core group of activists were ready to return in the fall for what looked like another year of turmoil. The struggle for student power and the protests against the war in Vietnam had reached new levels of tension. The divisions within the university and within the town of Bloomington were becoming increasingly evident. While few agreed on the value of student efforts to promote participatory democracy and to end the war in Vietnam, everyone knew that they had been through a year unlike any they had ever experienced.

During April and May, Americans had watched students at Columbia University battle New York City police as they took over ("liberated") campus buildings and forced the university to shut down when thousands of students, joined by some faculty, went out on strike. The Columbia protest sent shock waves through the academic community, both at home and abroad. During that spring, students around the world, from Paris to Prague, took to the streets. Administrators and board members were incensed. Students, even middle-of-the-road observers, understood that something revolutionary had occurred. And most parents were mystified—what in the hell was going on?

When pundits pronounced that student unrest and antiwar protests only happened in big cities or on large university campuses on the coasts, most Bloomington residents and IU students, faculty, and staff who had lived through the past year could only shake their heads. It was not just the edges of the nation that were frayed. Students at Indiana University proved that there was dissent in the very heart of the country.

The somewhat unlikely leader of that dissent at IU was Ted Najam, IU's student body president, who spent the summer of 1968 quietly at his parents' home in Bloomington. His father and mother were away and he was on his own in the town he had lived in since he was seven years old. His father was a professor in the French department and had been a dean at IU. Ted had gone to public schools in Bloomington before attending IU and was about to begin his senior year there, before going on to Harvard University's law school. Clean-cut, short-haired, conservatively dressed, a fraternity member, and a model student, Ted Najam was a trustee's dream come true as an undergraduate leader. After a year of Guy Loftman's often aggressive and combative style, board members welcomed Najam to their summer meeting like a long-lost son. That first gathering, Najam recalled, felt like a homecoming.[32]

As he prepared for the trustee meeting and for the year ahead, Najam spent the summer thoughtfully assessing the situation on the Bloomington campus. He believed that most students wanted to continue many of Loftman's students' rights programs. However, Najam wanted to try to promote peace with faculty and administrators by presenting these proposals in a more conventional tone—with reasonable rhetoric and reassuring phrases. Alone in the house, he sat at his typewriter and wrote a paper to present to the board at its August meeting, outlining his fears about the tensions between students and administrators that pervaded the campus, his own opposition to the war in Vietnam, and his hopes for promoting a spirit of reconciliation among faculty members and administrators.

Like his hero, President John F. Kennedy, Najam was a pragmatist and a good liberal. He supported the ideals of the civil rights movement, although he had never actively participated in it. As an undergraduate, he knew how popular Loftman's students' rights campaign was and how strongly committed many student activists were to it. He also sensed how easy it would be to bring many moderate students to open rebellion if the trustees adopted repressive policies. He wanted to avoid needless confrontation by explaining to the board that Bloomington students could be appeased by easing restrictions on women's hours, dormitory visitation privileges, and off-campus housing. The paper that he presented, "A Look at the Student Conscience," was a plea for IU's administrators "to make change gracefully, . . . for self-examination and change without substantial upheaval in its own social and academic order." He presented his paper in August 1968, while Bloomington and the rest of the world watched police beating students on the streets outside the Democratic party's convention in Chicago.[33]

Najam's proposals found a receptive audience. The board accepted his entire program. His earnest appeal to the trustees to accept the inevitability of changes in relationships between university administrators and students was convincing. They may not have liked the message, but they believed the messenger. They were much more willing to work with Najam than with his combative predecessor, Guy Loftman. In that one August meeting they rescinded all limitations on women's hours, allowed open dormitory visitation, and allowed any student who wished to, to live off campus. As trustee Jesse Eschenbach explained, "The board will get beat up either way we go. As long as we're going to lose blood, let's lose a ton of it.[34]

Eschenbach's words were prophetic, but, for the moment, any symbolic blood loss by trustees was largely overlooked by students beginning the fall term in an atmosphere of restless uncertainty. The board's acquiescence to their demands for control of their private lives was proof that change was in the air, but no one seemed to have any clear idea of its direction. Acting president Herman B Wells acknowledged that the university should not have used its resources to enforce parietal rules in his state of the university speech, adding, "One of the easiest things in the world is to say 'no' to change; one of the hardest is to provide for its reasoned and orderly occurrence."[35] However, the challenge for IU's student activists was to move beyond the successfully concluded campaign to change university policies on student life to larger, national concerns: the war in Vietnam.

About a hundred SDS members held a rally that fall to discuss IU's involvement in the war effort. They had already begun an investigation into several research projects funded under Project Themis, a Defense Department program aimed at supporting military-related research projects at state university campuses. They also decided to focus on military recruitment on campus and the ROTC program—both were easily recognizable symbols of IU's involvement in military affairs. As in previous years, SDS worked with members of CEWV and YSA in their campaigns. With some persistent nudging from former PRP member Mark Oring, student body president Ted Najam supported some New Left causes. At a September senate meeting, Najam announced his sympathy for "our brothers . . . sitting in again at Columbia." A confused reporter from the *Indiana Daily Student* who was covering the meeting wrote, "After deliberating on this comment for quite some time, and having decided that Ted didn't mean fraternity brothers, we find it all rather interesting."[36]

Writing about the New Left at IU in the fall of 1968, *Indiana Daily Student* editor Linda Kuntz found that members ranged from political moderates to radicals but that most were "deeply devoted to the ideals of freedom and democracy and have been driven to what some would call 'militantism' by the frustration and disillusionment of their ideals, these same ideals, incidentally, that were taught to them in college and high school." After interviewing many of the leaders of the antiwar movement at IU, especially from CEWV, she concluded, "Contrary to what at least some of my professors think these persons are not hippies . . . they are students of philosophy, or history, and government. They are idealists in the highest sense, who are disillusioned and frustrated."[37]

Part of the frustration many activists at IU experienced that fall grew from their continued difficulties in gathering a greater number of moderate students to their fold. In September and October they campaigned against a university policy that allowed campus security officers to wear guns on campus. Former president Stahr had banned their use after the Dow incident in 1967, but officers won the right to carry guns again after administrators agreed to that part of a new contract negotiated with union representatives of AFSCME Local 832 during the following summer. At a rally on campus between Ballantine and Woodburn Halls during the first week of October, Robert Johnson (former president of the Afro–Afro-American Students Association), Mark Oring, and Ted Najam made speeches arguing that campus police should not be armed. Oring said that officers should be given more training and higher salaries rather than weapons, although he hardly won fans in the force when he noted, "We hire the dregs of society to be campus police." The faculty council voted to disarm the police. However, thirty-seven campus security officers sued Oring in separate suits for $20,000 damages each for "false and malicious statements" for his "dregs of society" remark.[38]

The next week, recruiters from the U.S. Marine Corps faced about a hundred students in the union building, who challenged them to defend the war in Vietnam and the use of military force in U.S. foreign policy. The confrontation was peaceful except for a minor disturbance when someone set off a stink bomb in the afternoon and the building had to be cleared for an hour. The marines signed up eighteen men. Antiwar protestors declared the day a success because they were finally able to discuss national involvement in Vietnam with military recruiters.[39]

By the end of 1968, it was clear that the Progressive Reform Party was defunct. With its campaign issues effectively coopted by Ted Najam's victory as president the previous spring and without the enthusiasm and organizing skills of Connie and Guy Loftman, it dwindled to about twenty members, who criticized themselves for trying to develop a platform for a party "we consider almost dead" at their first meeting. There really was no other organization to take its place as an umbrella political party for activists to use for campus-wide action on student issues. Some, like CEWV, were directed toward building a broad constituency around a single goal—ending the war in Vietnam. SDS members focused on several campus political campaigns involved in ending university participation in military and government intelligence programs and on redistributing power within the campus community. The Du Bois Club and YSA were too sectarian to attract more than a small number of activists at IU in 1968. However, since most activists belonged to more than one group, membership lists tended to be overlapping and did not indicate how many people would participate in any given political event.

One of the great myths that has emerged from the Sixties is that most students took part in antiwar demonstrations. That certainly was not true on most American college and university campuses and it was especially not true at Indiana University. As historian Terry Anderson noted in *The Movement and the Sixties,* "student activists were a minority on every campus and concerning every issue throughout the decade." It is important to remember that during the 1960s Young Americans for Freedom, a conservative political group, and Youth for Christ, a fundamentalist religious youth group, had more members than SDS or any other leftist organization ever had. Opponents of the war were often isolated. Journalist Bil Gilbert visited a small town in Pennsylvania, for instance, where he found nearly unanimous support for the war. The only exception was one young high school girl who "was working at being a hippie" and who opposed the war. Gilbert observed that people talked about her in the same way witches were described centuries earlier. While that observation may sound extreme, it was not entirely out of line with mainstream conversations in the 1960s.[40]

The power that antiwar activists had came from the fact that they were usually the most intellectual, the most verbal, and the most energetic undergraduate and graduate students. They were generally more interested in the liberal arts, whereas most conservatives majored in more scientific and technical subjects like engineering or business administration. And they were on the offensive; they were the ones taking action. Conservative and moderate students found themselves reacting to activists' demonstrations, which made them less visible and, consequently, less memorable. But the fact remains that antiwar activists understood that they were a minority and that their struggle was one that placed them on the edges of the American political, social, and cultural spectrum.

Still, a core group of about two to three hundred undergraduate and graduate IU students continued to protest university policies and the war in Vietnam. They knew that despite the relaxation of campus rules, the structure of authority in the university remained virtually unchanged. Because of their public participation in demonstrations against the war and the military presence on campus, protestors came under increasingly close scrutiny by university administrators. Since IU officials were not particularly secretive about the fact that they were watching student activists, there was a sense of paranoia among some students. In hindsight, this all appears to have been a perverse kind of cat-and-mouse game. Yet, at that time and in that atmosphere, the idea that Big Brother was watching could be unnerving and personally destabilizing—even if the observer was no more than a hired student from the dean's office taking notes at an SDS or CEWV planning meeting.

One reason that students found observation so threatening was that the board of trustees had given administrators the power to expel any student who "actively engages in any conduct which includes violence or the threat of violence and which obstructs or disrupts university work or activity . . . or who engages in conduct which unreasonably interferes with the freedoms of movement of persons on any campus of the university."[41] Expulsion alone was a stiff penalty for planning or taking part in any activity as vaguely defined as those in the board's new ruling, but when expulsion also meant immediate loss of the student draft exemption and almost certain induction into the army, the punishment took on a whole new meaning. Protesting against university authority became an act of much greater significance when it brought the possibility of being killed in a war that was itself the object of the protest. An intensified feeling of "us" against "them" was apparent in the fall of 1968. Students and administrators lined up on opposite sides when they tried to talk about whose purposes the university was to serve. The middle "liberal" ground that Najam had staked out was increasingly suspect among student activists.

On October 17, 1968, Andrew Masiello came to IU to recruit students as civilian army personnel. SDS organizers decided to protest his presence on campus. They went into his office in Ballantine Hall and began to question him about national policies and the war in Vietnam. SDS leader Mike King announced, "We want to make their machine visible. We don't want military recruiters here. We don't want ROTC recruiters here. We don't want civilian personnel recruiters here." When questioned about army procedures in Vietnam, Masiello answered, "I too wish the war were over." When asked why he worked for the army, he replied, "They pay me every payday. Actually I'm a lousy salesman." Protestors knew that they were being watched by members of the dean of student's office with cameras and tape recorders. They also watched Masiello and listened to his responses, and realized that they saw "too much of ourselves" in him. "Were we any better . . . we, the potential recruitees, able to slide from our special student status into safe defense department jobs, avoid the war, or at least think we had. If the system needs its skilled computer programmers, we will possess the skill . . . we can live under the illusion that we control the computer." In the end, the protestors left Masiello's recruiting office and marched over to Bryan Hall "to confront the closed doors of the Open University." Acting president Wells agreed to meet with them later, but at least one student left the incident wondering, "Whose door do we wait outside and whose do we march in?"[42]

As it turned out, SDS members did not march in or out of any doors after the incident. They decided to present Wells with a list of demands for a meeting that began with the following statement: "We condemn all ties which link IU to the military apparatus: recruiting in our recreational facilities, learning how to kill in our classrooms, performing military research in our laboratories. . . . The choice is a simple one, if justice, humanity, and honor still mean anything at IU." Their demands included the use of the university auditorium for the meeting with Wells; aisle microphones for students' questions; and a meeting of at least two hours, with the stipulation that Wells speak for no more than ten minutes during that period. He declined to meet with SDS, arguing that allowing him to speak for just ten minutes out of a two-hour meeting was not fair.

Wells said later that he had wanted to meet with SDS but that advisors had warned that students would probably make it impossible for him to be heard. However, it is hard to imagine him submitting to the conditions presented by SDS. His record as president of Indiana University was one of quiet negotiations, well-placed telephone calls, carefully arranged meetings, and close personal involvement that resulted in mutual agreements to solve campus problems. Open confrontations under the limitations imposed by SDS demands were so uncharacteristic of Wells's style that his refusal to take part in the meeting should have come as no surprise to anyone who knew his record.[43]

In addition, Wells did not approach the issue of defense-funded research in the same way that SDS protestors did. From his point of view, faculty freedom to pursue research interests was of paramount concern. As long as the funding was legal and the project had professional merit, he saw himself as a protector of the faculty's freedom to perform research, regardless of whose ends that research might serve. Just as he had protected Professor Kinsey from attacks by those who found his interest in human sexuality immoral, so, too, would he protect those who were working in areas that served the defense department's needs in a war that students considered immoral. Wells simply did not see morality as an issue in these cases. What he did see was that the faculty had the right to obtain funds legally to pursue their professional interests, and that right was firmly ingrained in his own vision of his role as head of Indiana University. Wells answered SDS in an open letter published in the *Indiana Daily Student*. While he acknowledged that "sharp cleavages of opinion about the national involvement in Vietnam have brought pressures on the university," he stated that he would resist student "demands," a word he found inappropriate for discussions within the university community. "The questions raised by the S.D.S., I wish to emphasize, do not concern extra curricular activities or regulations affecting student life as have issues raised earlier by students. The S.D.S. demands invade the area of academic programs and the scholar's freedom to pursue his research interests." Further, he justified ROTC training because it was required at all land-grant institutions and IU administrators had decided that students who wanted to participate should have it available to them in Bloomington and not be forced to choose a land-grant university, like Purdue. He defended research funded by government support as necessary to many department programs and argued that all contracts were negotiated openly, concerned only unclassified projects, and were conducted under strict regulations. While admitting that students were correct in their claims that they were under administrative observation, he argued that university police were helping local authorities fight crime and he concluded that SDS fears of federal investigators were groundless. "I know of no secret police on campus."[44]

However, the FBI did have undercover informants at IU, as well as at other campuses across the country in 1968. New Leftists were targeted in 1967, but Hoover's agents had already focused on Dr. Martin Luther King, Jr., the Du Bois Clubs, and the Socialist Workers Party earlier in the decade. Hoover was especially concerned by the potential threat he saw from alliances between the civil rights and antiwar campaigns. After Dr. King announced his opposition to the Vietnam war at the Riverside Church in New York City in April 1967, Hoover ordered his agents to increase their efforts to infiltrate and undermine New Left organizations. As historian Kenneth O'Reilly observed, "Hoover constructed an unprecedented surveillance system—a system that reflected his belief that any movement for social change was dangerous."[45]

FBI agents infiltrated campus groups and tried to encourage interpersonal conflicts and paranoia, along with spreading misinformation about meetings and protests. They set students up for drug busts. One of their favorite methods was to write anonymous letters to the parents of antiwar activists, warning them of dire consequences awaiting their children, especially concerning their future employment. Hoover was particularly interested in alerting parents of daughters to the "depraved nature and moral looseness of the New Left."[46]

Bloomington was the primary focus of the Indianapolis FBI office. Reports to the Bureau's headquarters indicate that there were at least two paid informants at IU, one of whom had been elected to an office of a student group; "through this connection he is able to attend all of the open meetings and many of the closed meetings of the various New Left organizations at IU. He is also able to obtain information concerning their plans at IU." The FBI agents admitted, however, that they had been unable to penetrate any of the black student groups. The FBI included "all of the ringleaders of the New Left movement . . . on the Security Index of the Indianapolis Division." Local agents had instructions to interview New

Left leaders aggressively, "constantly reminding them that they are of security interest to the United States Federal Government." Other tactics, such as using "friendly news media" to observe and disrupt student meetings, were employed only when Bureau permission was specifically given. FBI agents had kept President Stahr informed of potential problems among student activists, and Stahr recalled that he had found their advice helpful and generally accurate. Students were sometimes suspicious of some members of activist organizations but never certain enough to confront them. Wells's denial of secret police on campus may have reflected his lack of direct knowledge, but it is unlikely that he was unaware of the FBI's interest in Bloomington's New Left leaders.[47]

In their zeal to confront the acting president, SDS members had misjudged the situation. Any possibility of talking with Wells about IU's involvement in Southeast Asian policies and the military's presence on campus, if indeed there had ever been one, was lost. Wells, worried about the university's position in negotiations with the state legislature's budget committee in the early 1969 session, urged the board of trustees to name a new president as quickly as possible. During the middle of November 1968, Joseph Sutton, vice president and dean of the faculties at IU, was made IU's thirteenth president, despite private warnings from former president Stahr that although Sutton had proven himself to be an able administrator, he had alcohol-related problems that could cause serious difficulties if he did not receive treatment. Shortly after the announcement of Sutton's selection was made, Wells left for Bangkok, Thailand, to receive an honorary degree.[48]

Student concerns about surveillance remained high. Their fear was not alleviated when Du Bois Club organizer Bob Grove was arrested and brought to trial on drug charges in November. Bloomington police said that they had been tipped off by Grove's landlord and, entering his apartment without a valid search warrant or Grove's permission to do so, found pipes thought to be used for smoking marijuana. Grove and his brother, John, had been among the first members of SDS at IU and Bob Grove's views against the war had been the subject of at least one extended interview by a Bloomington newspaper. Grove, a twenty-seven-year-old history student, was from Lapel, Indiana, a small farming community northeast of Indianapolis, and had become interested in politics during his service in the army in France during the Algerian revolt. After his discharge in 1958 he had joined the Socialist Party and organized civil rights demonstrations with the NAACP at Ball State University in Muncie, Indiana, where he was enrolled as an undergraduate. After corresponding with SDS national officers, Grove dropped out of school for a year to set up SDS chapters at Purdue University, Notre Dame, and Indiana State. Denied readmission at Ball State, Grove enrolled at Indiana University and, along with twenty or thirty others, founded a chapter of the Du Bois Club. Older than most undergraduates, Grove was known as a quiet, serious student; a local reporter wrote, "he doesn't look like a wild-eyed agitator." During the trial, Grove's landlord testified that he had seen communist literature delivered to Grove's mailbox and he "knew he was a criminal." Yet many students who knew Grove fairly well commented on his strong antidrug philosophy. In fact, Grove was remarkable, they said, because he was so straight, so committed to his cause that the hippie, drug lifestyle was alien to everything he advocated. The charges against Grove were ultimately dropped and most of those who knew him believed that the pipes had been planted and that his crime was political, not criminal.

FBI correspondence about Grove shows that Indianapolis agents had been aware of his activities at IU since he arrived on campus, but that they took special note of him after he helped found a secret Communist Party Club in the spring of 1968. After his arrest and trial, Grove left IU, and the FBI concluded that his departure, along with other events, eliminated that club, once "considered the largest single group with the greatest growth potential in the State of Indiana," as an effective political organization. Moreover, Grove's legal expenses had to be paid. Professor Orlando Taylor led members of CEWV, SDS, YSA, PRP, and other groups in raising money for his defense fund, and this effort diverted the energies of many activists from other causes. The trial only reinforced activists' fears that they were walking a fine line between freedom and arrest in Bloomington, regardless of who was watching them.[49]

Undaunted by the presence of observers or reporters on campus that fall, twenty free spirits organized a Revolutionary Insurgency Training Corps (RITC) at IU, armed with antiwar signs and toy guns. They goose-stepped their way through a ROTC brigade review shouting "sieg heil" and "end the war," and generally disrupted the event. An FBI informant described RITC as a group of about "one dozen students, mostly women, dressed in ragged portions of uniforms and helmets, carrying toy guns. They appeared to plan marching behind, mimicking and apeing the activities of the ROTC platoon. The stated purpose was to ridicule ROTC training and point out the university's involvement with the military establishment." Unfortunately for members of RITC, someone from the dean of students' office intervened before they could carry out their plan and told them that they were disrupting a class. After being threatened with expulsion from the university, they left the field peacefully.[50]

One member of RITC, Mike Kelsey, was a Vietnam veteran who had returned to IU to complete his undergraduate degree. A liberal Hoosier who had opposed the war before he had been drafted and sent to Southeast Asia, Kelsey's antiwar attitudes had hardened during his tour of duty with the Americal Division. When he came back to Bloomington, he participated in public protests against the war with somewhat less concern about being observed than others who still faced the possibility of the draft. But in talking years later about the atmosphere surrounding student politics, Kelsey reflected that before he left for Vietnam, it was generally acceptable "to call yourself a liberal." After he came back in 1968, he said, "liberal was kind of a dirty word." Students who opposed the war in Vietnam had less patience with the moderate middle ground, at least rhetorically, and had begun adopting a much more radical tone in their everyday speech. It may have been more style than substance, but they had begun to take a more sharply defined moral stance against moderates who sought to compromise with those who supported the war.[51]

RITC, defiantly unaffiliated with any organization, was one of the more light-hearted guerrilla groups formed to protest the university's involvement with the military. SDS, on the other hand, launched a rigorous attack on IU's collaborations with the CIA and the military in a report that outlined in detail verifiable links with clandestine intelligence units and classified military research. The first paper focused on the activities of Thomas A. Sebeok, Distinguished Professor in Linguistics, who was the founder and first chairman of IU's Program in Uralic and Altaic Studies. SDS researchers wrote that Sebeok, who had immigrated to the United States from Hungary in 1937, had applied to the CIA for a job in August 1950. The agency did not hire him, but it did accept reports from his IU graduate students when they were in Eastern Europe on research projects. Sebeok sold language training tapes to the CIA in the 1950s and directed a training program in the Albanian, Hungarian, and Russian languages held on the Bloomington campus for the U.S. Air Force in 1959, funded by the CIA.

SDS charges against Sebeok brought immediate denials from faculty members and Wells. History professor Robert F. Byrnes said, "the whole issue is phoney. It is set up by people who don't know how the structure works." Wells categorically denied the CIA connection: "The University has no connection whatsoever with the CIA. If I had a Bible here, I would swear on it." But when a student reporter asked him specifically about the Air Force Language Institute, Wells hedged: "That may have been CIA funded. I don't remember."[52]

Robert Byrnes was also a subject of SDS investigations. A former head of the CIA's Office of National Estimates and director of the CIA-funded Mid-European Studies Center of the Free Europe Committee, Byrnes helped establish IU's Asian Studies Program, first directed by Joseph Sutton, and the Russian and East European Institute. Since 1965, Byrnes had been director of the International Affairs Center and was primarily responsible for awarding grants to students interested in international study abroad. In 1967, *Pravda* had accused the CIA of influencing the award of grants made by the Inter-University Committee on Travel Grants, chaired by Byrnes, a charge he emphatically denied.[53]

In the mid-1960s, the Department of Defense funded Project Themis for university research in defense-related subjects. At IU that research concerned the use of languages and language behavior as indications of potential sources of international conflicts. Suspicions of shadowy connections with national intelligence agencies were common on most state university campuses in the 1960s, and the information that SDS researchers discovered confirmed many of them. Indiana University, they wrote, "offers intelligence men the truly perfect cover" because it was "isolated from mainstream politics, existing in a rural environment . . . the fabled groves of Academe come to life in one of the Crest-conquered All-American cities."[54]

When CIA recruiters came to IU in December, about two hundred students staged an all-night protest in Ballantine Hall, with the permission of the dean of students. The protest continued the next day with a "mill-in" in front of the recruiters' interview offices. When students tried to get CIA representatives to engage in a debate about agency policy, the recruiters refused because of national secrecy laws and left a day earlier than expected.

CIA recruiter Charles Minnick said that IU was not as bad as other schools, certainly not as violent as Columbia University, where in 1968 students had taken over buildings to protest institutional ties to agencies like the CIA. At IU, students continued to insist that they had a right to debate any representative who came onto the campus to recruit students, and they carried petitions for that right with over six hundred signatures to the president's office. President Sutton declined to meet with the students. He told them he would consider their petitions "in due course."[55]

Across the country, 1969 began in a dark, troubled mood. Indiana University and Bloomington shared that cloud of apprehension. In Indiana, the sense of rough times ahead was tinged by university officials' concerns about the mood of state legislators, who were to begin a new session that would decide university funding. With enrollment at the highest levels in its history, Indiana University desperately needed political and financial support from the state's leaders. But traditional reluctance to spend money on higher education combined with deeply rooted anger at what many state politicians perceived as outright acts of subversion and treachery on the part of student activists did not bode well for the university's future. A skilled strategist like Herman B Wells might have been able to head off the battle that loomed ahead. But Wells, having devoted nearly all of his adult life to working for the university, had been officially retired for six years and, except during his stint as acting president, he was often away from campus for both official and personal reasons.

Unfortunately, IU's thirteenth president, Joseph Sutton, while respected by many faculty members and other administrators, had neither Wells's sensitivity for Hoosier political imbroglios nor his long history of personal relations with many of the state's leaders. Moreover, alcohol-related problems continued to trouble him, and he was often unavailable for meetings with students and faculty. The events at Indiana University in the spring of 1969 reflected tensions that existed both nationally and locally. Indiana University faced political and cultural problems that were part of a much larger national and international arena and yet, at the same time, were deeply rooted in its own local history and traditions.

The semester began with an innovative proposal from a group of undergraduates, graduate students, and faculty to hold an election for the position of university chancellor. Since the board of trustees was responsible for filling that post, the election was more a symbolic gesture than substantive action, but it did serve to show administrators that there was some concern in the university community that other voices should be heard when decisions that involved the whole campus were being made. The New University Conference (NUC), composed mainly of a group of younger faculty members and graduate students, nominated Staughton Lynd, an outspoken critic of the Vietnam war who had been fired from Yale University and was then teaching at the University of Chicago. He came to Bloomington in the midst of a University of Chicago student demonstration against the administration for firing a popular woman sociology professor. He told his IU audience that the conversations about higher education that took place during the sit-in at the university's administration building were "the best intellectual discussion I have ever heard" and that he viewed disruptive sit-ins as legitimate expressions of democracy.

Two other candidates were nominated: Reverend William Dennis, a civil rights activist from Indianapolis, by the New Politics party, and Paul Boutelle, a socialist candidate for mayor of New York City and founder of the Freedom Now party, by YSA. Lynd advised IU voters to elect all three candidates, so that they could then act as a chancellor's committee to disarm the campus police, eliminate ROTC, and nominate African Americans to the board of trustees. Nearly two thousand people voted in the election, with Lynd getting about one-half of the all the votes cast. The board of trustees ignored the vote and confirmed John Snyder, a former vice president, dean of undergraduate development, and professor of history, as acting chancellor of Indiana University.[56]

Not long afterward, Snyder received the unpleasant news that IU's budget had been cut from the requested amount of $8 million to $6.2 million for the next two years. He told student reporters that he was "devastated" at the loss of $1.8 million for the university and warned that fee hikes and reductions in some programs would be necessary. The legislature's hard line against the state university might have made more sense if there had been a series of violent student demonstrations, building takeovers, or physical destruction of buildings on the campus. Yet, since 1965, the only person injured during a demonstration had been George Walker, the student hit by a police officer during the 1967 demonstration against Dow. The only building destroyed in Bloomington was the Black Market, owned and managed by an African-American graduate student, which was firebombed by the Ku Klux Klan in December 1968. Moreover, IU students had overwhelmingly voted for a moderate student leader, Ted Najam, whose campaign had been based on his respectability and reasonable approach to trustees, administrators, and faculty. Even fairly radical student activists like Russell Block acknowledged Najam's effectiveness: "Najam has provided a service to the University by bringing about change without unnecessary trouble. And I think that's good."[57]

What is striking about Indiana University during the years between 1965 and 1968 is the relative absence of confrontation between university and local authorities and students. The few times that violence did erupt, its instigators were not students. *Indiana Daily Student* editors decided that members of the legislature had become uneasy at recent reports of large student demonstrations at San Francisco State University, San Jose State University, and the University of Chicago and saw disruptions there as evidence for potential student violence in Indiana.

State legislators were especially alarmed at students' use of the strike in their protests against university policies and involvement in the Vietnam War. Since they were responsible for university funding from state taxes, they were sensitive to criticisms that a small number of activists could prevent the entire student body (the sons and daughters of Indiana taxpayers) from attending classes during these strikes. The first such strike to capture national media attention was the one at Columbia

University, a private institution in New York City, in the spring of 1968. The initial impetus for the students' demonstration was the university's attempt to build a gymnasium in a nearby black neighborhood, Morningside Heights, which would not serve the people who lived there. However, student leader Mark Rudd and others soon expanded the scope of the protest to include Columbia president Greyson Kirk's connection with the Institute for Defense Analysis (IDA) and its weapons research for the Defense Department and the war in Vietnam. Finally, the strike became a confrontation between institutional authority and students who saw themselves as revolutionaries, carrying copies of Chairman Mao's "Little Red Book" and pictures of Cuban guerrilla hero Che Guevara. Kirk called in New York City police to clear university buildings of student strikers; the brutality and violence of the police drove hundreds of previously uninvolved students into the strikers' camp. In the end, Kirk resigned, plans for the gymnasium were put on hold, university ties to the IDA were severed, and students gained increased representation on university governing boards and policy-making organizations. But even more significant was the shift to the rhetoric of revolution among student activists across the nation.

The student strike at San Francisco State University, part of the state university system, also attracted national media attention. African-American students formed the Black Students Union in 1968 and demanded that the administration establish a black studies department. With support from the Black Panther Party, they expanded their demands to include the abolition of admission requirements and tuition for blacks. After a black faculty member was suspended, African-American students declared a strike in November 1968. When students disrupted classes and committed acts of vandalism, the president called in the police, who came onto the campus swinging clubs. In the midst of the melee, the president resigned and was replaced by an outspoken conservative professor of semantics, S. I. Hayakawa. Taking a tough line, Hayakawa banned the use of microphones by student activists and went so far as to jump on a truck that students were using for a rally and pull the wires out of their amplifier. The strike lasted through the end of January 1969. Some students and members of the faculty were arrested, but in the end the administration agreed to establish a black studies department and to waive admission requirements for some students of color. The incident polarized California and the nation as well. Student activists confronted the intransigence of hardline university administrators, and mainstream Americans expressed their dismay at the chaos and violence they saw on tax-supported state university campuses.

Hoosier politicians were also uneasy at the relaxation of university regulations governing student living conditions. Republican state senator Danny Burton had tried to introduce legislation early in the session that would have stopped visitation between men and women students in university dormitories because he questioned the wisdom of subjecting students' morality to such temptations. Other legislators had tried to withhold scholarship money to any student who violated university rules. They also attempted to assess the university a fine of $1,000 for every student involved in an illegal campus demonstration. Aware of popular sentiment for voting rights, recently elected Republican governor Edgar Whitcomb vetoed a bill that would have allowed only married students to vote in Indiana state elections.

State legislators were generally frightened by IU students, despite the relative calm in Bloomington. They suspected that explosive social unrest was just around the corner unless stringent measures were taken to restrict university funding. But students and faculty disagreed with this logic. In fact, an *Indiana Daily Student* editorial concluded, the cutbacks that would be required because of budget reductions would increase students' frustrations and make demonstrations more, not less, likely. And as if to prove the point, soon after the announcement of the budget cut in March, a cartoonist took on the governor in the campus newspaper:

See the Governor of Indiana.
His name is Edgar Whitcomb.
Half of the Governor's last name is "whit,"
Proving that he's a half-whit.
Governor Whitcomb has restored my faith in democracy.
After Governor Whitcomb was elected,
I became convinced
That any American could be elected to public office.[58]

Students at IU did not react immediately to the budget cuts. They were also strangely silent in the face of the announcement later that month that the board of trustees was increasing tuition by a whopping 67% for both state residents and nonresidents. Throughout the month of April, most IU students faced the end of the term, final examinations, and the annual Little 500 bicycle race, which was either one of the world's great college weekends or, as some of IU's more cynical students called it, "The World's Greatest College Stupidity," depending on one's point of view. Many critics of the race were skeptical of the much-touted reason for its existence: ticket sales were used to provide scholarships for needy students. The Indiana University Foundation, the organization in charge of the event, kept its accounts secret, so the exact amount of money raised and contributed to scholarships was never public knowledge.

Student politicians concentrated on student government elections, and for the first time, activists were split between two parties. One, the United Student Movement (USM), was a mix of former PRP and SDS members, led by two African-American students and with about 120 core members. It supported black demands for a black studies program and wanted administrators to put student representatives on committees that hired, fired, and granted tenure to faculty. It advocated student control over all student publications and also demanded that the Indiana University Foundation make its accounts public.

About thirty students formed the main force of the Revolutionary Student Party (RSP), which was led by Russell Block and Allyne Kaplan. They presented a platform that was broader in scope but more detailed and more radical. Their "Nine Basic Demands" included getting U.S. troops out of Southeast Asia; supporting the California grape boycott; providing five hundred full scholarships for African-American students in the next academic year; opening Indiana University Foundation accounts to the public; banning all outside recruiters who refused to debate with students; supporting the black studies program demanded by the AAASA; and selling university-owned real estate in low-income areas in Indianapolis. At a rally in Dunn Meadow, Allyne Kaplan, RSP's candidate for vice president, injected a new feminist theme into the campaign when she charged that women at IU were second-class citizens and that women had to recognize their oppression. The whole RSP campaign was, Block stated, aimed at raising students' awareness of issues beyond the campus rather than actually winning the election. He dismissed student government as basically powerless but argued that "student power is a revolutionary force when it links up with forces fighting for liberation outside the campus. It is important to mobilize students around concrete demands that forge this link, touch their lives, and challenge the authority of the ruling class."[59]

FBI files contain a copy of a full-page advertisement in the *Bloomington Courier-Tribune* that featured a picture of Russell Block together with an endorsement from the Socialist Workers Party, one of the FBI's early targets in its COINTELPRO campaign to undermine the New Left. The advertisement also pointed out that Block had been convicted of disorderly conduct during the 1967 Dow demonstrations. It ended with a quotation from British historian Thomas Macaulay: "THINK THIS OVER: . . . the Huns and Vandals who ravaged the Roman Empire came from WITH-

OUT and your Huns and Vandals will have been engendered WITHIN your own country."[60]

The Independent Party, led by Ted Najam's vice president, Paul Helmke, ran a fairly conventional students' rights campaign. Student voter turnout was light. Out of about 6,000 votes cast, Helmke won handily with around 4,000; USM received about 2,000, and Block, whose Revolutionary Student Party received only about 150 votes, was characteristically philosophical about his defeat.[61]

The first sounds of alarm about the 67% tuition increase erupted at Purdue University, a campus composed largely of engineering, agricultural, and technical students, who were not normally vocal opponents of university authority. However, on this issue they were the first to protest, organizing rallies of between two and three thousand students for several nights running in mid-April, along with a boycott of classes that included at least six thousand students. Governor Whitcomb worried that the disruptions at Purdue were being instigated by "outside agitators." On April 24 around three thousand IU students gathered on the Bloomington campus to listen to Purdue representatives argue that all university students should band together and demand a budget freeze until the tuition problem could be resolved. When acting chancellor John Snyder tried to explain the fee hikes to an angry crowd in Whittenberger Auditorium, graduate student and former PRP leader Mark Oring won applause when he argued that IU should cut off any services to the state.

It is hard to imagine an event that could have radicalized Indiana University students more than the legislature's large tuition increase. Students perceived it as a direct attack on them by politicians who had made them an enemy of the state with no just cause. *Indiana Daily Student* editors warned Governor Whitcomb in anguished tones that "inside agitators are alive and growing. . . . The real disruption and disorder will come from the inside agitators—those people who cut their hair, go to classes, and haven't had to cross any state lines to riot and revolt at Lafayette and Bloomington. These are the loyal Hoosiers who have suffered all their young lives right here in Indiana. . . . they are the people who have had more than twenty years to build up resentment against a state that valiantly resists any kind of progressive change."[62]

On April 28, 1969, more than eight thousand students met in the New Field House to talk about the budget with university administrators. The mood was angry but nonviolent. Various ways to cut the budget were suggested from the floor. David Cahill, an early PRP leader and former student senator, advocated that faculty members donate their salaries to the university budget, that Founders Day and Commencement

Day ceremonies be canceled to save money, that all athletic scholarships be eliminated, and that ROTC be dropped. He brought the crowd to its feet. The *Indiana Daily Student* continued to demand an explanation for the tuition increase; its editors felt that students were being forced to pay for the governor's and the legislature's unrealistic tax policies and fiscal irresponsibility.[63]

Three thousand IU students celebrated May Day by rallying in front of Owen Hall for a boycott of classes for the next two days, shouting, "All strike, shut it down." The momentum of the protest was beginning to alarm some administrators and students. Acting chancellor Snyder said that a boycott was up to individual faculty members and students. Student body president Paul Helmke urged students to keep cool. African-American students joined the boycott the next day and declared that they would refuse to pay any tuition increase.

While Bloomington students were affirming their commitment to peaceful demonstrations, there was a fire in the library, then located in a building at the top of Kirkwood Avenue. With smoke pouring out of the windows and crowds gathered in front of its doors at the intersection of Kirkwood and Indiana, everyone's vision of student violence seemed to have come true. In fact, it was not what it seemed. Later investigations attempted to prove that the fire had been set by a disgruntled library employee, although its cause was never definitely determined. Members of the Bloomington Fire Department and the Indiana State Fire Marshall's Office announced that the fire was "definitely arson . . . started with flammable liquid . . . on ground level." Damage to books and property was estimated at $650,000. The scene, captured dramatically by local newspaper photographers, fueled resentment among many Bloomington residents, and Snyder warned the student senate about growing citizen antipathy toward protests in Bloomington.[64]

In an effort to calm student concerns, Snyder announced that any student in good standing who had financial need would receive aid from the university for the next academic year. Students, genuinely upset about the library fire, held a benefit dance in Dunn Meadow to raise money to replace damaged books. The event turned into a weekend of music, dancing, conversations about how to deal with local citizen groups, and teach-ins on the budget. In the evening, Dunn Meadow became a scene of tents and campfires, with students singing folk songs accompanied by guitars and sharing food, talk, and the warm glow of a common cause. Peace and love reigned on the grassy field of Dunn Meadow.[65]

By Sunday between eight and ten thousand students were in the field, and in a demonstration of unity, they voted to continue the boycott of classes. The next day the faculty met and, unified in opposition, voted to continue to teach. Trustee Frank McKinney advised President Sutton not to sign the diplomas of any students who missed classes during the tuition increase demonstrations. Vice president David Derge, acting for the president, urged students to return to classes.

In response, over five thousand students, most from Bloomington, marched from the IU campus to the state house on streets lined with policemen. They carried a coffin labeled "Education" and signs saying "State Education for Rich Only," "Death of Education," and "Indiana Needs Tax Reform," and they chanted "Save our Schools" and "Unity." The governor did not appear, but other state officials praised the crowd for its peacefulness. State senator Rogers told them, "You have frightened and angered many residents of this state. But in the process you have made quite dramatic the deficiencies in the state administration and the drawbacks in the state tax structure. . . . I have been here for 12 years and I have never seen a more impressive and orderly and, I hope, more effective march."[66]

On that same day, Indiana University celebrated Founders Day, a ceremony traditionally dedicated to honoring outstanding students. During the festivities, and in front of their parents and university officials, about five hundred of Indiana's highest-achieving scholars got up and left.

Both Chancellor Snyder and former president Wells praised the students for their peaceful exit, and Wells supported their demands for increased state support for education in order that universities not become a haven for the privileged classes. A local newspaper carried a photograph of the walkout showing three young white males, short-haired, wearing horn-rimmed glasses and raising their fists in the power salute. One girl summed up her feelings by saying, "It was an honor to walk out."[67]

Clearly, the tuition increase had aroused strong feelings among university students all over the state. Purdue University students had initiated the protests that activists in Bloomington carried on throughout May 1969. The issue was fundamental to the state's commitment to higher education and reached back to the first constitution, written in 1816, which had promised Hoosiers a free educational system, open to all. The controversy ignited tensions at all levels: from the governor, who was openly hostile to student activists; to faculty who opposed the strike; to administrators who praised students' peaceful protest but did nothing to rescind the fee increase; to bewildered parents whose sons and daughters were either the instigators, or the victims, or both, of the fee increase and the boycott; and to minority students who felt the brunt of the state's racial and economic discrimination. In the final days of the semester,

Spring 1969: Thousands of IU students gather in Dunn Meadow to support the class boycott during protests over tuition increases set by the state legislature. © Dave Repp.

students became more and more frustrated at their apparent inability to meet with anyone who could actually do anything about the problem.

On the afternoon of May 8, a group of about fifty students, administrators, and faculty met to try to come to some resolution that would end the boycott of classes. They broke for dinner and agreed to reconvene in the Ballantine Hall faculty lounge later that evening. At some point after they had done so, about 150 African-American students, led by Rollo Turner, came into the room. At about 11:00 P.M., Turner announced, "We're going to wait here until the board of trustees decides to talk to us." Members of the group, including well-known IU athletes, positioned themselves around the doors and windows of the lounge and waited. The lock-in began. One professor from the business school accused them of kidnapping. Professor Orlando Taylor, who came into the meeting shortly after Turner's announcement, told the group, "These students are here to discuss an issue dear to their hearts and futures. I urge that we be cool and do not pull rank." After recovering from the initial shock of Turner's words, everyone got down to business. Chancellor Snyder and William B. Harvey, dean of the law school, began talking earnestly about the university's budgetary problems. Money was collected for food, and faculty and administrators were escorted to bathrooms. Students standing by the windows were afraid that the police were watching. They pulled down the windowshades and closed all the windows and doors. The lounge got very hot. Everyone agreed that the police should not be called and, according to one student observer, "a rather odd community then developed—faculty members stoutly maintained they were having a fine time." Another labeled the event "Beautiful Ballantine" and wrote, "Thursday night was the most beautiful thing that has ever happened at Indiana University."[68]

Not everyone agreed with that assessment. Vice President David Derge had left Ballantine Hall earlier in the evening and was in his office at Bryan Hall when the lock-in began. However, he was in contact with Chancellor Snyder by telephone during the meeting and with the police as well. The students in Ballantine Hall were unaware that President Sutton had called the head of the safety division, who, in turn, called the governor. Gov. Whitcomb ordered two platoons of the state police to Bloomington, and placed two hundred National Guardsmen on alert. Sutton got a court injunction against the black students that required them to release everyone in the building and leave the premises or be arrested on contempt charges. The mayor of Bloomington mobilized his police department, as did the Monroe County sheriff. By 2:30 A.M. the IU Safety Division staff and the Monroe County Civil Defense Police Unit were in full riot gear and ready to move onto the campus.[69]

Students learned from an anonymous telephone call that the police would come into Ballantine Hall if the African-American students did not open the doors. Snyder and other administrators promised the students that they would do everything possible to arrange a meeting with the board of trustees. While police waited in their cars, Bloomington mayor John Hooker and chief of police James East went into Ballantine Hall to assess the situation. They observed that the students and their "hostages were milling around the building and seemed to be treating the whole situation as a joke." Taking administrators' words in good faith, the students agreed that they had accomplished what they had set out to do and everyone went home.

The next day, eight hundred students came to a meeting in Dunn Meadow. They voted to end the boycott. On Sunday, May 11, four of the trustees came to Bloomington to talk with students, faculty, and administrators. They discussed the state's commitment to higher education, changes to the tax structure, and the university's budget for the coming year. Rollo Turner and Robert Johnson called the trustees' visit "administrative chicanery." Others were even less charitable: "What we have here is not a failure in communication. The administration has simply chosen to ignore the real anger felt by students against an outrageous tuition increase. Derge, Snyder, and the whole ugly bunch are well aware that 'outside agitation' is not the problem—the problem is power, a conflict of interests, a complete breakdown in the facade of the 'university community.'" For many who had called for peaceful demonstrations, the entire episode had been a dramatic illustration of students' apparent powerlessness. "We are tired of being patted on the head for our 'responsibility,' and being ignored. We are tired of nice p.r. efforts that do not attack the power that has attacked us. We are tired of 'responsible' actions that are not responsible to us."[70]

Although the faculty members and administrators who had been in Ballantine Hall had decided that "the student action threatened no kind of physical violence to anyone present or damage to university property" and refused to bring any legal action against them, the Monroe County sheriff, Clifford Thresher, was not of the same mind. He called for a grand jury investigation of the incident, and despite vigorous student protests, indictments were brought against Professor Orlando Taylor, Rollo Turner, Kenneth Newsome, Joel Allen, and five other students. The students were charged with "riotous conspiracy" and faced sentences of two to ten years in prison and fines up to $2,000. The irony of the indictments, especially for African Americans Turner, Newsome, and Taylor, was that the statute invoked was one that had been created in 1905 to deal with criminal acts of the Ku Klux Klan.[71]

Once Taylor had been indicted, his nomination for vice chancellor was withdrawn and the opening of the Black Studies Institute, which had been promised for the following year, was delayed for another year. The editor of the *Indiana Daily Student* called the black studies program the "victim of institutional violence" on the part of IU trustees. "It was an ego thing. They had to show the critical taxpayers around the state that they were the power elite at I.U." For other student critics it was "the old game of the privileged and the powerful standing upon the backs of the poor and the powerless." For African-American students at IU, the tuition increase protest had been, strangely, a mixed blessing. They saw how effective their acts and words could be and they won respect from other students for their willingness to take risks to force administrators to listen to them. At the same time, they lost two of their most important spokesmen—Orlando Taylor, who left for Washington, D.C., and Rollo Turner, who accepted a teaching job at the University of Pittsburgh—and the prospect of soon having their own academic program. Still, at the end of that tumultuous spring, activists held out the hope that "the movement must tighten the belt of a frayed rather worn collective psychology, for as Rollo Turner has often pointed out, 'the struggle is just beginning.' Dig it?"[72]

In the end, the lock-in was a dramatic illustration of just how divided the university community had become. Students—both black and white—were outraged at the arbitrary way in which administrators exercised their authority. Faculty found themselves on the sidelines of an issue that threatened the viability of higher education in the state. Administrators charged students with that most disruptive of all crimes—disrespect. And they allowed politicians to intervene in what was clearly a campus controversy.

By the summer of 1969, students at Indiana University shared with other students across the country a sense that things would never be the same again. The end of the 1960s marked the end of an era in their personal histories as well as the collective history of the country.

In the past two years, the war against the war in Vietnam had reached a point at which it threatened to tear the country apart. President Lyndon Baines Johnson, the politicians' politician, had retired to his Texas ranch, his dreams of a Great Society destroyed by protestors against a war he never planned or understood. His two primary critics, Dr. Martin Luther King, Jr., and Senator Robert F. Kennedy, had both been gunned down by assassins and had become martyrs to the cause of peace and civil rights—causes that he himself had worked for throughout his political career.

Students had organized the most dramatic antiwar protests in

American history—and yet the war went on and Richard M. Nixon had been elected president in 1968 as a representative of the "silent majority" of citizens who supported the war and opposed the protestors. In the Midwest, most students talked about revolution but continued to protest nonviolently. However, state legislators and local elected officials acted as if students' rhetoric of revolution were, in fact, reality. In Bloomington, the irony was that state legislators, angry about student strikes over war-related issues on other university campuses (e.g., Columbia University and San Francisco State University), slashed Indiana University funding, which resulted in, not surprisingly, a student strike.

The last two years of the decade also saw the emergence of the FBI's COINTELPRO program aimed at the New Left, using surveillance techniques that fundamentally threatened First Amendment freedoms. Not since the days of McCarthyism in the 1950s had so many Americans been subject to infringements of their rights to free speech and a free press. The long arm of the Federal Bureau of Investigation reached into every part of the country, from Boston, Massachusetts, to Bloomington, Indiana. In the late 1960s, paranoia on the part of students who took part in antiwar protests was not necessarily a delusion.

For any student who hoped for peace and for an end to the bloodshed and bitterness that the war in Vietnam had brought to this country, the late 1960s were marked by some very dark clouds. Looking back, it may be difficult to understand that many people thought that the war would never end. Thousands of young Americans gathered in Woodstock in August 1969 to celebrate peace, love, and drugs, but at the same time, thousands more were fighting and dying in Southeast Asia. And even for the most cynical citizen, the assassinations of King and Kennedy seemed to mark the end of any hope for a peaceful resolution to domestic racial tensions and political opposition to the war. From the violence of the streets of Chicago during the Democratic national convention in 1968 to Dunn Meadow during the tuition protests in Bloomington in 1969, students in the heartland were trying to find a way to "give peace a chance."

CHAPTER 4

A Precarious Peace

During the last academic year of the 1960s, students faced a series of challenges. President Richard Nixon, like most Americans, recognized the inherent class and race inequities of the selective service system, and therefore instituted a new draft lottery that was based on birth dates and called for younger men to be drafted before older ones. The first drawing was December 1, 1969. Although students still received deferments, this new policy removed some of the injustices that had provoked protests. The challenge for antiwar activists was to maintain the same level of personal commitment to the cause, even though many men no longer faced the threat of being drafted.

Another reason that fewer men were being drafted was President Nixon's policy of Vietnamization of the war, which called for increased financial aid and armaments for the South Vietnamese army along with a gradual withdrawal of American combat troops. While this might seem likely to have placated the antiwar movement, it did not. Activists rose to the challenge and organized the largest antiwar demonstration in American history on November 15, 1969, when over seven hundred thousand people marched against the war in Washington, D.C.

In the late 1960s and early 1970s, some antiwar activists reached out to include factory workers in their movement. Most Americans think of the 1960s as a time of division between students and workers. However, the student movement grew out of Old Left worker alliances and SDS received much-needed support in its early years from union leaders like Walter Reuther, head of the United Auto Workers, and Myles Horton, founder of the Highlander Folk School, an experimental labor educational center. During the late 1960s, students at Harvard, Boston University, MIT, and Indiana University joined picket lines with workers at General Electric, a major player in the military-industrial complex.[1]

As activists in the antiwar movement succeeded in reaching out to a broader spectrum of Americans, they also experienced the beginning of a backlash. In the spring of 1970, when students across the nation demonstrated against President Nixon's decision to widen the war by invading Cambodia, they had to acknowledge that many of the so-called "silent majority" applauded the Ohio National Guardsmen who killed four and wounded eleven at Kent State University. The 1970s began on a note of desperation and anxiety. Moreover, some activists had begun to quarrel, not with conservative opponents, but with one another, arguing over who was more, or more properly, revolutionary. The war against the war was turning on itself, and it looked like the students who began it would become its first victims.

Chaos during fall registration was nothing new at Indiana University, but in 1969 there was more than the usual pandemonium of 29,800 students scrambling to get into classes. Anger at the tuition increase still smoldered and activists encouraged registrants to write "no more bullshit" on their computer cards—"at least let them know what you think of the increase." While enrollment was not as high as had been forecast earlier, there really was no way to know what effect the fee hike had had on deterring students from entering or returning to Bloomington. But the memories of the previous spring had a definite effect on the mood of those young Hoosiers who had the financial means to come back to, or start, school.

Students resented the fact that all the peaceful demonstrations and protests had elicited no response from the trustees or the administration other than praise for students' "responsible" actions. Fees went up anyway. The promise of adequate financial aid for all needy students was questionable. The administrator who had made that commitment to students, John Snyder, had resigned his position as chancellor of Indiana University to accept a job at a university in California. Students who tried to work out a work-study plan discovered that in order to earn enough money to support themselves on university wages they could only go to school part-time. Students who applied for loans at Fletcher National Bank (owned by trustee Frank McKinney) found their applications denied.[2]

The board of trustees added to student discontent by passing a tough new student code of conduct that called for suspension or expulsion of any student guilty of "violation of any rule, regulation or policy governing student conduct," including those that prohibited intentional damage to university property, occupation of university buildings, refusal to vacate university buildings, rioting, bomb threats, or possession of alcohol or firearms. This code reflected a reactionary trend among university officials across the nation. In Pennsylvania, for example, conservative legislators gave officials in the Department of Education the power to deny financial aid to students who had been convicted of disrupting classes.[3]

At a meeting with students that fall, two of the trustees admitted that they had passed the student conduct code because of political pressure from the state legislature, but maintained that they had succumbed to that pressure only after waiting for over a year for the faculty to produce a code of conduct. It was the faculty's failure to do the job, the trustees argued, that pushed them to write a new code that would satisfy legislative demands for rigorous disciplinary procedures.[4]

Beneath their frustration at the failure of protests over the fee hike to bring any tangible results, students were nostalgic for the sense of solidarity that the previous spring's protests had produced among their ranks. One student editor felt that "there seems a depressing note in the air. Fond memories of the Spring Semester boycott are being chilled by stark reality." On a more positive note, another editorial writer urged students not to forget Bloomington's version of the legacy of the Woodstock festival. Praising the "Spirit of Dunn Meadow," this student editor insisted that, "embryonic as last spring's confrontations were, the ideas then expressed must not be aborted. The demands of this student community and youth across the land need the creative attention which was expressed at Woodstock." As they walked down Kirkwood Avenue past the vacant lot where the Black Market had been firebombed by the Klan the year before, some IU students expressed their despair at the absence of the "throng of beards and long hairs, blacks and whites" and "the atmosphere of togetherness and comradeship" that used to reach out to those who walked past.[5]

Something was wrong with Indiana University, but no solution was acceptable to everyone. In the eyes of many members of the New Left, the university administrators' responses to student protest over the tuition increase had proven that peaceful demonstrations were ineffective and that, as an institution, the university was inherently undemocratic. From that perspective, the lesson to be learned was that "moderates and liberals at I.U. have chosen to be part of the problem instead of part of the solution." With the students who had headed the Ballantine lock-in still under indictment and with new regulations threatening even more suspensions and expulsions of student protestors, some activists called on their fellows to fight local repression "in the courts, in papers, on the streets with leaflets . . . keep up the pressure." Fearing that university administrators and moderate faculty and students would try to ignore activists who were familiar from past confrontations, they wanted "to make clear that they will remain a vocal part of this community. Action is the answer to repression."[6]

As a veteran of earlier battles with IU administrators, Robert Johnson expressed another point of view. Surveying the recent history of student protests, Johnson worried that members of IU's New Left were falling into the competitive trap of "I'm more revolutionary than you." In a plea for unity, Johnson urged protestors to try to build an inclusive movement, not a revolutionary vanguard. Repudiating Marxist revolutionary rhetoric, he argued that American students should look into their own history for theories of insurgency, "use the past in order to bring clarity into the present, get away from jargon. . . . One of the main problems of American culture is the self-imposed isolation that the alienated spirit assumes in its own selfish defense." It was this kind of thoughtful, sensitive appeal that made Johnson a respected spokesperson for student activists. He understood instinctively that the majority of IU students would be persuaded to join the opposition to the Vietnam war if they could see that it represented a divergence from American democratic principles and national interest.[7]

IU activists' frustration in dealing with educational authority mirrored the sense of futility that antiwar protestors across the nation felt as nonviolent demonstrations and marches seemed to bring only increases in American military involvement. When two leaders of feuding SDS factions came to town to present their organizational strategies for future campaigns against the war, Bloomington protestors were eager to hear them speak. Their debate, sponsored by the New University Conference (NUC), concerned the use of planned street confrontations between antiwar protestors and Chicago police in a three-day demonstration to be held October 8 to 11. Mark Rudd, leader of Columbia University's student demonstrations in 1968, represented the SDS Weathermen faction. He spoke to an audience of about three hundred, inviting Bloomington students to participate in the so-called "Days of Rage," the beginning, as he saw it, of the coming revolution. Les Coleman, from Harvard University and spokesperson for the Revolutionary Youth Movement 2 (RYM2), argued against using violent tactics and for peaceful organization of Americans against the war.

Rudd's call for street fights with armed police did not win much support either at IU or at most other universities. For the most part, Bloomington activists remained committed to a more reasoned approach to political protest. Coleman's insistence on peaceful organizing was more appealing to the Bloomington audience, even though some found his style "vitriolic" and "excessively emotional." After listening to Coleman and Rudd, local activists saw the debate between the two SDS speakers as largely irrelevant to the problems they faced in Bloomington. They did not want to be used as "cannon fodder" in Chicago. Nor were many persuaded that the national SDS organization, scarred by "immature, emotional infighting," was a promising vehicle for building a broad-based peace movement. IU students who wrote about the debate emphasized that "blowing into Chicago for a weekend is not going to bring the palace down. Mass mobilizations only have effect if they are coupled with consistent work, before and after. We want to be able to talk to the troops when they come back home." Another observer thought it was time to stop "ego tripping" and learn to talk to ordinary people, face to face. Criticizing SDS "vanguardism," Mike King, an undergraduate from Hammond, Indiana, commented,

> If the revolutionary movement is to be maintained and built throughout the country, self-appointed leaders had better curb their romantic souls and dig in for a long siege of relative obscurity and simple, diligent work, learning from and teaching the people.
>
> It is important, then, for Bloomington radicals who have previously subsisted on mass meetings and collected speeches to begin to know each other and *work* together consistently, that we might build a new community that means more than common dope and common music. Radical 'leaders' had better begin to integrate their public politics with no-longer-private lives and learn what liberation is all about.

Just as most IU students were, like King, unimpressed with national SDS leaders, Mark Rudd was equally critical of IU students, commenting that they were "reactionary . . . people who just sit on their ass and talk about revolution."[8]

Although there was not much enthusiasm for guerrilla warfare in Chicago, students from CEWV organized a War Moratorium on October 15 with support from university groups and organizations from the Bloomington community. Supporters included Clergy and Laymen Concerned about Vietnam, the Committee for a Sane Nuclear Policy (SANE), the Women's International League for Peace and Freedom (WILPF), the NUC, the Women's Liberation Front, the Young Democrats, YSA, the office of Afro-American Affairs, the Draft Project, the YMCA, SDS, the student government, the United Students Movement, and the Revolutionary Student Party. When students announced their plans for a day of antiwar meetings, the faculty council voted that graduate students should follow their own consciences concerning their teaching responsibilities. Professors said they would not penalize students who skipped that day.

The day before the official moratorium in Bloomington, about seventy-five members of SDS demonstrated in front of the Aerospace Research Applications Center, an old quonset hut on campus built during World War II, and Rawles Hall, the ROTC building. After a brief march and a few speeches in front of Rawles, Army Lt. Col. Robert Jones asked them to leave because they were disturbing classes. That evening WILPF sponsored a film, "A Plague on Your Children," about the effects of the biological and chemical warfare being conducted in Vietnam. Around 9:00 P.M. nearly four thousand people gathered around Showalter Fountain for a candlelight parade to Dunn Meadow protesting the war. Students marched from campus dormitories and others came from town with candles in hand, some laughing softly and joking as they walked. But as they reached the meadow, which soon blazed with light from the small flames, the crowd, long-haired students next to straight adults, became quiet until someone began singing "Give Peace a Chance," followed by "We Shall Overcome." Jerry Rubin gave a brief speech; an early leader of the antiwar movement and founder of the Yippies, he was currently on trial in Chicago for his part in demonstrations during the Democratic Party's convention in 1968. The spirit of Dunn Meadow lived on in a brief interlude of candlelight and music.[9]

While antiwar protestors sang songs of peace in the autumn night, other members of the community were attending the first of the year's five Patten Lectures, an endowed series of talks given on the Bloomington campus each year by an invited scholar. In 1969–70 the Patten Lecturer was Clark Kerr, former president of the University of California and current chairman and executive director of the Carnegie Foundation Commission on the Future of Higher Education. Kerr was well known to many in the audience for his role in the Berkeley Free Speech Movement in 1964. The lights dimmed in the auditorium and Kerr stepped up to the podium to give his lecture, titled "The Higher Learning and Its Discontents." At about the middle of Kerr's speech, a male figure in a devil costume leaped on stage, threw a cream pie into the speaker's face, and raced off into the darkness. There was a moment of panic. No one was sure what had happened and some feared Kerr had been hurt. The audience gasped and stirred in their seats. Stunned, Kerr took out a handkerchief, wiped the creamy filling from his face, and then continued his lecture. At the end of his remarks, he won a standing ovation from his audience when he told them he was "wondering, facing the next four lectures, whether or not to have dessert before I come."[10]

Former University of California chancellor Clark Kerr delivers the first Patten Lecture of 1969. *Arbutus*, 1970.

Jim Retherford, a former IU student and ex-editor of Bloomington's underground newspaper, *The Spectator*, was the pastry hurler. His original plan had been to flee out the back of the auditorium before anyone could catch him. Unfortunately Retherford tripped and was caught by auditorium attendants. The police came, placed him under arrest, and took him to the Monroe County jail. Students who were still gathered in Dunn Meadow heard the news of his arrest minutes after it happened. Jerry Rubin, who knew Retherford, proclaimed him a hero. SDS member Joel Allen began collecting money for Retherford's bond. About fifteen hundred students marched from the campus to the county jail to seek his release. They found him guarded by an officer carrying a shotgun and, as a reporter for one of Bloomington's daily papers described the scene, "a thin brown line of deputies" from the

After the pie-throwing incident at Kerr's Patten Lecture, James Retherford (in a devil costume) is carried on supporters' shoulders outside the Monroe County jail. © Dave Repp.

sheriff's department augmenting the blue uniforms of Monroe County Civil Defense Auxiliary Police. Retherford walked out of jail shortly after midnight and was lifted onto the shoulders of his supporters as they walked back to campus.[11]

Retherford and his defenders charged that Clark Kerr, who had coined the term "multiversity," and the Patten Lectures represented the "epitome of the Academic Experience, pompous, dignified, matter-of-fact, uninvolved, supercilious, stuffed-shirt," and that the pie in Kerr's face was an attack on "pomp and self-important dignity." Not everyone thought that Retherford's idea was a particularly good one, but most agreed that a charge of assault and battery was ludicrous for an attack involving a cream pie. New Left critics called Retherford's prank "an emotional, slapstick gesture . . . a kind of frustrated guilt acted out." Local reaction was stiffly critical. Throwing a pie at Kerr was hardly likely to win awards for good behavior from the Bloomington citizens who had been outraged when students had booed and heckled Secretary of State Dean Rusk in 1965. One local editor wrote,

> Surely all mature persons must have reacted with disgust to the pie-throwing incident in Woodburn Hall. Subjecting a distinguished speaker to that

kind of abuse goes against the grain of the majority's sense of fair play and good manners. . . . The administration has the support of almost all of us in strict enforcement of the student code. . . . They must act or we soon will have campus anarchy.

The Bloomington city council passed an antimoratorium measure and voted to support President Richard Nixon's war policies. Official civic commitment to patriotism and politeness ruled the day.[12]

Moratorium Day, October 15, 1969, began with music and speeches in Dunn Meadow. Methodist bishop James Armstrong told the crowd that he believed that the United States had to "stop playing God with the rest of the world." However, the frustration and tension that had been building throughout the fall started to crack student protestors' peacefulness. In the afternoon about a thousand students held a "mill-in" in front of the Bloomington draft board. An unidentified woman broke one of the windows in the door of the building. Protestors marched back to campus, chanting defiantly, "Ho, Ho, Ho Chi Minh, Viet Cong is gonna win." They stopped at Rawles Hall, the ROTC building. Again, an unidentified participant broke a window. Someone tripped the fire alarm. The day ended with a teach-in about the Vietnam War in Woodburn Hall.

Nerves were frayed and it showed. The minor physical damage done to two buildings was only the outward manifestation of the anger that was building within IU's antiwar movement. No one claimed responsibility for breaking windows and no one was arrested, but no one was especially happy about it either. These outbursts indicated the frustration that many activists felt at the absence of any reciprocal response from university administrators. Nonviolent tactics only seemed to bring more bureaucratic harassment, more resistance, and more repressive rules from the university, and resentment from some community leaders as well.[13]

As the lights dimmed before Clark Kerr's final Patten Lecture, Pam Gockley, an IU undergraduate, walked up to the podium and tried to make a statement, but she was arrested and taken out of the auditorium before she was able to say anything more than "Good evening, ladies and gentlemen." About one hundred students in the audience left the auditorium and went over to the chemistry building, where CEWV was meeting. They explained what had just happened to Pam Gockley and passed around two hats to contribute to her bail fund. The students then returned to the lecture hall and asked for more contributions from the audience.[14]

At a hearing early in 1970, Gockley read the speech she had tried to make at Kerr's lecture to officers of a university misconduct court. Pam Gockley was an engaging, idealistic, and intelligent young woman. Observers reported that even the hearing officer smiled as she read what she had wanted to say to Kerr and his Bloomington audience months before:

> Good evening, ladies and gentlemen.
>
> Don't get uptight . . . we don't get uptight when somebody plops a pie in our face in order to show us something about ourselves that we hadn't learned through our practical methods of communication.
>
> Tonight is Clark Kerr's last lecture. . . . He has been a sport throughout this whole thing. . . . We brought a special pie for Clark Kerr to throw at a well known campus freak, Jim Retherford. Does anyone want to live out your fantasies, break through your inhibitions, turn your dreams into reality? Want to throw a pie at a freaky?
>
> We promise not to charge you with assault and battery. [15]

The prospect of Kerr actually accepting Gockley's offer was unlikely but the possibility that he might take part in such a reprisal seemed to be at least a good-natured attempt by a few students at mending fences.

Antiwar protestors across the country began organizing a massive march to be held in Washington, D.C., on November 15, 1969. At a planning meeting of the Bloomington CEWV in October, members were concerned when Larry Bizarri, an IU Safety Division officer, showed up as students wrote their names and addresses on a sheet of paper passed around the room. Bizarri waited until everyone present had signed and then left, taking the list with him. Soon after, faculty and students attending a meeting of the NUC noticed that safety division officers were outside the house as they went in, taking down their license plate numbers. Despite some fear, over six hundred IU students made the trip to Washington and another three hundred organized a local march from Dunn Meadow to Bloomington's World War Memorial on the courthouse square.

As the marchers drove out of Bloomington on Highway 37 toward Washington, they saw Indiana state police officers in patrol cars taking down their license numbers. A local newspaper reported that Bloomington and Monroe County law enforcement officials had agreed to supply Washington, D.C., police with the names of all known Bloomington protestors who were attending the march.

In addition to the cars filled with people, two buses were carrying IU students east as well. As they met other buses on the way to the march, someone would shout out, "Where are you from? Want to trade food? See you in D.C.!" The IU contingent was made up of liberals who hoped that the march would help to stop the war, along with a few more radical protestors who saw the march as only a small step toward more revolutionary goals. On board the buses, there was a "jolly weekend out atmosphere," although political raps went on far into the night.

Once the Bloomington contingent arrived in Washington, they were overwhelmed at the enormous size of the crowd. As one student described the scene, "It's impossible to see where the crowd begins or ends—We keep coming, rank upon rank . . . THIS IS IT!" The sight of nearly half a million people gathering to protest the war was an exhilarating experience.

> The elation flowing from a national action is a powerful phenomenon. To be among thousands of brothers and sisters moving almost as one in a common cause, seems almost more important, more beautiful, than the specific cause itself. We all need such therapy, radical therapy that renews our rage and hope, rather than directing us to adjust . . . to a monotonous and powerless condition.[16]

The crowd watched as protestors carrying placards with the names of soldiers who had died in Vietnam marched silently from Arlington National Cemetery to a peace memorial below the Capitol building. Marchers put over thirty-five thousand signs into caskets arranged on the lawn. At a confrontation outside the Justice Department building, some IU students got caught in a fight with National Guard troops, who filled the air with tear gas. The sounds of sirens seemed to come from everywhere. It was an emotional, passionate event and one that provoked some from Bloomington to an even deeper commitment to the movement to end the war.

> The march proved that it is possible to assemble warm bodies to protest the war. It proved that a great deal of people are fed up with Vietnam and want out. But the majority of marchers only saw things wrong without seeing the connections between the problems. . . . If we expect the war to end, if we want to form a revolution, we have a fantastic job ahead of us. Singing "Give peace a chance" isn't enough. We must march, we must talk, and write, and convince people, expect repression and fight it. We must commit ourselves totally, or there will be no peace, no change, no hope for life.[17]

While marchers in Washington experienced dramatic mass action, those who stayed at home demonstrated their own hopes for peace by participating in a "March for Life." About three hundred students and members of WILPF, the YMCA, and Clergy and Laymen Concerned about Vietnam walked silently from Dunn Meadow down Kirkwood Avenue to the War Memorial, where some laid wreaths. Paralleling the Washington, D.C., march, protestors wore placards with the names of Indiana servicemen killed in Vietnam, and members of WILPF read the names aloud as the marchers went past the memorial. Back at Dunn

Meadow, Rabbi James Diamond, director of the Hillel Foundation, spoke to the demonstrators. He condemned the false sense of national pride that consumed Americans who branded protestors traitors, drawing an analogy with the vilification of Old Testament prophets. It was a quiet ceremony compared to the drama that Bloomington students experienced in Washington, D.C.[18]

The end of 1969 saw the beginning of closer relationships between student activists and Bloomington's working class. Even though activists were convinced that the war in Vietnam was just as threatening to workers as it was to students, relations between IU's activists and Bloomington's working class had often been strained. During the late fall of 1969, workers on strike against the local General Electric refrigerator-freezer plant provided IU students an opportunity to prove their point. Around 1,100 members of the International Brotherhood of Electrical Workers (IBEW) participated in a national strike for cost-of-living wage increases. Inflationary pressures on the economy brought on by the war were eating into workers' take-home pay, and the union's efforts to negotiate new contracts had broken down in October. Out on strike, Bloomington GE workers found little support in the town's newspapers, whose editorials had not been enthusiastic about their demands. *Indiana Daily Student* editors chose to run a derogatory cartoon showing a beer-drinking, potbellied worker calling for a strike because it beat working. In contrast, the Student Mobilization Committee (SMC), the successor to CEWV, prepared a supportive leaflet that explained the connection between the General Electric strike and the antiwar movement. After noting the presence of labor leaders and workers in the latest march on Washington, the SMC voiced its support for the local Bloomington strike because "it aims a powerful blow at the U.S. war machine and because we are opposed to forcing American workers to sacrifice their standard of living to prosecute a war which the American people do not want and do not support, a war which corporations are making huge profits off of."[19]

Activists at the *Spectator,* Bloomington's underground newspaper, issued a sixteen-page special strike supplement that included an article by Staughton Lynd on steelworkers' efforts to organize in Indiana and a statement from the IBEW Local 2249 president on the Bloomington situation. Activists formed a Student Strike Alliance and held a benefit concert to raise money to buy Christmas food and toys for strikers' children. Members of IU's Women's Liberation held a pot-luck dinner for strikers and their families that brought about forty workers and fifty students together for the evening. Although the two groups had some trouble mixing, everybody liked the country music played by two well-known student musicians, David and Bernella Satterfield. About a dozen students joined the picket lines outside downtown stores that sold GE products and 150 students voted to boycott those stores. Bill Holliday, a union activist, spoke at a December meeting of the IU Young Democrats, who voted to support the strike. It was a small, tenuous step for cooperation between students and striking workers. General Electric, one of the country's largest defense contractors, was, in the eyes of many New Leftists, "as logical a target for the antiwar movement as Dow Chemical." Students understood that not all the workers who were out on strike were opposed to the war. However, they saw that the strike was affecting the corporation's productivity, so it was a blow against the system that produced the war. It was also a strike against one of the most pervasive effects of the war—inflation that cut into everyone's ability to benefit from a booming economy. For the first time, a few students and factory workers were able to collaborate in a fight against a common enemy—the war that threatened workers' standard of living and students' lives.[20]

As the year ended, student activists were both optimistic and increasingly anxious. The antiwar movement was gaining support, both nationally and in Bloomington. Local clergymen and women's groups had joined with the existing student protest organizations. African-American and white activists were trying to work together more closely. However, the administration and police were taking even more repressive measures to stop students from expressing their opposition to national policies and university rules. The new student conduct code made most acts of protest potential causes for suspension. Obvious police surveillance during the planning sessions for the November peace march and the marches themselves had been unnerving. One writer noted the "Draconian law enforcement displayed here," citing Jim Retherford's recent charge of "assault with the deadly pie incident, . . . and Bizarri's theft of the C.E.W.V. list," concluding that "you start to get paranoid and rightfully so. This university is out for everyone's ass who has the nuts to say something different and it's time we get together and defend ourselves against our freedom's impending death." In its last issue of the 1960s, the staff of the *Spectator* (who were also engaged in a battle with university officials, who had banned all university organizations from buying advertising) wished readers a happy new year and encouraged them to "Keep on truckin', Keep on fightin'."[21]

When activists returned to campus at the beginning of the new year, they continued their efforts to forge stronger bonds between the antiwar movement and Bloomington's working-class community. The strike at General Electric continued and two veteran IU protestors walked picket lines at the local plant. Jim Bingham, a former IU student, an early member of the Fair Play for Cuba Committee, and one of the "Bloomington 3" whose arrest for "assembling to advocate the overthrow of the state of Indiana" had made headlines in the early 1960s, had been working with union leaders throughout the strike, and graduate student Robin Hunter, an early SDS and PRP organizer, joined him on the picket line. The FBI had been watching Robin Hunter for months and concluded, in an underhanded compliment, that he was "the brains, what little there are, behind the YSA."[22]

The strike was settled during the first week of February, after 1,175 employees had been off the job for five months. Later that month Bingham and Hunter, along with Robert McHenry, vice president of IBEW Local 2249, were indicted for conspiring to commit arson by burning garbage trucks that went into the plant. City officials did not release details about the conspiracy charge because the act of arson had not been accomplished. When students learned about the arrests, seventy demonstrators marched peacefully in front of the business school building where General Electric recruiters were interviewing students for jobs. They protested university support of GE's recruiting efforts on campus but left when they were barred from meeting with the company's representatives. Other students organized a legal defense fund for Hunter and Bingham to raise money for their bonds, set at $2,000 each.[23]

In the midst of these protests and arrests both on and off campus, New Leftists once again faced the problem of what to do about student government. Ever since the PRP victory in 1967, some had hoped that they could provide the leadership that would make students' voices a meaningful part of the university community. On the other hand, many felt that student government had been so ineffective in the years since Loftman's victory that it was a waste of time to even get involved in elections. However, those who argued for another attempt at an activist coalition won enough support to create the United Student Movement (USM) and nominated Keith Parker, a junior from Indianapolis who belonged to the Black Panther Party, for president and Mike King, a junior from Hammond, Indiana, and editor of the *Spectator,* for vice president. USM hoped that with this combination of African-American and white radical leadership, it could pull together as many activists as possible into one student party.

Parker, a premedical student who hoped to become a pediatrician, answered questions about his links to the Panthers by saying, "Sure, I'm a panther. That's cool. But I'm also a student, a male, a Methodist—all these other things." King, an English major, worked in Hammond steel mills, along with his father, during summer vacations. Tall and lanky, he had a quirky sense of humor. As editor of Bloomington's underground newspaper, the *Spectator*, he was prone to provoke as well as to amuse his readers. He defended his reputation as a radical at the *Spectator*: "We've elected too many nice guys. . . . most people think I'm crazy . . . but maybe you have to be crazy to be interested in student government."[24]

The USM ran a populist campaign with radical rap. Charging that the university was being turned into "an elite institution" and that "the only way we are going to accomplish anything . . . is to involve people, not revolutionaries, not radicals or conservatives, but people," Parker and King customarily ended speeches and articles with raised fists or capital letters: "ALL POWER TO THE PEOPLE." They put out a fourteen-point platform that called for tuition assessments based on each student's ability to pay; student participation in setting all university policies; student control of campus police, the student newspaper, and the student union; abolition of the Student Conduct Code; and adequate wages for all university employees. Before the March elections, Parker and King wrote, "Education must be taken out of the hands of the pig administrators and put back in the hands of the people. Dig it, reflect upon it, and when you are ready to deal with it, vote USM."

Opposition candidate Tim Morrison of the Independent party lacked Parker's and King's flair for speeches and campaigning. After the votes were counted, Parker, with 2,289 votes, and his opponent, with 1,717, had won the most votes out of the 5,830 ballots cast—a sharp decline from 1967, when over 10,000 students had voted. Some students were beginning to wonder whether student government had much of a future at IU. There was some talk of a run-off, but Morrison conceded the election and the USM candidates took office. Indiana University was the only major campus in the country to elect a member of the Black Panther Party as president of the student body.[25]

Throughout the spring term, students against the war in Vietnam saw even more clearly that they had to come together in their efforts to protest U.S. policies and get American troops out of Southeast Asia. In February 1970, several groups, including WILPF, the Black Panthers, Clergymen and Laymen against the War, YSA, and Veterans for Peace, met to raise money to defend GIs who had been charged with antiwar acts on military posts at home and abroad. The guest speaker was a founder of several underground GI newspapers. He said that the men had been inspired by listening to tapes made by Malcolm X. Charges were dropped after peace activists supported the GIs and charged military officials with violating their civil rights.[26]

At a March meeting of an umbrella group called the Coalition against the War, members of several campus organizations voiced the same goal: "unilateral withdrawal of all U.S. troops—now." They were also unanimous in their commitment to nonviolent action: "We are not interested in violence, destruction, or alienation of those who disagree." The coalition included the Student Mobilization Committee, which had succeeded CEWV in a reorganization the previous fall, and the Bloomington Veterans Committee for Peace in Vietnam. Led by Bill Wiley, a former member of the Air Force and a graduate student in political science, the Veterans Committee had begun to recruit members in earnest after the November 1969 Washington Moratorium and worked with the national organization Veterans for Peace to bring ex-military personnel to the antiwar movement. YSA, back after a period of inactivity, also joined the coalition.[27]

One of the goals of the coalition was to organize a Week of Action in Bloomington—a series of daily antiwar events. Veterans for Peace distributed literature in Ballantine Hall. Clergy and Laymen Concerned about Vietnam sponsored antiwar films. And there was the by now almost traditional gathering in Dunn Meadow on April 15, 1970, with local musicians and speeches by leaders of coalition groups and others, such as the NUC and the Socialist Workers Party. About one thousand people showed up—not as many as were at the previous spring's protests against the fee hike, but the Dunn Meadow mood returned. As one observer described the scene, "The tribe is reborn. . . . Dunn Meadow is a symbol of the Revolution of Life Styles. It is the communal ground and ancestral home for the young. It is IU's continuing Woodstock . . . the spirit of freedom. Some people say that youth has lost its heroes. We are all heroes. Every man striving and yearning to be free is a hero. . . . It's good to be young and it's good to be a little crazy." That evening some of the students returned for a candlelight march to honor the men who had died in the war. About two hundred marchers walked from dormitories through a barrage of conservative, pro-war hecklers who threw eggs at them from windows above the streets.

The crowd of antiwar protestors, holding their flickering lights cupped in their hands, stood together on the grassy field on a beautiful spring night. Everyone was quiet. Keith Parker made a short speech, but the mood was more religious than political. The juxtaposition of that beautiful Bloomington spring and the horror of the war they were protesting caused one student observer to reflect,

> It is difficult and almost hypocritical to try to write one more statement of feeble protest against American aggression in Asia. I sit in Bloomington,

watching a southern Indiana springtime spread its glory as though nothing had happened. . . . War is an ugly rumor in Bloomington, and we are so ashamed of our impotence that we cease to talk about destruction in the hope that we will simply escape. . . . thank God the war is 10,000 miles away.

As you walk about Bloomington this precious springtime, as you swim, smoke dope, play baseball, ride a bicycle, do all those things American college students are most free to do, imagine a daily war that would bring to Bloomington what Asia has felt for more than a decade.

Imagine fighting back now. For the Vietnamese people.[28]

Just as the writer of those words contemplated the beauty of nature in southern Indiana, thousands of other Americans across the country had begun to focus their attention on the environment. Certainly the devastating effects of defoliants such as napalm on the Vietnamese countryside led activists against the war to consider the ways in which our own environment was being damaged. Authors such as Rachel Carson, who wrote *Silent Spring* in the early 1960s, had warned about the dangers of pesticides to birds and plants.[29] And the fragility of the earth was made clear when Americans watched pictures of our planet—in beautiful shades of green and blue against the black backdrop of space—captured by the astronauts who landed on the moon in 1969.

Senator Gaylord Nelson of Wisconsin proposed that Americans should celebrate Earth Day on April 22, 1970. His idea was that citizens could take part in debates and information sessions modeled on earlier antiwar teach-ins. Some twenty million people from coast to coast enthusiastically joined together to promote clean air and clean water by picking up trash along roadsides and in lakes and ponds, planting trees, or protesting against smog produced by automobile emissions. At the University of Wisconsin–Madison, environmental activists handed out flyers about the benefits of recycling, returnable bottles, and biodegradable products.[30]

Senator Nelson came to Dunn Meadow to initiate the Earth Day ceremonies at IU. Amid booths from Planned Parenthood, Environmental Action, and Bloomington Recycling, and after a brief piece of guerrilla theater by members of the Women's International Conspiracy from Hell (WITCH), Nelson spoke to the crowd about the use of dangerous chemical herbicides by U.S. armed forces in Southeast Asia and the need to end pollution of the Earth's environment by stopping the war ("the first environmental war in American history"). He urged the Bloomington audience to work to end pollution within their own community and to vote for politicians who would work for the environment.

The impulse to put good environmental theory into action prompted students at the University of California, Berkeley, to take over an abandoned university construction site near campus and begin planting grass, trees, and flowers on it. An atmosphere of peace and love prevailed as they turned what had been an eyesore into People's Park, a place of beauty. Unfortunately, university administrators saw these students not as happy gardeners but as illegal trespassers. On May 15, 1970, police entered the park and put a fence around it. Students tried to retake the park and were confronted with tear gas, which spread all over campus. Police fired shotguns into the crowd and one student was killed. Berkeley's People's Park became the rallying cry for increasingly alienated activists.

In Bloomington, students expressed their commitment to the environmental cause by creating their own People's Park on the site of the former Black Market. Landowner Larry Canada had razed the burned-out buildings and tried unsuccessfully to sell the property. Students plowed the dirt, planted flowers, vegetables, and other plants, and called for donations so that the land could be used by everyone in Bloomington as a peaceful gathering place.[31]

Then, in the midst of a balmy evening before May Day, students were shocked by President Nixon's announcement that he had ordered U.S. troops to invade Cambodia. About two thousand angry students made their way to Dunn Meadow and listened as Parker spoke about the need to continue the struggle against the war and racism with nonviolent action. Mike King led a large number of students down Kirkwood Avenue, past the freshly dug earth of People's Park, to the town square, circling the county courthouse. Tension was in the air, and King and Parker managed to get most of the crowd back to the campus, where they stopped in front of Kirkwood Hall. Although there were some calls to "trash" Rawles Hall, the ROTC building, Parker and King, along with Finley Campbell, a Democratic party candidate for Congress from the seventh district, preached nonviolence and most of the demonstrators left the scene. However, after Parker, King, and Finley left, about five hundred demonstrators went back to the courthouse. Along the way, someone broke a window of the Monroe County State Bank, and when the marchers got to the courthouse, several men gathered on the lawn were "noticeably irritated by the action of the students." There was a shouting match. One of the men charged at Thomas Veller, an undergraduate, swinging a golf club at him. Veller was arrested for disorderly conduct. His attacker was held at the jail for a few hours and then released. By 4:00 A.M. Bloomington streets were quiet, except for a few heated discussions continuing in some corners of the square.[32]

On May Day 1970, Parker called a meeting to organize a protest dem-

A WITCH (Women's International Conspiracy from Hell) demonstration captures a cameraman's attention during the first Earth Day celebration in 1970. © Dave Repp.

First Earth Day, April 1970. *Arbutus,* 1971.

onstration against the Cambodian invasion. Most of the students were part of Parker and King's USM, but there were a few representatives from YSA, graduate student and labor activist Robin Hunter among them. At the demonstration that afternoon, Parker presented the crowd of fifteen hundred with five demands: that the university officially repudiate President Nixon's Southeast Asian policy and terminate all ROTC programs; that IU administrators admit African-American students in proportion to their percentage of the state's population; that the IU Foundation make public its accounts and supply information on government contracts; and that the university should contribute to Bobby Seale's defense fund. (Seale, a member of the Black Panther Party, was on trial in New Haven, Connecticut, at the time.) Finally, Parker demanded that the administration respond to the demands by Wednesday, May 6, 1970.

Not everyone was happy with the inclusion of a demand for Bobby Seale's defense. YSA members and others favored focusing on a single issue, the latest expansion of the war in Vietnam, and argued that the Cambodian invasion was the main reason students were in the streets. They wanted to stick with that single issue so that they could make the broadest appeal to the community. Nevertheless, the crowd of students endorsed Parker's speech and began marching out of Dunn Meadow. Midway across campus, a bus filled with university police stopped in front of the marchers and about forty officers dressed in full riot gear stepped out at double time, on their way to provide protection for administrators in Bryan Hall. The students, surprised at the sudden rush of police in front of them, also began to pick up the pace. Parker, King, and others led the crowd away from Bryan Hall to the nearby Student Building to avoid confronting the police. Parker told them, "We can accomplish our purpose of presenting our demands without anyone getting ripped up." But the possibility for violence then seemed real to one observer, who described the scene as "40 scared cops vs. 1000 scared students."[33]

Parker and King went over to Bryan Hall to present their demands to President Sutton, but he was out of town. They did talk with Vice President David Derge, who relayed Sutton's message to them: "I will not accept or consider demands of any kind." Parker and King returned to the protestors, and with the university chimes playing "We Shall Overcome" in the background, Parker told them that the administration was "so freaked out they don't know what to do."[34]

On Monday, May 4, 1970, four students were shot by National Guardsmen at an antiwar demonstration at Kent State University in Kent, Ohio. When rally organizers met with dormitory residents Monday afternoon, they were confronted with questions about what would happen if police or local pro-war groups attacked student demonstrators. Pam Gockley, who spoke with students in Wilkie Hall, came away from the meeting feeling that the rally should be canceled.

In fact, it nearly was. Sometime during the night of May 4, an unidentified thief stole fifty automatic shotguns and six handguns from Stewart's Speed Shop in downtown Bloomington. Students suspected the Ku Klux Klan, while downtown the rumors had students as the culprits. Parker and King began to have doubts about pulling students into a situation where they might get hurt or killed, and they called a press conference to announce that the rally was canceled. At the last minute, however, they decided that since students had approved the rally, they could not unilaterally abandon it, and canceled the press conference. The demonstration was on for May 6, 1970, with Parker and King urging students to "keep people around you from going crazy."[35]

No one went crazy. Around eight thousand students in Dunn Meadow listened to speakers, then marched north to the athletic field (a route designed to lead students away from Rawles Hall, on the other side of campus), and broke up peacefully. Parker began the rally with his plea for nonviolence:

> We saw what happened at Kent State when four very beautiful people were murdered. We have witnessed helicopters over our campus, the mobilization of police, the mobilization of the Ku Klux Klan, and of reactionary provocateurs on this campus. This rally will still be held. . . . We don't want to have a Kent State here. We don't need any more martyrs to our cause. We have a duty to ourselves and to humanity to speak out against injustice. To be silent is to endorse it.

The biggest ovation went to political science professor Bernard Morris, who climbed up on the speakers' platform in Dunn Meadow on crutches (he had been injured in an accident earlier) and said to students,

> I'm told the University is supposed to be above politics. Well, I don't know if it's above, beyond or beneath politics. I join you in condemnation of Nixon's strategy of terminating the war by widening it. It is strategically unsound, politically self-defeating, and morally indefensible. We must have no more Earth Days, no more anti-pollution days, no more goody-goody anti-litter diversions until the war is ended.

Everyone in the crowd stood up and shouted their approval.[36]

The next day, the faculty council declared a day of mourning. The killings at Kent State and their own students' peaceful demonstrations for an end to the war seemed to have penetrated the collective professorial conscience. While the faculty did not go so far as to cancel classes,

IU students march on May 6, 1970, two days after the National Guard's killing of four students at Kent State University. *Arbutus,* 1971.

they did endorse the student-led teach-ins that had been planned for that day. Political science professor York Willbern, secretary of the faculty council, announced that the university community needed "to give concentrated attention to divisions in the country and to how a university can properly study and work to resolve these divisive questions."[37]

IU students joined thousands of other college and university students on 136 campuses across the country in boycotting classes. President Sutton told the press that while no classes were to be officially canceled, "I just couldn't be more proud of the way our students and faculty have behaved during this crisis." On Founders Day, just as had happened the year before, honors students walked out on the ceremonies to protest the war.[38] Jody Lanard, a straight-A student, led the walkout after she announced, "I cannot stay here while students are being repressed in the name of law and order." Three hundred of the six hundred students being feted followed her, some holding signs that read "There are four dead honor students in Kent."[39]

After the antiwar rally, the YWCA and the union board conducted a campus-wide referendum on Parker's demands, which resulted in a resounding vote against the war and for some kind of continued strike action. Of the 17,450 students who voted, 12,345 said they opposed President Nixon's decision to invade Cambodia, while 5,575 expressed support. Slightly over 12,000 students supported a Congressional cutoff of funds for the war, with 4,780 opposing it. Nearly 10,000 of IU's students felt that classes should be canceled to protest the war, while 7,137 did not. Approximately the same numbers favored and opposed university repudiation of President Nixon's war policies: 9,857 favored it, and 7,285 did not. When asked if the university should admit African-American students in direct proportion to their percentage of the state's population, students split almost evenly: 8,371 favored such a policy, 8,545 opposed it. When asked whether the IU Foundation should make its records and accounts public, student support was fairly strong: 12,234 in favor, 4,651 opposed. However, students were not in favor of university contributions to Bobby Seale's defense fund (13,170 against funding, 3,356 for), nor did they want ROTC programs to be abolished (9,481 for keeping ROTC, 7,361 against).[40]

The results of this referendum provide important insight into Hoosier students' attitudes at the beginning of the 1970s. First, the majority of them opposed the war in Vietnam, although they did not generally support canceling classes in order to demonstrate that opposition, or any official university repudiation of the war. Moreover, by a slim margin, they did not approve of abolishing ROTC classes as a way of expressing their opposition to the war. Second, their antiwar stance did not translate into widespread support for increased educational opportunities for African-Americans or for support of black political causes. While most students could unite around their opposition to the war, racial issues continued to be divisive.

Hoosier students reflected a national move to the left end of the political spectrum. A Harris survey conducted after the Cambodian invasion showed that more students referred to themselves as radicals than had ever done so in the 1960s (11%) and that the proportion of liberals had doubled (to 40%) during the decade. All across the nation, students debated the best way to show their opposition to the war and to President Nixon's policies. The debate usually came down to one question: to strike or not to strike.[41]

Students went on strike on 350 campuses across the country, and antiwar protests resulted in the closing of 500 campuses, 50 of them for the rest of the academic year. At Michigan State University, 12,000 students joined the strike action. At Pennsylvania State University, 18,000 students turned out for a referendum on whether or not to strike and 11,000 voted to substitute antiwar teach-ins for regular classes.[42]

At Indiana University, USM leaders Parker and King called a mass meeting to discuss strike action. The first proposal was to picket Bryan Hall in order to shut it down, an act that could have triggered a dangerous crisis.

Everyone knew of Governor Whitcomb's hostility toward student strikes, and no one doubted that he was capable of calling out National Guardsmen to enforce his policies and keep the administration building open. President Sutton and Chancellor Carter would then be caught between the governor and the students. Once again, fortunately, everyone's worst nightmares never materialized. With about six hundred students peacefully standing around the administration building, police arrested eight picketers. After the arrests, students left quietly. There were some picketers at Ballantine Hall, but after administrators talked with Parker, King, and others, a deal was made to keep university buildings open if Sutton and Carter would meet with students in the auditorium that afternoon.[43]

The university auditorium was packed, and closed-circuit television cameras relayed the meeting to large classrooms in the school of journalism and Ballantine Hall. The two administrators expressed sympathy for students' concerns about the war and praised their peaceful demonstrations. Both of them rejected student demands to shut down the university. They acknowledged that nearly ten thousand students had voted to cancel classes in the May 11 referendum. However, they pointed out that there were approximately fifty-five thousand students on all of the university's campuses and they felt that as long as any students wanted to attend class it was their duty to keep the classrooms open. At the same time, the two university officials acknowledged the reasonableness of students' concerns and agreed to work with the faculty council to consider various options for dealing with students who missed classes while taking part in peaceful demonstrations.[44] They disclaimed any university responsibility for national policies in Southeast Asia. Parker had demanded that there be no heckling during the meeting, and his attack on Sutton was more or less focused on giving students more power within the university. A few students criticized those who had picketed Ballantine Hall because they had yelled at anyone who tried to get into the building to attend classes. As the meeting drew to a close, students' main concern was that striking students not be penalized with low or failing grades—a crucial issue but one that the faculty council had to decide, not the president and chancellor.[45]

During the session, there were reports of local townspeople attacking students around Showalter Fountain. A group of about a hundred citizens and university employees, calling themselves "Neighbors and Citizens of Bloomington," were led by Spike Dixon, a trainer in the athletic department. These "Neighbors and Citizens" had driven to President Sutton's house in a car cavalcade to express to President Sutton that they "were behind him 100%."[46]

Ten days after the shootings at Kent State, two more students were killed at Jackson State University, an all-black campus in Jackson, Mississippi. Parker speculated publicly about the murders, "I question whether these are really shootouts or shoot-ins. They are always justified as a 'mysterious sniper.' He's an invisible dude." About thirty people, mostly graduate students, began a fast in Dunn Meadow for peace and for the students killed at Jackson State. They planned to fast for a week, but rain and threats of violence from hostile townspeople forced the group to leave after two nights.[47]

There was a second teach-in on May 18, 1970, organized primarily by faculty and the student government. Before a crowd of about 1,700, leaders at the meeting urged students to get involved in local Democratic Party politics. Indiana Senator Vance Hartke, an opponent of the war in Vietnam, appealed to students to campaign for local representatives who would join him and his antiwar allies in Congress and in state assemblies as well.[48]

On May 22, 1970, final examination week began. The strike, the teach-ins, the fast, and the demonstrations were over. The faculty council had voted to adopt several grading options so that students who had participated in the strike would not be punished.

The Bloomington campus remained unscarred, unlike others across the country. Students at Kent State University firebombed the ROTC offices, as did students at over thirty other universities, from Berkeley to DePauw. At the University of Wisconsin, students broke the windows of a classroom building and set the trash on fire. But with a Black Panther leading protestors and a white Hoosier radical behind him preaching unity, IU activists disdained "mad dog adventurism," saying that they were "disciplined people who are not fools to face bullets with our flesh." Despite stolen guns, racist Klan leaflets, and a few fistfights, no one in Bloomington was killed or even seriously injured. Even with all the threats and all the fears, antiwar protesters, university administrators, faculty, and supporters of the war had managed to keep their emotions and actions balanced and maintain a precarious peace in the community.[49] After students left Bloomington and other campuses in the spring of 1970, most of those who had been involved in the antiwar movement realized that the killings at Kent State had changed it. Even though IU remained peaceful—at least on the surface—that was not the case elsewhere. In March 1970, members of the Weathermen who had been trying to construct a bomb in an apartment in New York City succeeded only in blowing themselves up. Later that summer, activists at the University of Wisconsin blew up a physics laboratory and killed a young graduate student.[50] For a few, the movement had become a self-destructive path toward nihilism.

However, the majority of student activists continued to oppose the war, though with new perspectives and different agendas. The decade of the 1970s marked a turning point for women, who took the lessons they had learned in SDS, the Student Nonviolent Coordinating Committee (SNCC), and elsewhere and applied them to their own struggles, both against the war and for gender equity. Many students looked at the war in Vietnam as not only immoral but also destructive to both human beings and their environment, bringing in a new "green" theme. Students who had joined picket lines with workers in the 1960s continued to protest against the war because it undermined the economy and working-class people. African Americans continued their fight against the war as part of their ongoing struggle for racial justice. The movement in the 1970s was different than it had been in the 1960s: less dominated by white males, and more varied in voices, philosophies, and agendas.

CHAPTER 5

Student Rights, Civil Rights: African Americans and the Struggle for Racial Justice

African-American students at Indiana University were part of a national civil rights movement that reached its height during the 1960s. This movement, more than any other in modern history, shaped the vision that university students—both black and white—had of themselves, their country, and the world.

The Student Nonviolent Coordinating Committee (SNCC), which was the most important student civil rights group during the early sit-ins and freedom rides in the South, had around three hundred members at its founding in 1960. At the height of the movement, during the Mississippi voter registration drives of the mid-1960s, probably not more than a few thousand students were involved. But numbers do not really tell the story of the civil rights movement and its importance to American students.

The civil rights movement was a moral crusade to make Americans live up to the ideals of their Constitution. Leaders of the movement, such as Ella Baker, the "founding mother" of SNCC and officially executive director of Dr. Martin Luther King's Southern Christian Leadership Conference (SCLC), Bob Moses, James Forman, Diane Nash, and Ruby Doris Robinson, all founding members, spoke of "a beloved community" that included brothers and sisters who worked for and shared a common vision of an America based on principles of peace and justice. This idea spread from campus to campus as students debated, in class and late into the night in dormitory rooms, Mahatma Gandhi's principles of passive resistance and nonviolence, existentialism's ideas of the value of an authentic existence, and religious principles concerning humanitarian compassion.

Indiana University provided a challenging environment for black students because of Bloomington's roots in southern culture and the strong influence of the Ku Klux Klan in Indiana history and politics. At the same time, the university itself, especially under the leadership of Herman B Wells, had proven to be relatively enlightened in its policies regarding students of color. Defying a Midwestern tradition of isolationism, Wells was a confirmed internationalist. He dedicated much of his presidency to making IU a world-class institution, open to students and scholars from around the world. He understood, when many Hoosiers did not, the debilitating effects of racism on the effort to achieve intellectual excellence. When black students came to IU during the 1960s, they found more racial tolerance than at many other Midwestern universities.

At the same time, black students could not avoid evidence of racism within the university community and Bloomington and especially the obvious presence of the Klan. White students might brush off racist remarks or Klan leaflets. But African Americans, especially those from the South, took such things seriously. They were very well aware that the atmosphere that bred racial epithets also bred death threats. Moreover, because their numbers were so small, they felt especially vulnerable whenever they challenged the all-white university administration in a state that harbored dark elements of racism and bigotry.

IU's African-American students found themselves in an ambiguous position during the 1960s. They came to IU because they wanted to improve themselves, to become leaders in their communities and their professions. And, in many ways, IU offered them exceptional opportunities to achieve these goals. However, they faced discrimination every day— not just in the classroom, but at the grocery store, the bank, and the bars. The bravery of the SNCC freedom fighters in the South was not lost on IU students. While they were not a part of the early struggles for civil rights, eventually, they, too, had to make their stand for justice.

The assassination of Dr. Martin Luther King, Jr., on April 4, 1968, provided the catalyst for black students at IU, and at many other Midwestern universities, to organize. They circulated petitions for racial equity on campus and for courses and programs on their own history, literature, and culture. In fact, IU's administrators and faculty approved a black studies program before those at any other major American university. This early initiative on the part of IU leaders was not lost on students, who appreciated the leadership of Dr. Orlando Taylor, the proposed director of the program. Professor Taylor taught communications studies and was a favorite of many black students. Tall, outgoing, and highly energetic, he was one of the few black faculty members at IU and was often called upon to speak to community groups about race relations.

Toward the end of the decade, black students on many campuses became increasingly militant, adopting former SNCC activist Stokely Carmichael's call for black power. In the spring of 1969, for instance, black students at Cornell occupied the student union building to protest the administration's delay in creating a black studies program; when they finally left the building, they did so carrying guns, with bandoleers of ammunition slung over their shoulders. Black students at IU, while determined to fight for their rights, did not abandon peaceful protest, mainly because they wanted to retain the moral high ground that nonviolence provided. Moreover, they maintained relationships with concerned administrators and faculty throughout their years of protest on the Bloomington campus.[1]

Historically, black-white relations in Bloomington had been less hostile than in other Indiana towns. During the 1920s, the Ku Klux Klan, with its vicious message of hatred on racial, religious, and ethnic grounds, played a prominent political role. With nearly three hundred thousand members, the Klan dominated state government. In Bloomington, the Klan made its presence known by marching through the black community, where most of IU's twenty black students rented rooms. However, there were no lynchings on the courthouse square, as there were in Marion, Indiana, in 1930. Bloomington did not have a sign at the city limits that warned blacks to be out of town by sundown, as some small Indiana towns did as late as the 1950s. And no one ever murdered a black woman on the streets of Bloomington, as happened in nearby Martinsville in 1968.

Still, Bloomington's attitude toward blacks had ranged from indifference, to intolerance, to outright hostility. These attitudes derived from the southern culture that many white settlers brought with them when they arrived in Indiana. While most of the whites who settled in Monroe County were not slaveowners, they had adopted some of the racist views that slaveowners held of blacks. After moving north, they had only sporadic contact with blacks, and these views, formed in the antebellum past, solidified during the late nineteenth and early twentieth centuries.[2]

A small black community in Bloomington grew up alongside the university campus. During the early 1900s, black homeowners and businessmen lived in an area known as Bucktown, on the east side of town between the courthouse square and the campus. As the university expanded, whites bought property in those blocks and black residents moved west of the square, restricted to that area by discriminatory practices on the part of many Bloomington realtors. One of the most important places on the west side was the Second Baptist Church, the largest black institution in Bloomington. Reverend Ernest D. Butler, who became the church's minister in 1959, was a frequent critic of white business owners and politicians who discriminated against blacks. In the early 1960s he launched a campaign to get city officials to hire black employees, especially public school teachers, and to eliminate unfair housing practices. Elizabeth Bridgwaters was another prominent member of Bloomington's black community. Her grandfather, Preston Emmanuel Eagleson, had been an outstanding athlete at Indiana University in the 1890s and in 1897 had become the first black to receive a master's degree from IU. When Elizabeth Bridgwaters applied for a position at the university in the mid-1960s, she was offered a job as a kitchen helper; she had advanced to production supervisor by the time she retired in the 1980s. Convinced of the need to help black children, she became the first black elected to the school board. However, Butler and Bridgwaters were exceptional. Most educated blacks left Bloomington if they wanted to advance themselves, leaving behind a small community that had few leaders and that was, for the most part, cut off from the campus both geographically and socially.[3]

For blacks born in Indiana, the Bloomington campus of Indiana University was affordable and, despite its problems, offered the best chance for an education that would be a ticket to better careers and opportunities. For high school graduates from southern states, Indiana was one of the closest northern universities, and no matter how racist it appeared to many, its academic strengths outweighed its racial problems. Moreover, some progress had been made toward better race relations by the mid-1960s. During the years when William Lowe Bryan was president of the university, black students and their problems were largely ignored. With Herman B Wells at the helm, however, things began to change. Quietly and without much fanfare, Wells started to remove overt signs of racism on the Bloomington campus. In the early years of his administration, "reserved" signs were placed on tables in the student union, and everyone understood that these were "reserved" for blacks. Without saying anything publicly, Wells had the signs removed, and soon students sat wherever they pleased. In addition, he persuaded the barber in the union building to cut black students' hair. Some university sports had been segregated until Wells supported black students' rights to play on all varsity teams and to use the university swimming pools. Wells also initiated a program that brought teachers from Stillman College, an all-black school in Tuscaloosa, Alabama, to attend classes at IU's School of Education during the summers, boosting the number of blacks in Bloomington significantly during those months.[4]

Despite these relatively progressive steps, black students at Indiana University in the mid-1960s lived in a world separate from whites. African Americans made up a little over 6% of the state's population during the 1960s. At IU, they made up only about 2% of the university's student body—four to six hundred students out of about twenty-six thousand. They often found themselves alone in otherwise all-white classrooms, highly visible and conscious of their separateness. Their professors were nearly always white. There were fewer than ten black faculty members at IU and there were no blacks in the upper levels of the administration. If they had academic or personal problems, their only official recourse was usually to a white professor or administrator. Black students were overwhelmingly more likely than whites to drop out of school. Nearly half of those who entered left before graduating.[5]

Partly because of the pressure they felt in the classroom and on campus, African-American students often lived with or near each other, on and off campus, so that they could give each other the support and sense of community that they needed to survive. Many preferred to live in groups in the dormitories, especially Briscoe Hall, or in one of three black fraternities. There was only one integrated fraternity, and it was the only fraternity founded at IU—Kappa Alpha Psi, organized by black students in 1906. Sixty years later, Ray Stubbs, a civil rights activist, was initiated as its only white member.[6]

There is no evidence that black students at IU took part in the sit-ins or the freedom rides of the civil rights movement in the early and mid-1960s. Given the urgency of the cause, this absence of activity might seem surprising. However, the reality of the times makes it less so. First, young black students who managed to enroll at Indiana University were part of an emerging middle class. For a young black man, a college degree was, according to sociologist Dr. Harry Edwards,

> a 'union card' that enables him to get a better job than blacks from the lower classes, but also a sanctuary within which he can feel safe from the humiliations and insults heaped upon most Black Americans by whites. . . . [I]t provides . . . some compensation for an undesirable accident of birth that he was born Black in a white racist society.[7]

Many of these young people were the first in their families to go to college. The majority received financial aid, but even with that help, they and their families were making tremendous financial sacrifices to make their college experience possible. No matter how much they wanted to join up with the civil rights workers in the South, the cost was nearly prohibitive. SNCC volunteers had to pay for their own transportation and had to be able to support themselves, even if minimally. Black students also had to figure in the cost of lost opportunities and the consequences of jail records. For these representatives of an emerging black middle class, the civil rights movement of the 1960s was a sign of hope but also an effort toward a distant goal—much admired but not always acted upon.[8]

Moreover, black students at Indiana University did not face the same kind of inequities that students of color faced on other campuses. In Mississippi and Alabama, blacks were not even allowed to enroll at public universities. Other Midwestern universities were open to black students but often provided an extremely hostile environment.

For example, at the University of Missouri, white students flew the Confederate flag at football games and a local deputy pulled a revolver on a black student for responding by unfurling a black nationalist flag. At that same campus, members of the Kappa Alpha fraternity wore Confederate uniforms on horseback in homecoming parades. They paid blacks to follow them dressed as servants and slaves. At the University of Kansas, tensions between the Lawrence Police Department and African-American students remained high throughout the 1960s, ultimately resulting in the shooting of Rick "Tiger" Dowdell, a member of the Black Student Union, in 1970.[9]

However, black students on IU's Bloomington campus were well aware that, while their situation might not appear to be as difficult as those of their peers at other Midwestern and southern campuses, they, too, had to face the indignities of racism. As they walked along the main streets of the Bloomington campus, they passed the imposing houses of all-white fraternities and sororities. They watched as impeccably dressed Greeks rushed to class, assured of their own social standing in a world that seemed made to order for them. Greeks had friends in the right places. Herman B Wells was a loyal Sigma Nu, and Elvis Stahr belonged to Sigma Chi. The problem that the Greek system posed for black students was not really one of housing—most African-American students did not want to join white fraternities or sororities, and most could not have afforded the house bills and dues even if they had been allowed to join. Rather, the all-white Greek system symbolized university administrators' acceptance of organizations whose very existence was based on racial exclusion.

At the same time, African-American students were wary of student activists, even though many of those activists were outspoken advocates for civil rights and criticized the Greek system and the university's sanction of discriminatory policies. However, not many black students saw the activists' call for participatory democracy as relevant to their own needs. Most black students found that they had to work harder than their white counterparts to stay in good academic standing. Many black males were on ath-letic scholarships that required long hours of practice. Black students who faced these daily demands, along with the effort of simply being a black student at a nearly all-white campus, regarded student causes as far re-moved from their lives. They did not have time, energy, or interest to spare for issues like women's hours and control of student government.

African Americans had good reason to be suspicious of members of the New Left who tried to recruit them. They did not want to be branded radicals in Bloomington, where conservative social values dominated both the black and white communities. They knew that many Hoosiers were outraged by the sight of integrated social groups. In a region where hostility toward blacks was often only thinly submerged beneath a veneer of civility, the price of integration was usually paid by blacks. It might be cheap if it was just taunts and jeers from whites in passing cars. But those taunts could turn to threats and physical violence. Blacks in Bloomington were well aware of how vulnerable they were to white racists.

Aside from a natural caution about associating with white students, black students wanted to maintain their own integrity. They were proud of who they were and of their heritage. They did not want to look as though they were trying to "be white." Nor did they want to be used as symbols of white liberalism on issues of race. They wanted to have their own voice at IU. They wanted to succeed with their integrity intact.

In the spring of 1968, African-American students organized the Afro–Afro-American Students Association (AAASA) to improve commu-nication between students from Africa and black Americans on campus. They elected Robert Johnson, a graduate student in sociology, as their first president. Johnson, a thoughtful, soft-spoken intellectual who cared deeply about problems of racism and poverty in America, was respected by a wide cross section of students and faculty. A native of Lafayette, In-diana, Johnson had graduated from Franklin College, where he had been an excellent scholar and athlete. He was one of a few students at IU who worked with both black and white activists. Although no one doubted his integrity or his commitment to racial justice, the fact that he lived with his white girlfriend created some tension within the black student community.[10] Nor did AAASA go unobserved. Shortly after Johnson or-ganized the group, the FBI opened a file on it.[11]

Johnson described AAASA as seeking "to cooperate with individuals and organizations dedicated to the eradication of those impediments to human progress," such as racism and segregation. Black students who joined AAASA, he explained, wanted to discover an "anchored sense of identity. . . . In order to counter the distortions of their history as Americans, black students are turning increasingly to an examination of the contributions people of color have made in an oppressive environment." They also wanted to discuss questions that black students across the country were posing to themselves and to their white peers: "How long must we wait for acceptance by the majority? What must we do to further prove that we are worthy of acceptance? Do we want to be integrated into society under prevailing conditions?" AAASA members wanted to take part in a process of "exerting the will of human dignity by individual action, by ethnic assertion, by multiracial coalition, or by any means that speak to humanizing this often inhumane system we inhabit."[12]

Another reason for the founding of AAASA was the increase in racist remarks and threats in Bloomington, and the decreasing willingness of black students to tolerate them. The Ku Klux Klan asked city officials for a parade permit to march through downtown streets. Judge Nat U. Hill refused to grant the permit on the grounds that the parade might lead to violence and incite riots. Johnson and other AAASA members were quick to see that if the Klan could be banned from marching, so, too, could any other group. They protested the ban, saying that they were offended by the cancellation since it was based on rumors that AAASA "had planned a violent action." Actually, AAASA wanted the Klan to march, so that their message of hate would be clear to everyone. At the same time they wanted to mount a peaceful counter-demonstration in order to clarify the differences between the two groups.[13]

Thwarted in their efforts to march in Bloomington, leaders of the Klan asked university officials to allow them to hold a debate under the auspices of the IU Forum, a lecture series. President Stahr urged Forum organizers to cancel the debate because, he argued, it would be insulting to black faculty and students. In an open letter to Stahr, AAASA members demanded that he take more concrete measures, hiring more black faculty and admitting more black students, as well as introducing a black studies program.[14]

Stahr responded to these demands in a speech at the National Conference on Negroes in Higher Education. He told his audience that he did not think predominantly white universities should hire black faculty away from all-black colleges, because they were often vital to their own institution's existence. He did not want to recruit more black students until he felt "reasonably confident that we have learned effective methods of instruction, geared to meet the special need they may have—so that they are likely to succeed, not fail, when they do enroll." He admitted that IU had "a long way to go" toward achieving these goals and announced that he was searching for "an outstanding Negro scholar-administrator" for his staff.[15]

After hearing about Stahr's speech, AAASA members decided to respond by marching to the president's house on April 1, 1968, even though they knew he was not in town. The president and his family lived in a lovely home, surrounded by gardens, in the middle of the IU campus. AAASA member Clarence "Rollo" Turner led the marchers across the green lawn. A native of New Jersey and a graduate of Central State University in Ohio, Rollo Turner was a Ph.D. candidate in sociology. Short and stocky, he was feisty by nature and street-smart from his early years around New York City. Plagued by problems with his eyes, Turner was rarely seen without his dark glasses, which made him more threatening to some IU administrators. He was a natural leader, and black students admired and respected him because he said out loud what many of them thought privately. One student reflected later that if Robert Johnson was the brains behind AAASA, then Rollo Turner was its voice.[16]

AAASA members sat outside Stahr's house for six hours. Even though the group was nonviolent, Mrs. Stahr and her children remained inside, terrified of the group of black students on the lawn. One of the students' demands was that Stahr abolish the university committee on discriminatory practices, because students had no say in its membership. Finally, Stahr sent word that he would agree to disband the committee. Upon hearing of Stahr's decision, Turner agreed to disband the group outside the president's house. Turner told AAASA members, "The point has been made here that black students can come together as a group of black people, stay together as a group of black people, can make a point as black people. It is time to go home."[17]

A few days later, on April 4, 1968, Dr. Martin Luther King, Jr., was assassinated in Memphis. As the news swept across the nation, presidential candidate Senator Robert F. Kennedy was campaigning in Indianapolis. He was scheduled to address a black audience in the heart of the city and many of his advisors, fearing violence, urged him to cancel his speech. Kennedy refused and delivered an eloquent encomium to Dr. King and to the American people. Looking out over the crowd, he spoke without a prepared text:

> What we need in the United States is not division; what we need in the United States is not hatred; what we need in the United States is not violence or lawlessness; but love and wisdom, and compassion toward one another, and a feeling of justice toward those who still suffer within our country, whether they be white or they be black.[18]

In contrast, Robert Johnson reflected the feelings of many black students about Dr. King's assassination when he wrote, "My first reaction was pure outrage. . . . [C]oming at a time like it does, it will do away with the faith in non-violence." As a memorial to Dr. King, African-American students formed an Ad Hoc Committee against Racism (AHCAR) with the following program: abolish racism in fraternities and sororities; employ a full-time black human relations officer on campus; recruit more black undergraduate and graduate students; establish black history and literature courses; demand that the IU Foundation provide scholarship funds for underprivileged black students; and waive entrance requirements so that more black students could be admitted to IU. The committee issued a statement that noted "a lack of and a lag in communications between the administration and the remainder of the University family on human rights issues." While black students remained hopeful that King's vision of racial justice could still be achieved, many worried that nonviolence would no longer work in America's "violent, racist society."[19]

In May 1968, African-American students at IU felt increasingly frustrated at their inability to focus administrators' attention on the inequities that they faced on the Bloomington campus. Dr. King's assassination only heightened their sensitivity to that lack of attention.

White fraternity and sorority members saw no reason to cancel Indiana University's annual rite of spring—the Little 500 Bicycle Race. The race had been created by the Indiana University Foundation as a spinoff from the Indianapolis 500 automobile races, and money from ticket sales was used to provide scholarships to needy students. Since the foundation never allowed outside investigators to look at its accounts, no one could verify the exact use of the event's revenues. Nevertheless, "Little 5" had become one of the world's greatest college weekends, and thousands of fans flocked to Bloomington in May to watch young men on bicycles race against each other in teams representing fraternities and other groups. The races were accompanied by parties where large quantities of beer and other forms of alcohol were consumed, sometimes leading to various forms of public embarrassment. The Little 500 remains one of Indiana's most significant contributions to the popular culture of American undergraduates.[20]

Watching white fraternity members race bicycles in laps around the university stadium while fans cheered and drank beer seemed more appalling than ever to these members of AAASA who had been fighting the racial exclusion policies of IU fraternities and sororities. This was the year, they decided, to make their stand. Rollo Turner and Robert Johnson joined forces with Kenny Newsome, a popular athlete, to stage a demonstration that would shut down the Little 500. They organized fifty black students to sit in on the stadium field on May 8, 1968, and issued an ulti-

Clarence "Rollo" Turner during African-American students' shutdown of the Little 500, May 1968. *Arbutus,* 1969.

matum: no one would race until IU's fraternities eliminated the racially discriminatory clauses in their charters. As they put it, "The declared bigots will not ride on Saturday, or nobody will ride on Saturday." In a statement to the press, Rollo Turner emphasized that in the tradition of Dr. King, the demonstration would be nonviolent. However, he said, if they were attacked, the demonstrators would defend themselves.[21]

President Stahr, fully aware of the public relations damage that would result if the Little 500 was shut down, began negotiating with all of the fraternity presidents on campus, trying to arrange for the elimination of discriminatory clauses. Meanwhile, it began to rain in Bloomington and the stadium field turned into a lake of mud. The demonstrators huddled together under makeshift shelter, refusing to give up. For thirty-eight hours they waited. Some were afraid of attack by groups like the Ku Klux Klan. Armed mostly with sticks and lead pipes, they knew they were no match for any serious assault. But Rollo Turner was fairly confident that they were safe. He knew that university officials remembered the criticism of campus police after the Dow demonstration in 1967 and would try to maintain order. Moreover, Vice President Joseph Sutton and Chancellor Wells, along with faculty members Orlando Taylor and John Joyner, had come to the stadium to assure the demonstrators of their concern for their well-being. Students, black and white, came to offer support. Local high school and grade school students sneaked into the shelters at night, bringing food and other supplies. It became an extraordinarily emotional experience for the protestors and it tied them to each other for years to come. For this group of university students, the shutdown of the Little

500 was a dramatic statement. By putting their bodies on the line, they were finally able to communicate the depth of their feeling about the cause of racial justice. They were willing to challenge authority in order to gain recognition for their cause. And in the aftermath of Dr. King's murder, they demonstrated peacefully.

The FBI kept a close watch on the Little 500 shutdown. Agents sent in detailed memos of the events and enclosed handouts from members of the United Anti-Racist Movement (UARM), a group of white students who supported the protestors. One FBI agent noted that the UARM was controlled by the IU Committee to End the War in Vietnam and led by white activist Mark Ritchey.[22]

Race officials postponed the race until the next weekend because of the rain. University administrators had ordered that no fraternities would be allowed to participate if their charters contained discriminatory clauses. Throughout the week, Bloomington fraternity officers called national officers in order to get rid of these clauses. Every fraternity complied except Phi Delta Theta, whose team was duly excluded. Jeff Raff, the president of Phi Delta Theta and a member of its team, was personally committed to racial equality, but he had been unable to reach agreement with the national leaders of his fraternity. He was bitterly disappointed not only at having to sit out the race but also by the uncompromising policies of his fraternity's leaders. The race was held without incident, and was won by the team from Phi Gamma Delta. In a symbolic gesture of brotherhood, the team leader tossed their trophy up into the stands to Raff. As the crowd looked on, Raff refused to accept it.[23]

When students returned to campus in the fall of 1968, they learned of the murder of an African American in a nearby town. On September 16, 1968, Carol Jenkins, a young black woman, was selling encyclopedias door to door in Martinsville, Indiana, about thirty miles north of Bloomington. During the afternoon, an assailant attacked her and stabbed her through the heart with a screwdriver. Local police were never able to find the murderer. Many blacks believed that the Klan was involved, but no one could prove it. Jenkins's murder heightened fears of white violence among African-American students at Indiana University.[24]

At the University of Illinois, members of the Black Student Union occupied a building to protest broken promises of financial aid, improved admission policies, and adequate housing.[25] But at IU the first confrontation between African Americans and the administration centered on the election of the homecoming queen in the fall of 1968. In August, the Miss America pageant in Atlantic City, New Jersey, had been disrupted by women charging, among other things, that the all-white contest was racist. They also argued that women were no longer willing to follow white male ideals of feminine beauty. To make their point, they thew girdles and copies of *Playboy* magazine into a trash can. Among the signs they carried was one that said, "Miss America Is Alive and Angry— in Harlem!"[26]

In Bloomington, five African-American contestants for homecoming queen complained that they had been discriminated against in the selection process because only one of the five judges, Professor John Joyner, was an African American. They charged that the criteria used to choose the winner were biased against nonwhite candidates. Armed with a statement prepared by members of IU's anthropology department, Rollo Turner went before the Joint Committee on Discriminatory Practices, chaired by Professor Orlando Taylor, to argue the case. He told its members (and acting president Herman B Wells) that all judgments about beauty are influenced by cultural values and by race, class, and ethnicity, and that the contest was inherently racist. He challenged the committee to abolish beauty contests because they demeaned all women, especially those whose physical attributes were neither shared nor valued by the majority population. After consulting with Wells and with representatives from the alumni association and the student union board, Taylor announced that the contest was void and that there would be no homecoming queen, because the contest had been based on racial standards that could not "fairly consider entrants of different races and ethnic groups whose physical and behavioral characteristics depart materially from the dominant segment of society, which in this case means an American white standard." Wells agreed, saying that "the customary procedure is no longer adequate in representing a campus grown cosmopolitan and which itself represents people of nearly every national origin, creed, and color."[27]

Once again, Wells's leadership proved to be decisive in averting a crisis. He understood that this was not a battle worth fighting and that, indeed, black students had positioned themselves on the moral high ground. As an educational leader committed to making Indiana University an international institution, Wells saw no point in maintaining a campus tradition of homecoming queens when it so clearly flew in the face of racial equity. When questioned about the incident over twenty years later, Wells remarked, "I never cared much for queens anyway."[28]

Apparently, Wells's feelings were shared by others on campus, as the president of the union board announced that the Miss Indiana University pageant would be canceled that year and the staff of IU's yearbook, *The Arbutus*, decided not to elect a queen for the first time since 1930. Because there was no homecoming queen, no Miss IU, and no *Arbutus* queen, the 1968 yearbook was the first ever not to have a special "queens" section. Steve Mayes, editor of *The Arbutus*, brushed off the decision to not have a yearbook queen, saying, "We were only having a contest to more or less follow tradition. We weren't really symbolizing anything special."[29]

While the campaign against campus queens did not mark a significant change in race relations at IU, it did indicate that African Americans had made their point to the university community—that promoting white ideals of physical attractiveness at the expense of other racial and ethnic groups was antiquated and insulting to students who came to Bloomington from across the country and from all parts of the world. In 1968, many students at IU had faces and bodies that were beautiful, but different from those of the latest sweetheart of Sigma Chi.

That fall, Rollo Turner decided to open a store on Kirkwood Avenue in collaboration with other African-American students and faculty. He called it the Black Market and sold books, records, artwork, clothing, and jewelry imported from Africa or made by African Americans. Located on property owned by local political activist Larry Canada and his wife, Kathy, the Black Market fit in well with the surrounding small shops selling incense, posters, pipes, and other items popular with local members of the counterculture. Turner saw the Black Market more as a consciousness-raising operation than as a profit-making enterprise. He never made money on it, but felt it was important to keep the store as a center for African-American and African students who had few other places to gather in a friendly, congenial atmosphere. As the only store in Bloomington that offered African products, it would, he hoped, help to "eliminate misconceptions about black people and expose blacks and whites to African culture."[30]

When students gathered at the Black Market after it opened that fall, one of the things they talked about was the arrival of three members of the Black Panther Party on campus. The party members spoke at IU on their way to Indianapolis to hold a rally for blacks who had been sent to jail in Evansville the previous summer for causing disturbances. According to FBI informants, there were about 325 students in the audience, half African American, half white.[31]

Even though most black students at IU were convinced that nonviolent confrontations were more effective than carrying guns, they were attracted to the Panthers' style and bravado even when the speakers argued that universities like IU were creating a new group of "Toms" and that "the sole means, the total means, of liberation is the gun." Robert Johnson was in the audience, and despite his distrust of their call for in-

Students gather at the Black Market. Courtesy Indiana University Archives.

creased militancy, he concluded that "the Panthers do not play. Their rhetoric and their actions are straight, hard and angry." He warned white New Leftists to "quit arguing about the revolutionary/non-revolutionary nature of their program and begin to see the suppression of the Panthers—quit playing school boy games." Johnson joined the Panthers in their rejection of black participation in the Vietnam war. "We will not kill other people of color being victimized by white racists."[32]

Although IU's African-American students listened to the Panthers and were sympathetic to the anger behind their words, the Black Panther Party was not a continuing presence on campus. Blacks were more interested in trying to resolve the problems they saw before them every day— that is, IU administrators' inattention to minority recruitment and retention programs. Robert Johnson talked to members of the University Lutheran Church, urging them to use their influence to encourage administrators to admit students who might be educationally disadvantaged. Johnson was joined in his efforts by Professor Orlando Taylor. In a speech to the Bloomington Optimists Club, Taylor expressed his frustration at the lack of progress he and other African Americans had made at IU and in Bloomington. He remarked that he felt it was "inappropriate for a black man to tell a white audience about racism. The racial crisis has been developed by whites: slavery, lynching, and discrimination against black Americans."

He concluded that the answer to the problems of racism at IU and in Bloomington would never be solved by one black man talking to an all-white audience. The way to achieve racial justice was to pressure university administrators to recruit more students of color, to hire more minority faculty, and to create a new position, a vice president of the university who would have real power to deal with race relations.

IU officials responded to Taylor's concerns by offering him a position as vice chancellor and head of a new Black Studies Institute that would be the first of its kind at a major state university. For the first time, Taylor felt that some real progress in improving race relations was possible.[33]

But in the same days in which Orlando Taylor saw some hope for African Americans at IU, local newspapers reported sightings of burning crosses outside of town. Two men who said they belonged to the Ku Klux Klan visited the editor of the *Indiana Daily Student* and warned him that he should stop criticizing the Klan, because they were "family men and hard-working people." Moreover, they added, the Klan was well organized in Monroe County. African-American students reported receiving telephone death threats. The director of the IU Safety Division arrested, then released, a local man who explained that he had indeed made the threats but that he assumed the students knew he was joking. Black students were not so sure. The memory of the Martinsville stabbing was still fresh. Moreover, they knew that early in November, a student from Africa had been attacked by several whites as he walked alone from the library toward his dormitory. A karate expert, the student left six of his assailants sprawled on the sidewalk in front of Eigenmann Hall.[34]

If there were any doubts that racism was a serious problem in Bloomington, those doubts were dispelled on the day after Christmas, 1968. Early that morning, the Black Market was firebombed. Witnesses reported seeing a white man in a car throw something through one of the store's windows. Police investigators said the object was a Molotov cocktail. No one was injured, but the store was completely destroyed. The next day a local newspaper carried headlines proclaiming "Flames Hit Hippy Haven," but the editor of the student newspaper wrote that December 26, 1968, was "a day of shame for Bloomington. . . . [T]he firebombing was deplorable. . . . [T]here is a need for this community and this university to bring full-scale action to fight racism." Police began an investigation into the crime. Students started a fund drive to raise money for Rollo Turner, whose inventory, valued at about $2,000, was uninsured. At the beginning of the spring term, over two hundred students gathered in front of the burned building and put a sign over the gutted doorway saying, "A Coward Did This." Turner, obviously angry, said he

The Black Market after the Klan bombing. Courtesy Indiana University Archives.

would now tell blacks to "live by the law of God, an eye for an eye, and a tooth for a tooth." Kenny Newsome, one of Turner's closest friends, agreed, saying, "I'm tired of amens. Too long we've been kicked, too long we've been talking, too long we've been signifying."[35]

By the end of January, student groups and some community organizations, including the Women's International League for Peace and Freedom, the Bloomington chapter of the ACLU, and the Quaker Peace Committee, had collected over $3,000 so that Turner could pay off the store's debts. Turner was grateful for the money but told contributors that he was not going to reopen the Black Market. It was time, he said, to get on with his life and to focus his attentions on his graduate studies, his duties as a teaching assistant, and his campaign to establish a black studies program.[36]

Nine months later, Bloomington police arrested two local men, Carlisle Briscoe and Jackie Kinser, along with William Chaney, Grand Dragon of the Ku Klux Klan, in nearby Ellettsville for transporting over three hundred pounds of dynamite. Under interrogation, Briscoe and Kinser confessed to starting the Black Market fire. They were sentenced to prison terms of one to ten years, but Judge Nat U. Hill ordered Kinser transferred to the Norman Beatty Memorial Hospital in Indianapolis to receive treatment for mental disorders.[37]

Throughout 1969, African-American students continued to face other aspects of racism at IU. For some men, discrimination in university athletic programs was increasingly troublesome—especially after African-American athletes demonstrated at the Olympic games in Mexico City in 1968. Harry Edwards, who had called for a black boycott of the games, came to Bloomington during the spring semester of 1969. He brought to students at IU the same message that he had brought to other college campuses across the country. Edwards outlined the racism that most black athletes faced in college athletics and he urged black players not to serve as beasts of burden for white coaches and players. His words were well received, especially by those who had made sports history in 1968 by being part of the first IU football team to play in the Rose Bowl. When those players returned for practice the next fall, hopes were high that IU would repeat the victories of last year and make a return trip to Pasadena.

However, black players had a different point of view. Following the example of black athletes at other college and university campuses that fall, IU's black football players submitted a list of eight grievances to Coach John Pont, an Ivy League transplant and friend of President Stahr. The players complained that African-American players were disciplined more strictly than white players; that they received inferior medical treatment; and that they were harassed and demoralized by the discriminatory attitudes and remarks of the coaching staff. Coach Pont ignored the list.[38]

By November, black players had had enough. They announced that they had decided to boycott the game and deliberately missed two practice sessions, which, under Pont's rules, meant automatic dismissal from the team. Coach Pont and his coaching staff, along with white members of the team, were outraged. But Robert Johnson, a former football player himself, supported his comrades. He called IU's white quarterback, Harry Gonso, nothing more than a "foul-mouthed punk" and criticized Pont for keeping good black players on the bench so that whites like Gonso could make the headline-grabbing plays. Coach Pont denied all charges of racism.[39]

Within a few days of the announcement of the boycott, four of the black players decided to go back to practice and join their teammates, who were getting ready for a game against the University of Iowa. The IU team had done well in the season so far. Hopes were high. Their decision was a setback for the ten black players who continued the boycott. They decided to call a meeting with students to explain their grievances and to ask for support.

Clarence Price, a defensive back from Indianapolis, maintained that to return to the team or to stay out was a matter for players' own consciences. He insisted that lack of playing time on the field was not the issue, and reiterated the grievances that the players had originally stated. Black members of the cheerleading squad and the marching band joined the boycott. Its effects became clear as IU lost to Iowa, to Northwestern, and finally to arch-rival Purdue University.[40]

In the end, Coach Pont negotiated a settlement with the black players. In the spring of 1970, three of the ten boycotters were dismissed from the team for "an expressed negative attitude." The Faculty Committee on Race Relations investigated the dismissals and decided that the "root of the problem is the extreme difficulty blacks and whites have in communicating effectively, respecting their different cultural values and styles." Since most white activists were consumed with antiwar protests, the problem of racism in college athletics did not attract much attention. Those who did consider the situation saw racism in college athletics as merely a symptom of the larger problem of the role of profit-making and fund-raising that plagued universities across the country.

The African-American football players' boycott was a classic illustration of the gap between white New Leftists and black activists. For white students, the problem of athletics was often dismissed because it was too far removed from their own antiwar playing field. But for blacks, racism in athletics was an affront to their dignity. It was real. It was personal. And it had to be confronted.[41]

In May 1969, Rollo Turner, along with other student activists, occupied Ballantine Hall to force the faculty and administrators convened there to meet with students concerned about the imminent tuition increase. Rising tuition threatened African-American students' ability to remain at IU and made it more difficult for would-be students to enroll. Turner made sure that the building's doors and windows were guarded by black athletes. Their very presence made his demands appear serious to some, threatening to others. Turner and his friend Kenny Newsome, a basketball star, paid a price for their display of courage and concern. Both were indicted, along with Dr. Orlando Taylor, for their parts in the occupation. Taylor's indictment was an especially painful blow. University administrators decided that because of the charges brought against him, he could no longer be considered for vice chancellor or for director of the Black Studies Program. Taylor resigned and left Bloomington to teach at Federal City College in Washington, D.C., and later at Howard University. IU's Black Studies Program was put on hold while administrators conducted a national search for a new director.

Black activism was not lost on white New Leftists. The challenge that black students issued was one that they could neither deny nor ignore. There was a constant tension between black and white activists at IU throughout the 1960s. On the one hand, black demands represented a radical challenge to white university authority, and one with a valid claim to the moral high ground. And yet white New Leftists clung to their own intellectual, often romantic, views of political and cultural opposition to the dominant elite. What happened at Indiana University was a fortuitous combination of black and white activism. White activists at IU, like their counterparts throughout the country, embraced the cause of racial justice along with their own agenda of peace and individual empowerment as part of a larger vision of grass-roots democracy. Black activists at IU joined the larger student movement after they realized that they were powerful enough not to be drowned out by a white majority. The spring 1969 protests against the tuition increase, which was much more threatening to most black students than it was to most whites, highlighted the willingness of black students to take risks in order to make their point. That single protest drew black and white student activists together and provided them with a common cause. Indiana University was the only campus to elect a member of the Black Panther Party president of its student body, as IU elected Keith Parker in 1969. While Parker's allegiance to the Panthers might have disturbed some IU students, his role in both opposing the war in Vietnam and fighting for racial justice represented a true fusion of the goals of black and white student activists at IU in the 1960s.

CHAPTER 6

The Women's Movement: An Idea Whose Time Had Come

The women's liberation movement of the 1960s grew out of the first coalition of black and white abolitionists, before the Civil War. Those ardent women and men succeeded in abolishing slavery with the passage of the Thirteenth Amendment (1865), but women were denied the right to vote that the Fifteenth Amendment (1868) gave to black men. Women organized their own suffrage campaign and succeeded in passing the Nineteenth Amendment, which gave the vote to all Americans regardless of sex, in 1920.

The next coalition of black and white Americans began after World War II with the civil rights movement. The second struggle for racial justice spawned a second wave of the women's movement—for equal rights for all citizens, regardless of race or sex.

The first evidence that women recognized that they were victims of discrimination came in 1965. Mary King and Casey Hayden, two young women active in SNCC, wrote an essay titled "Sex and Caste: A Kind of Memo" and distributed it at a meeting. It was discussed but not taken seriously. However, the memo made its way into other organizations and was the catalyst of a serious dispute at the 1967 meeting of SDS, where men disparaged women's criticisms—and women walked out. That was the beginning of the end of SDS.

Civil rights activists succeeded when Congress passed the Civil Rights Act in 1964, outlawing discrimination based on race or sex in jobs and public accommodations. This act also created the Equal Employment Opportunity Commission (EEOC), which had the power to investigate complaints of job discrimination and to withhold funds to public agencies that practiced discrimination. Betty Friedan, author of the pathbreaking *The Feminine Mystique* (1963), and others formed the National Organization for Women (NOW) in 1966 to push for reforms under this legislation.

The logical culmination of this effort was the campaign to pass the Equal Rights Amendment (ERA): "Equality of rights under the law shall not be denied or abridged by the United States or by any state on account of sex." The ERA, introduced in the Senate by Indiana's Birch Bayh, passed both houses in 1972. Indiana ratified the amendment in 1977. However, after a strong campaign by antifeminists led by Phyllis Schlafly, who claimed that it would be harmful to women, the amendment failed to pass the required number of state legislatures and died in 1983.

Despite the failure of the ERA, second-wave feminism achieved some remarkable successes. Using a technique developed by SDS for its Economic Research and Action Project to organize poor people, women across the country formed consciousness-raising groups. In these groups, usually of ten to fifteen, women met in private homes or community centers to talk about personal and political issues. Through these conversations, women realized that "the personal is political"; that is, power relationships in the family reflect political power. They examined the patriarchal system and the ways in which women were dominated by men in society, in the economy, and in politics.

One of the most emotional subjects to arise in these groups was abortion. As more and more women realized millions of women were seeking abortions and being victimized by illegal practitioners, the campaign to legalize abortion became one of the central goals of women's liberation. The 1973 Supreme Court decision in *Roe v. Wade,* legalizing abortions, was a significant victory. Along with abortion rights, women wanted to gain control over their own bodies through safe and accessible methods of birth control. They also sought protection against domestic abuse. And they continued to fight for equity in the workplace.

Just as African Americans discovered that their history, literature, and culture had been left out of traditional texts used in schools, so, too, did women. Feminists began to demand that colleges and universities introduce women's studies so that women could reclaim their place in history and American culture.

The women's movement of the 1960s affected nearly every aspect of American life. Women asserted their rights as human beings and as citizens at home, in the classroom, in the workplace, in courtrooms, and in politics. It was the logical outcome of the civil rights and antiwar movements. It was, indeed, an idea whose time had come.

The history of the women's movement at IU is deeply rooted in the lives of the women who were part of it. Women's issues went to the core of both university and community traditions. Women who challenged authority in order to gain control over their lives were also challenging the power structure of the university, traditionally male-dominated, conservative, and, despite Herman B Wells's best efforts, often quite insular. Women at IU who took part in the liberation movement defied cultural traditions that instructed them to be compliant, as well as solidly entrenched political and intellectual authorities whose power was buttressed by respect for male dominance. At the same time, women had to address problems of male-female relationships, often arousing serious conflicts among the very people whom they had supported and who, in turn, had been their most valued sources of support. The women and men who experienced the full impact of the movement went through intense and sometimes quite painful changes. The liberation of women—and men—at IU was one of the most positive contributions of Sixties activists.

The women's movement at IU began in 1969 and grew quickly, because the ground had been well prepared. Women had been working for years in Bloomington's antiwar and student political campaigns, often quietly and effectively behind the scenes. In fact, the student protest movement at Indiana University, although dominated by male undergraduate and graduate students, had begun by addressing women's issues.

When Guy Loftman and the other students who organized the Progressive Reform Party (PRP) decided to concentrate their energies on abolishing women's hours, they promoted a cause that nearly everyone could support. Women's hours affected men and women in different ways, but the restriction of personal freedom offended nearly everyone at some time during their undergraduate or graduate years at IU. Sporadic opposition to Loftman's crusade came from some members of Associated Women Students (AWS), a group of women undergraduates who were elected by their living units and the dean and assistant dean of students (at that time, Robert Shaffer and Virginia Rogers). The deans and AWS were principally responsible for making the rules governing women's lives at IU, and losing the right to establish hours for women meant, at least from some points of view, less influence within the university bureaucracy.

By the middle of the 1960s, the university's parietal role was on the wane. Former president Herman B Wells later reflected that women's hours were on their way out even before he assumed his duties as interim president in 1968. The campus was getting too large, there were too many students to oversee, and the current student population had been raised in a more permissive culture.

Still, most students were willing to abide by traditional rules governing their behavior. When the *Indiana Daily Student* asked students whether there was a sexual revolution on campus, both men and women agreed that IU was still a place where a sexual double standard was generally accepted. Student editors concluded that "an alarmingly large number of students admit they haven't spent much time thinking about the situation and accept University policy as a matter of course."[1]

The first chair of the Progressive Reform Party, Lynn Everroad, a sophomore student senator, explained PRP's opposition to women's hours as part of its dissatisfaction with "a university which hands us 'knowledge' in mass classes, which covers us with a morass of rules and regulations, and which tries to force our character development along predetermined lines." Members of PRP, she explained, wanted to "re-integrate the academic community with the outside world," and part of that process was to give all women at IU the freedom to control their own lives, their own time, and their own behavior—sexual and otherwise.[2]

The women students of the 1960s were not the first at IU to struggle against sexism. After World War II, veterans and their wives and families crowded into house trailers that had been hastily organized on courts near campus in a kind of "veteran village." These adult students presented challenges to IU administrators because they were in a hurry to complete their education and demanded a variety of special services, such as child care and health facilities. Women who had served their country in the military complained about living in restrictive dormitories, so the dean of students allowed them to live off campus. However, administrators did not see veterans as typical undergraduates. They were, in Herman Wells's words, "a very special lot." And university rules about women's hours remained in force during the 1950s and 1960s.[3]

Many students in the 1960s saw university parietal rules as irrelevant. Wells commented later, "It was probably not by chance that such a feeling had manifested itself soon after the national call-up of youth to bear a large share of the responsibility for the American defense of Vietnam." The issue of women's hours was just part of a much larger struggle by students to gain control over their lives—lives that often seemed to spin out of control once students left campus.[4]

While PRP leaders felt there was a wide base of support for abolishing women's hours, it was difficult to arouse IU students to endorse the change. Student government held an all-woman referendum on the issue in February 1966. Out of over ten thousand women on the Bloomington campus, only 3,115 voted, and fewer than half of them voted to abandon women's hours. Over two hundred supported the existing system, and the rest wanted some variation (hours during the week with unrestricted weekends, or "free" nights during the year). Most of the voters were freshmen, and they cast the majority of the votes against women's hours. The biggest disappointment was the low turnout. Everroad declared the referendum irrelevant, arguing that IU women had been suffocated by dorm rules for so long that they were passive and unresponsive. Activists' fight to stir women from their apathy and "to help in building . . . a dynamic community profoundly committed to maximum educational opportunity for every student" had only begun.[5]

Later that spring, AWS voted to abolish hours for all undergraduate women except freshmen. After PRP candidates Loftman and Hunter won seats in the student senate, they succeeded in getting a resolution passed recommending the elimination of women's hours. Dean Shaffer responded by telling students that nothing would happen that semester because parents, alumni, and trustees who were strongly critical of changing university policies had not received enough information. He said that he had received letters from parents who told him they would not send their daughters to IU if the rules on women's hours were relaxed. Parents who opposed relaxing the restrictions pointed out that there was no organized entertainment in Bloomington after midnight and that unrestricted hours would "force students to make their own entertainment. We feel this is unnecessary."[6]

Dean Shaffer told students that he was against abolishing hours for sophomore women because he did not think they were ready for the "responsibilities of unlimited hours," given the "fact of the 'sophomore slump' and the adjustment problems of this class are well known to faculty, counselors and other staff members of the University." He urged women to begin selling the plan to their parents over the summer, adding, "It would be much more effective if undergraduate women were arguing for their own freedom instead of letting graduate men protest for them."[7]

In 1966 students were divided on the issue of abolishing women's hours. In an editorial titled "Students Can Help Troubled University," the *Indiana Daily Student* urged students to drop their demands to abolish women's hours because of a serious communication gap with Hoosier voters, who thought the university was "overrun by communists, LSD users, and homosexuals." The student editors expressed sympathy for IU administrators who were "caught in the middle" between outraged citizens and "leaders in the leftist campus organizations," who were not Indiana residents. As if to demonstrate just how heterosexual IU males were, five thousand of them ran through all the women's residence halls in late May, screaming, "We want panties!" Overwhelmed, one campus policeman said, "It's like a herd of wild animals—worse than anything we were ever warned about."[8]

Shortly after the spring panty raid, SDS and PRP leaders, along with other student government officers, submitted the following bill to the student body:

> WHEREAS: Women are not inferior to men and should not be treated as inferior, and such treatment is a clear violation of the Civil Rights Act of 1964, and, . . .
> WHEREAS: The Student Senate and the AWS have passed resolutions . . . and nearly all student leaders have reasoned with the Administration and have gone through "proper channels"—all to no avail; and,
> WHEREAS: Due to lack of real pressure from the Student Body during the past semester, the Administration has seen fit to continue its double standard policy; and,
> WHEREAS: It is now obvious that only direct pressure from the Student Body can effect administrative decisions;
> THEREFORE BE IT RESOLVED THAT: The undersigned ask YOU to participate in "STUDY OUT" on the Library lawn from 6:30 p.m. until 7:30 p.m. Monday evening, May 30. (bring your books please.). . . .
> This demonstration is a token—it is a warning—it is a premonition of the massive demonstrations which will occur unless this absurd, degrading, and intellectually indefensible policy of discriminatory confinement is abandoned.[9]

The "study-out" attracted a small, quiet, serious group of protestors who sat and read together without getting much attention. Nonetheless, the issue had received enough notice that it was on the agenda for the summer meeting of the board of trustees in June 1966. The dean of students surveyed other Big Ten schools. The University of Illinois had the most restrictive policies, with curfews for women in all classes at 10:30 P.M. on weeknights and 1:00 A.M. on weekends. Purdue was the most liberal, with unlimited hours for all sophomores, juniors, and seniors. The rest of the schools fell in between, with varying restrictions for each class. As historian Beth Bailey has observed in her study of women at the University of Kansas, "as rules relaxed . . . they became more complex." There were different hours for underclassmen and upperclassmen, special hours for orientation week and finals week, individual late permissions and group late permissions. As the system grew more complex it also appeared more arbitrary.[10]

At the urging of AWS, IU administrators reluctantly agreed to make some changes in women's hours. After a summer of conferences with trustees, alumni, and parents, Dean Shaffer extended senior hours privileges to junior women for the fall term of 1966.

Women worked within PRP for a wide range of changes in university policies, including abolishing hours for all women, allowing more women to move off campus, and removing dress restrictions in residence hall dining rooms. Some, like folksinger and political activist Bernella Satterfield, had considerable experience in New Left activities. Satterfield, along with her husband, David, had been one of the founders of SDS at IU, and she was practiced in the art of building grass-roots support through dormitory education programs. Connie Kiesling managed PRP's spring campaign, and with a budget of about $200 she put together a combination of telephone callers, speakers, rock and roll concerts, and a few posters that won her party the election with the biggest voter turnout in IU's history. Right before spring break, Connie and Guy Loftman, PRP's candidate for student body president, were married. A Hoosier who had grown up in a conservative family, Connie had come to IU to study music. She spent much of her freshman year getting involved in IU's political scene, singing in weekly folk music club meetings, talking all night long with friends in her dormitory, and finding a new way of looking at life from the New Left. She quit school in the middle of her sophomore year and put all of her considerable energies into PRP politics and her relationship with Guy. While most of her work was behind the scenes, she was outspoken about the university's "rigid, conservative system of controlling education and students' personal lives" and a strong advocate of "seeing changes take place on this campus which have been needed for a long time." Loftman said he owed his victory to her organizational skills, adding that "she isn't capable of keeping quiet when it comes to political issues."[11]

When activists took over student government in the spring of 1967, the issue of women's hours was at the top of their agenda. Loftman supported AWS president Lisa Purdy's argument that AWS had the power to legislate rules for women and to abolish hours for freshmen and sophomores with parental consent. In challenging the dean's authority, Purdy said, "Almost every administrator now admits that control over the social and personal lives of a university's students is rapidly diminishing" and that student self-government was "an inevitable end."[12]

In the midst of the women's hours campaign, AWS elected officers, and the new president was opposed to challenging university authority. Nancy Ellis, unlike her predecessor, felt that the university should continue to regulate hours for freshmen women. Moreover, she worried that if restrictions on women were removed, AWS would lose many of its responsibilities. However, sensing that students would continue the fight, the board of trustees granted some concessions and voted to abolish hours for sophomore women with parental permission.[13]

For activists at IU, having one of their own as student body president meant that an opportunity for real change had arrived. The campaign for student rights, with its emphasis on ending policies that discriminated against women, was gaining momentum. Loftman never wanted students to forget, however, that the point of raising the issue of women's hours was to encourage students to connect personal concerns with public issues. When he argued for action against rules that applied only to women, he was trying to make the point that "the heart of a democracy is in the rights of the minority rather than the rule of the majority. . . . If one woman does not want them, she should be free to decide for herself."[14]

Women's issues were part of the 1968 spring election campaign, as New Leftists continued to push for an end to hours for all women students and extended their list of reforms to include open visitation for all students in university residences and the right of all students to live off campus. The new student body president, Ted Najam, presented the board of trustees with the message that the university was no longer standing *in loco parentis*. In one sweeping motion, the board gave women the right to live wherever they wanted, to come and go as they pleased, and to entertain male friends in their rooms. By this time, both Connie Loftman and Guy Loftman were out of school, although they remained in Bloomington. When asked later to name the most significant issue of the New Left at IU during the 1960s, they answered emphatically, "women's hours."[15]

Women participated in campus politics, but not many were on the speakers' podiums at rallies and protests. As historian Sara Evans observed, during that time of intense antiwar and racial protests the New Left was made up of "strong women in a movement that was increasingly alienating for women." Frustrated with the macho atmosphere of organizations like SDS, women kept trying to find ways to express themselves without being criticized or scorned by male leaders. Evans commented, "Separatism was in the cards logically, for the new left was focused on the need for all oppressed groups to organize themselves. . . . [But] women in the new left also resisted. They kept trying to find a way to be equal within the very insurgency that had built the foundation for their growing self-consciousness." Student activists at Indiana University were a minority. Women activists were a minority within that group. Their ambivalence about breaking away from their male comrades grew in part from their admiration of and respect for each other. In the end, however, the need to express their own ideas in their own voices won out.[16]

The women's movement at IU began definitively on February 22, 1969, when Marlene Dixon, who taught in the University of Chicago's sociology department, came to speak at the Bloomington campus. One of the founders of the Women's Caucus of the New University Conference, Dixon was an outspoken leader of women's rights in academia and a teacher who devoted most of her energies to her students rather than to publishing articles for her own professional advancement. Citing her lack of published research, members of the University of Chicago's Division of Social Sciences had decided not to renew her academic contract. However, university students argued that it was Dixon's protests against the university's discriminatory policies toward women and minorities that caused her dismissal. They staged a sit-in at the administration building to protest the administration's refusal to discuss racial and gender issues.

After the demonstration, Dixon came to IU to talk about the plight of junior faculty whose professional lives were at the mercy of more senior colleagues and whose rights to free speech were restricted by the powers given to more senior professors by the hierarchical structure of the university. After Dixon spoke to a general audience, she asked to speak to IU's women's caucus. The women in the audience looked around at each other in confusion and finally told her that there was no such caucus. Hearing that, Dixon sighed audibly, looked around the room at all the women seated there, and asked them to get together later for a separate meeting.

At that meeting, Dixon urged Bloomington women to "consider the role of women, the history of women's movements in this country (which like Black history has been largely ignored or trivialized in history books) and our own political activity on this campus and in various radical groups." She talked about how women in the university community had to fight to receive equal treatment; about the necessity for women to get together to support each other, especially in consciousness-raising groups; and about the movement that was building everywhere to win respect for women's rights at work and at home.

It was an idea whose time had come. Charged by Dixon's call for action, the women at that meeting started to hold weekly discussions in living rooms all over Bloomington. The Bloomington women's liberation movement had begun.[17]

By the spring of 1969, women at IU were pouring their energies into improving their lives. At the weekly meetings, one of the big surprises was how different it was to have a meeting without men present. For the first time, women talked about their own histories and their immediate problems, and began venting the steam of suppressed anger at their own and other women's burdens, both at home and in their working lives. It was, many remember, an exhilarating experience to find out, first, that they were not alone, and next, that they could join together to try to solve some of the problems they faced. They excluded men because, as one woman wrote in a position paper, "we have repeatedly discovered that women find it very difficult to talk about women's liberation in a spontaneous, unapologetic manner in the presence of men unless they know them to be completely sympathetic."[18]

Since no one in Bloomington had ever participated in this kind of women's group before, they followed advice sent to them by friends in other parts of the country where groups had already formed. Sitting in circles, they asked one another what their own views of women were; how they saw themselves in their relations with men—husbands, fathers, employers, sons; what bothered them most about these relationships; and what they wanted to do with their lives. The women themselves were, for the most part, connected with the university in some way, as undergraduate or graduate students, faculty, staff, or wives of male students or faculty. Some were single or married women who worked or went to school; others were full-time wives and mothers. For many, these gatherings were like religious experiences. Opening up private lives to public scrutiny for help and sympathy was so powerful that it was like becoming a new person. Those living rooms provided warm, supportive environments where participants could have spirited intellectual discussions or erupt in emotional outbursts. Group members kept all of their conversations confidential, and they soon learned to trust one another completely. They talked about affection and sympathy, anger, and sometimes bewilderment during the meetings. When one woman told her group that she was being physically abused by her husband, the group became so outraged that they went to confront the man and, when he tried to leave the room, quite literally forced him to stay and listen to them.

Women talked about everything: abortions, daily problems with housework and child care, male co-workers, husbands, boyfriends, lesbian relationships, feminist philosophies, Freudian psychology, and Marxist economic analysis. Common problems received uncommon attention. The unspoken was made clear. The last year of the Sixties was the year that women found their voice in the university community.[19]

The politics of the women's movement were personal in every sense of the word. Women pursued liberation in the kitchen, the bedroom, and the office. At home, women began to demand that their husbands and lovers share in household chores. They found, in their male partners, a remarkable lack of enthusiasm for the idea that "participatory democracy begins at home." One woman writer made a list of the most common masculine excuses for avoiding household chores. They included "I don't mind sharing housework, but I'm not very good at it," "Show me how," "I don't like dull, boring, stupid jobs. I hate it more than you," and "We have different standards." She concluded her article with the following words: "I was just finishing this when my husband came in and asked what I was doing. Writing a paper on housework. Housework? he said. *Housework?* Oh my god how trivial can you get. A paper on housework." The revolution, she warned her readers, did not end with men doing dishes—that was only the beginning.[20]

With confidence and enthusiasm, women confronted their problems, formed committees, and set about to right those wrongs. They formed a group for sex education and went to work in the dormitories to help women learn about their own bodies. They distributed birth control information and began asking for contraceptive devices at the university health center.

During their weekly meetings, women talked about their own abortions and the incredible difficulty of finding a doctor who would perform one, so graduate student Ruth Mahaney began an abortion counseling center. Since abortion was illegal in Indiana, the women who worked at the center assumed that their telephone lines were tapped by FBI agents or other law enforcement officers. The telephone counselors had to ensure that callers said they wanted an abortion at the beginning of the conversation, or the counselors could be prosecuted for a felony. Abortion counselors put up signs in women's bathrooms, passed out cards with their telephone number, and talked to anyone who would listen about what they were doing. The center got calls from women in small towns outside of Bloomington, from undergraduate students, and from housewives in town. Local ministers and doctors offered help when they could. Once an abortion counselor began assisting a woman, she stayed with her through the abortion (either a legal one out of state or, more usually, an illegal one locally) and continued to offer advice and support for as long as she needed it. The number of illegal abortions in Bloomington was thought to be as high as three hundred a year, and each cost between $400 and $700. Advocates like IU graduate student Margie Stamberg argued that until women were freed from the restrictions of unwanted pregnancies, they would remain slaves to laws made by male legislators. Making abortion legal was one of the main goals of the women's movement.[21]

One of the women's movement's most ambitious campaigns was the attempt to revolutionize day care for children. Women would never be free to pursue other personal and professional goals as long as they were the primary caretakers of their children. When veterans enrolled at IU after World War II, university administrators recognized their need for help with child care and organized staff and facilities for that purpose. However, in the late 1960s, students who promoted cooperative day care centers were unsuccessful when they asked the university for assistance. The trustees denied their request for the use of university facilities or for released time for employees to work at the center. But the women found space at the Unitarian Universalist Church and began to care for about twenty children.

Nancy Brand, a recently divorced mother of two who had come to IU to do graduate work in history, and Sonja Klawitter, a faculty wife and mother of two children, were early leaders in the cooperative day care movement. They approached the problem first as a matter of absolute necessity. They both needed to find affordable child care that met their needs. But they also wanted an alternative to the traditional form of care. Most American families depended on mothers to be constant companions to their children, thus eliminating any opportunities for women to go to school or work. Granted, a few families were wealthy enough to hire someone to take care of their children or could send them to commercial day care centers. But the majority of women who had children did not have the opportunity to pursue both family and education or career.

The philosophy of the cooperative day care movement was to liberate the family—to free women from constant child care, to allow children time with other children and adults, and to expand men's roles in their children's lives. The parents who worked at the Bloomington day care center hoped to involve both fathers and mothers, as well as other adults, in providing every child with "competent care and healthy, stimulating surroundings regardless of the financial status of his or her parents." When Brand and Klawitter began the Bloomington Cooperative Day Care Center in 1969, it was staffed by twenty-two parents and seventeen other volunteers. Everyone worked four or five hours a week, five days a week, and the center was open from 8:00 A.M. to 5:00 P.M., taking care of fifteen to twenty children, aged four months to eight years. Parents contributed about $8 a month to maintain the center. They met with other adult volunteers every week to discuss the center's operation. Decisions about how the center was run were made democratically and collectively. The day care center demanded a high level of emotional commitment from participants.[22]

Undergraduate women who were a part of the liberation movement and who had been members of student groups began looking for alternative political organizations that would allow them to express not just their opposition to the war but their opposition to gender discrimination as well. In the spring of 1969, a small group of student activists broke off from the United Student Movement (USM), a political party that supported Mel Yancey, an African American, for student body president and Mike King, a white activist, for vice president. Even though USM's platform advocated free day care for the children of university students and employees and affirmed the rights of women to control their own bodies, this dissident group met to form the Revolutionary Student Party (RSP), nominating Russell Block, a graduate student in German who had been active in the antiwar movement at IU for several years, for president and Allyne Rosenthal, a junior English major who had been active in SDS with her former husband, Dan Kaplan, for vice president.

The RSP platform had nine points, none of which directly addressed women's issues, but Allyne's place on the ticket spoke louder than words. The daughter of politically active liberal parents, Allyne had grown up in Cleveland, Ohio. Her parents had taken her to civil rights marches as a child and encouraged her to join in discussions of current events over dinners with friends and family. She came to IU because she thought she might want to major in music, but switched to the English department. SDS was one of the first groups she joined when she arrived, and it was an important part of her life. But she saw herself as always in the shadow of her boyfriend, then husband, then ex-husband, and after her divorce she wanted to find a way to express her own views in her own way. She shared Block's belief that their new party should try to connect IU students to national issues. But she also wanted to show women that they could be effective political leaders. In a campaign speech, she told students, "Women are second class citizens. . . . [W]omen must recognize their oppression and discrimination." In a direct plea for students to work to legalize abortion in Indiana, she said, "our sisters are suffering now under the oppressive rules enacted by male legislators." The two candidates were more concerned that RSP publicize its radical platform during the campaign than that they win the election. They received token votes from 151 students in an election that USM lost as well. RSP's split from the larger New Left group represented a difference more in style than in substance. Most student activists generally agreed on basic issues. Still, putting a woman near the top of the ticket was a breakthrough.[23]

Jane Dillencourt, one of IU's leading antiwar organizers, attended the last SDS convention, in June 1969, and reported that the national organization had collapsed into hopeless factionalism and that the meeting was "generally unrelated to chapter realities." If SDS was no longer a meaningful political organization for many IU women, that void was filled by the New University Conference (NUC).

Organized in 1968 in Chicago by young faculty members and gradu-ate students as a means of expressing their political views within academic communities, the NUC had a less flamboyantly macho operating style than other groups, and it addressed the needs of more mature students and professionals who were becoming increasingly disillusioned with not only the revolutionary rhetoric of younger radicals, but the unyielding au-thoritarianism of university hierarchies. For Martha Vicinus, a young fac-ulty member in the English department who had been a union organizer for University of Wisconsin teaching assistants, the NUC allowed her to express her politics, organize her friends, and create a warm social circle that was a haven in a sometimes heartless academic world. Allyne Rosenthal found in the NUC opportunities for leadership and women mentors who could provide much-needed support as her marriage ended and she began a new life. Ruth Mahaney had been active in the Committee to End the War in Vietnam and was attracted to the NUC's antiwar philos-ophy as well as to its broader efforts to reform the university into a more humane institution that recognized the value of women's roles in society. For Ruth Mahaney and others like her, the message of women's libera-tion at IU was developed within the framework of the NUC's national philosophy, which called for "struggle for the liberation of all peoples. . . . [I]t must therefore oppose imperialism, racism, economic exploita-tion and male supremacy."[24]

Although women in Bloomington took their movement seriously, they never lost their sense of humor. Early in the summer of 1969, a quick-witted university secretary noticed an announcement in campus mail of an all-male administrators' dinner, to be held at a restaurant east of Bloomington, the Pic-A-Chic Ranch. Copies of the announcement were circulated among IU women, and a group of guerrilla activists who called themselves WITCH (the Women's International Terrorist Conspir-acy from Hell) decided that the opportunity was just too good to pass up—a group of male administrators eating at a place called the Pic-A-Chic Ranch! The situation cried out for action. They organized a car pool and drove down to the restaurant. Stopping in a wood next to the Pic-A-Chic, they put on witches' regalia. Then they ran from the woods to where the men were already eating at tables on the lawn, and "moving among the overstuffed males, they chanted their curse and sprinkled a generous helping of garlic on their victims." After a few wild moments of cackling, cursing, and howling, the Bloomington debut of the WITCHes ended as they ran back into the woods and drove off in their cars. The dinner guests were amused ("Are they part of the entertainment?") and a little be-wildered by the action, although most of them never stopped eating.[25]

English professor Martha Vicinus, feminist and founding member of the New University Conference. *Arbutus*, 1971.

While IU administrators were laughing at the WITCHes in Bloomington, another group of women were working on a report that many men would find not so amusing. Affirmative action for women was an essential element of NOW's agenda, and a group of NOW members had decided to concentrate on discriminatory practices against women in employment (especially wage disparities) and education (admission policies and hiring and promotion practices in schools). They based their campaign on the Civil Rights Act of 1964, which created the Equal Opportunity Employment Commission, and especially on its Title VII, which outlawed sexual discrimination in employment. In 1967 President Johnson had amended the original executive order to include sex as well as race in EEOC considerations.

In 1968 these members of NOW formed the Women's Equity Action League (WEAL) and began researching and publicizing the disparities in pay between male and female workers performing essentially the same tasks, as well as discrepancies between women's and men's admission rates to higher education and professional schools. Hiring and promotion policies at colleges and universities were special targets, as they revealed great deficiencies not just in the number of women faculty hired but also in their pay and promotion to both tenure-track positions and tenure itself. This issue was especially important to taxpayers, since everyone—men and women—paid to support state universities, but the faculties of those institutions were overwhelmingly male. Activists determined that if institutions received public money then they should hire the public, which meant that the proportion of women hired in state universities should reflect the proportion of women taxpayers.

Calling themselves Concerned University Women, several IU faculty members started gathering information about university hiring and salary policies. The results gave them a sobering look at what was going on within the academic community. Instigated by English professor Martha Vicinus and administered by psychology professor Margaret Peterson, the report found that in 1970 the total number of faculty members was 1300, of whom 138 were women. Most of the women were at the lower academic ranks: 26.9% of all the instructors were women, but only 5.2% of full professors. From 1967 to 1970 the percentage of women on the IU faculty had remained relatively constant, about 10%. According to figures obtained from United States Office of Education publications, this was below the national average percentage of women faculty, which was 14.6%. The report also proved that from 1967 to 1970, the university paid its women faculty an average of $130.53 less per month than men of comparable status. Overall, the faculty was about 90% male and women who were hired usually taught for at least six years before receiving any kind of promotion, compared to slightly over four years for their male counterparts. Confronted with these carefully gathered statistics, university administrators and faculty admitted that discrimination against women had taken place and made a verbal commitment to address the problem.[26]

In addition to addressing inequity in academic salaries and promotions, women faculty members began to talk about the need for increased emphasis on women's issues in university courses. They began by collecting syllabi of women's studies courses from other colleges and universities across the country. They found "a great intellectual ferment," as women everywhere were "attacking the ideological roots of their oppression, the neglect or misrepresentation of their sex. . . . They are discovering their history, their artists, their movements and their heroines." In planning their own course, women professors decided to begin modestly with an interdisciplinary seminar that would be offered in the fall of 1970. However, their vision of a women's studies program was much larger in scope and promised to expand women's intellectual opportunities at Indiana University in the next decade.[27]

That spring the national committee of the NUC held its quarterly meeting in Bloomington. The theme of the meeting was women's liberation. The women of the NUC told men that male chauvinism, subtly expressed but present nonetheless, was a problem within the organization. Instead of breaking off, however, the women wanted to stay in the NUC and work within its structure. The group agreed that men would be in charge of child care at the next national convention, in June, and that all committees would be made up of equal numbers of men and women.

In 1970, the Bloomington women's liberation movement celebrated International Women's Day, March 8, with an evening of readings titled "I'm Everywoman and I'm Proud," featuring the words of women like Victoria Woodhull, Elizabeth Gurley Flynn, Sojourner Truth, Mother Jones, and others. African-American and white women joined together to learn about women that many had never heard of before and were touched by their bravery, courage, and strength and disturbed at the knowledge that much of women's history remained unknown, untaught, unappreciated.[28]

While these women were strongly committed to each other and to the movement they were building, most of them would not have agreed with the radical feminist argument that women should break away from existing political parties and antiwar organizations and form their own groups. Women writers quoted Roxanne Dunbar's *No More Fun and Games* and argued about Dunbar's separatist message in the pages of Bloomington's underground newspaper, the *Spectator*. But the *Spectator* staff, like the movement itself, was made up of men and women who put in long, exhausting hours, working together in a frantic, almost manic atmosphere. From time to time, women would express their annoyance at some of the more glib sexist comments that appeared in *Spectator* columns. Mike Bourne, the paper's music critic, drew angry responses from women when he wrote about female musicians in ways that emphasized their sexuality over their musical abilities. The strain on everyone who worked at the *Spectator* increased during the spring of 1970. Furthermore, the women's movement began to affect more women personally, especially those who were politically active.

Feminist writers in New York City took over *The Rat*, one of the best-known underground newspapers, early in 1970 and created a women's collective. Robin Morgan wrote a farewell essay to her New Left brothers ("Goodbye to All That") that was reprinted across the country. In Bloomington, during the last months of the semester, women writers took over the final issue of the *Spectator* before its summer hiatus and devoted the entire paper to the women's movement. The writers ranged from young undergraduates to women on the faculty. Some were quite emotional, filled with anger and pain.

I don't want to BE anything. Except Wendy. Except a human being. And that is a hurtful, painful thing to be in this society, especially if you're a woman. Because this society, created by men, perpetuated by men, slaps my humanity in the face at every step. Because this society . . . tells me I am less than a human being. . . . It tells me I am a cunt.

. . . 'my struggle is not born of a Marxist-Leninist analysis,' but of an ache starting deep in my gut. An ache felt by all women—of disappointment, of hurt, of emptiness, of self-contempt, of bitterness, and, yes, of hatred. . . .

These are my politics.
I am not a revolutionary.
I am a woman . . . fighting for my survival.

Priscilla Zirker, an instructor in the English department, gave a rational, detailed analysis of women's oppression in a capitalist economy. African-American writers Patricia Haden, Donna Middleton, and Patricia Robinson discussed the ways in which black women were systematically excluded by all men, both black and white. While some writers were more explicitly hostile toward men than others, the newspaper's final issue was an emotional explosion that had been building for a long time.[29]

CHAPTER 7

Bloomington and the Counterculture in Southern Indiana

When most students think about the 1960s, they usually think of hippies, or, in academic language, the counterculture. The stereotypical hip lifestyle that embraced "sex, drugs, and rock and roll" has become powerfully associated with that decade. Like most stereotypes, it has some truth, but there is also much more to the story of the Sixties counterculture.

One of the most important aspects of the hip movement is its connections with earlier expressions of dissent from mainstream America. Many American historians find the hippies' ancestors in the bohemians of the 1920s, and most would agree that the 1960s counterculture was the direct descendant of the 1950s Beat movement. All of these groups of writers and thinkers challenged the values and institutions of the majority of American citizens. And, since America was created by a group of revolutionaries who challenged British values and institutions, nothing could be more American than these various expressions of cultural rebellion.[1]

Yet the work ethic continued to maintain a powerful hold on the minds of most Americans. Individualism, materialism, and commercialism were and are the trinity of our conception of success. Those who proposed an alternative vision of communalism, spiritualism, and socialism were obvious threats to the political and economic order. Instead of concentrating on hard work and profits, cultural rebels advocated concentrating on spiritual fulfillment and pleasure. It is not surprising, therefore, that the Beats and the hippies were ridiculed in the mainstream press, criticized by those in power, and ultimately targeted by government investigators. They were dangerous people—you could tell that because they were having such a good time.

Although the hippie became the symbol of the Sixties, not everyone who took part in the political movements of that decade was a hippie or agreed with hippie values. Many student activists who belonged to civil rights and antiwar groups saw free-spirited hippies as frivolous and self-indulgent. Student protestors were angered by hippies' disdain for organized action and criticized them as irrelevant distractions from their cause. Hippies, on the other hand, looked at protestors as just another aspect of the society they despaired of. Signing petitions, taking part in marches, and occupying university buildings were not techniques that could change the system because they were part of the system. The only way to change America, hippies maintained, was to change yourself. Don't do things differently—live differently. Or, in Timothy Leary's famous phrase, "Turn on, tune in, drop out."

At the same time, there was a symbiotic relationship between these two groups that often worked to their mutual benefit, especially in places like Bloomington and other Midwestern university towns, where activists were a fairly small minority. In these situations, "politicos" and hippies used each other's talents and energies. Activists could count on hippies to show up for demonstrations, whether out of sympathy for the cause or curiosity about the scene. Protests sometimes came with rock-and-roll bands and they nearly always provided an opportunity to take part in some kind of guerilla theater for the benefit of local reporters and cameramen. Hippies relied on activists to raise money for their fines and legal fees; drug busts were a constant hassle for advocates of alternative lifestyles.

During the 1960s, hip people seemed to be everywhere, even in small to midsize towns like Millersburg, Pennsylvania, and Lawrence, Kansas. However, some areas were more hospitable than others to members of the hip movement, and Bloomington was one of them.[2]

A Hoosier of the 1960s, if asked to describe Bloomington, would probably have included the word "hippie" somewhere in the answer, perhaps saying, "That's the town where all the hippies live" or "It's a hippie town." At first glance, Bloomington might not have looked like the state's counterculture capital, with its quiet courthouse square next to IU's heavily wooded campus. But, on closer inspection, there was something different about some of the people on the streets. Many of them wore their hair a little longer than normal, and a few did not look like the other Hoosier college students. Local artist Wendel Field, for example, remembered that for a while when he was a student at IU he dressed completely in white. More typically, a lot of people wore old jeans or overalls, and many women favored long skirts and handmade tops, scarves, and headbands. In addition, small groups of people walked together with little smiles on their faces and odd, knowing looks in their eyes. On Kirkwood Avenue there were small shops with strange names: a record store called The Other Side, an ice cream shop known as Pill Village, African imports at the Black Market, and a place that sold exotic pipes and posters, Go for Baroque. There were street musicians and vendors selling copies of Bloomington's underground newspaper, the *Spectator*. Off Kirkwood Avenue, students— some of them unmarried couples—lived in aging houses divided into apartments. When the weather was warm and windows were open, guitar and drum music could be heard, and there might be a whiff of marijuana in the air. Bloomington was not as well known as Berkeley, California; Madison, Wisconsin; or Ann Arbor, Michigan; but it was an unusual sight for many of the state's citizens. When Dan Kaplan first came to Bloomington from his home in Gary, he had never seen anything like it.[3]

The most obvious evidence of Bloomington's counterculture is in the pages of the *Spectator,* an underground newspaper published from 1966 through 1970. Underground, or alternative, newspapers sprang up all over the country during the 1960s. The first ones appeared in New York City (the *East Village Other*), the Bay area (the *Berkeley Barb*), and Chicago (the *Seed*). Initially, they focused on news about the Vietnam war that was not being published by mainstream newspapers. However, there was more to the new journals than that—these papers were collectives of like-minded writers and artists who wanted to be the voices of their community. They wrote about issues that were important to them and to their friends: rock and roll, drugs, the antiwar movement, the Black Panthers, abortion rights, and New Left politics. Uninterested in profits and never sticklers for accuracy, these papers ran on contributors' manic energy, raw enthusiasm, and passionate opinions. In other words, they were on the other end of the journalistic spectrum from the *New York Times.*

By the early 1970s, many of these papers had gradually faded, along with much of the antiwar movement. But others became part of a new alternative press movement, like *Mother Jones,* or went mainstream, like *Rolling Stone.* As Abe Peck commented in his history of the underground press, "The papers changed minds, and lives, and showed people that they could fight city hall. They ran the news that didn't fit when nobody else would. They provided an alternate history for a decade and beyond."[4]

The story of the *Spectator* reflects, in many ways, the collective stories of the people who produced it. The *Spectator* was remarkable in the world of underground newspapers because it came out regularly for four years. Many papers in other towns and cities came out sporadically and disappeared after only a year or two. Moreover, the people who worked on the *Spectator* were articulate and literate, with a healthy sense of humor about what they were doing, qualities that were reflected in the articles. The *Spectator*'s staff was dedicated to producing an alternative view of the news—local, national, and international—and at times they exercised their First Amendment freedom in the face of pressure and harassment. When the *Spectator* folded in 1970 because of financial problems, hassles from local and federal authorities, and general exhaustion, Bloomington's counterculture lost one of its most visible and articulate means of expressing dissent from mainstream society. And everyone in Bloomington lost a sometimes witty, often caustic newspaper whose writers followed the advice of Ray Mungo, founder of the Liberation News Service: "Tell the truth, brothers, and let the facts fall where they may."[5]

From its very beginning, the *Spectator* was an experiment. The only other student newspaper was the *Indiana Daily Student* (or the *Daily Stupid*, as some called it), a laboratory paper for the Ernie Pyle School of Journalism. The *Indiana Daily Student* was supervised by professors and its editorials usually reflected the administration's views on campus issues. When the *Spectator*'s founders got together to talk about what kind of paper they had in mind, they agreed that it would be an entirely student operation, with no faculty controls. It would present all philosophical and political points of view with a strong emphasis on literary content, which reflected the personality of one of the first editors, Jim Retherford. Born and raised in Brookville, Indiana, Retherford studied the history and philosophy of science at IU as well as pursuing his love for classical opera. He was, according to one of his friends, Chris Scanlon, "intellectually curious," with a questioning mind, a real interest in the world around him, and an engaging personality. With his black-framed glasses and unruly dark hair, Retherford was a blend of his own conception of a New York intellectual and a Hoosier version of a California prankster. Some people, like his friends Allen Gurevitz and Chris Scanlon, found him completely likeable. Serious politicians worried about his penchant for the frivolous. Artists thought he was too political.[6]

In the beginning, *Spectator* staffers played by the rules and asked the university publications board for permission to publish. The paper was founded in February 1966, in university-owned offices in the travel services building on campus. However, as the war in Vietnam escalated, articles on philosophy and literature gave way to antiwar editorials. Guy Loftman, one of the founders of SDS, and other campus activists were on the *Spectator*'s editorial board and, along with Retherford and other writers, they saw the paper as a means of involving students in campus politics and national events. But Retherford also got along with poets and artists. The tug of war between political and cultural activists was apparent within the paper's first months, and it contributed to the *Spectator*'s vitality. There were always arguments between activists who saw social change as political action and those who insisted that the only way to change the world was to change people's minds, worldviews, and lifestyles. This tension was present across the country in the 1960s and Bloomington was no exception.

Yet in Bloomington, as in most college towns, there was no great rift between so-called "politicos" and "hippies." The two groups respected each other's ideas, agreed on some points, and agreed to disagree on others. Allen Ginsberg picked up on this spirit during his trip around the Midwest in 1966. College students turned out in large numbers to hear him read poetry and talk about his own experiences. Ginsberg hoped to close the rift between hippies (who he felt had a vision of a new culture) and activists (who knew how to organize) so that all the restlessness, the dissatisfaction, the feeling that something had to happen that he sensed among Midwestern students could be mobilized into a larger movement.[7]

By the beginning of the fall 1967 semester, university administrators were less and less comfortable with what was going on over at the *Spectator*'s offices. Many people in town did not care much for the paper either. There were two daily newspapers in Bloomington, the *Herald-Telephone* (or the *Horrible Terrible*, as some called it) and the *Courier-Tribune*. Both were afternoon papers, both were politically conservative, and both supported American foreign policy in Vietnam. The editor of the *Herald-Telephone* called the *Spectator* "the organ of the New Left chorus," and he was right. The Spectator subscribed to both the Underground Press Service and the Liberation News Service, which provided national news stories not covered by mainstream press agencies.

During the fall of 1967, *Spectator* editorials supported demonstrators who protested the presence of Dow Chemical representatives on campus and Secretary of State Dean Rusk's speech at the IU Auditorium. IU administrators decided that the newspaper should not operate from university-owned offices, because it did not receive financial backing from the university's general operating fund. *Spectator* staffers moved their files and equipment into an abandoned World War II quonset hut away from the main part of the campus and continued to criticize the university administration's policies on women's hours, the presence of ROTC on campus, and racial discrimination. Finally, vice president and dean of the faculty Joseph Sutton decided it was time to get rid of the *Spectator* once and for all. He told the staff that they had to get out of the quonset hut and off of university property. *Spectator* staffers argued that they had no other office to go to on such short notice. Sutton had no patience with their excuses. One night in March 1968, he went over to the quonset hut with a fire ax in his hand and offered to "help" *Spectator* staffers to move. Accompanied by a few other university administrators, Sutton threw out files and equipment.[8]

Overnight, the *Spectator* became an underground newspaper in both senses of the word, moving into an empty basement in an apartment house on Third Street where the art director lived. Editor Jim Retherford lived next door. From then on, the *Spectator* was off campus, unofficial, and free to challenge authority in every possible way. In an attempt to limit hassles from officials, staffers decided to incorporate and dutifully paid state taxes. With the support of an unpaid staff of anywhere from fifteen to ofty, writers and artists expressed their opinions about war and peace, drugs and sex, rock and roll, and anything else that got their attention. They may have been down—in the basement—but they were not out—of ideas at any rate.

Jim Retherford faced challenges on all fronts. The FBI was investigating him for violating draft laws. He was also concerned about finding a printer for the paper. Wade Mann, owner of the *Scott County Journal* in Scottsburg, Indiana, had been printing the *Spectator*, but rumors circulated that he had been pressured by arch conservative Eugene Pulliam, who owned the *Indianapolis Star*, to get the students to tone down their political rhetoric. Mann sold his company, and the *Spectator* eventually took its business to another firm in Ohio. The increased driving time from Bloomington was a problem, but one that could be handled.

A more threatening crisis was brought on by the IU board of trustees in February 1969. Increasingly irritated by the *Spectator's* editorials against IU administrators and university policies, board members ordered all university organizations to stop advertising in the paper and threatened to cut off funding to any group that continued to do so. They also banned the *Spectator* from being sold on campus. The board's ruling brought cries of outrage from students across the political spectrum. The editor of the *Indiana Daily Student* wrote, "In an intellectual community, the suppression of radicalism is more dangerous than anything that could be printed in the *Spectator*." The student senate voted a protest against the trustees' ban and urged student organizations to continue to advertise in the *Spectator*. *Spectator* staff members argued that the board's policy hurt writers and artists in Bloomington who had no other outlet for their ideas

THE SPECTATOR, December 17, 1968   page 3

HEADITOR'S NOTES

The administration has clearly escalated its war on dissent since last year, having even eliminated the classic means of symbolic protest developed for civil rights actions—the sit-in. Students are going to be seriously frustrated by this course of events, and I.U. has asked for it. It is going to get hard to catch anybody. It is going to be desperate.

BOBBY: WHAT'S IN A NAME

Spectator "Headitorial."

and work. Mimi Bardagjy, a longtime *Spectator* contributor, defended the underground paper as necessary because it provided "a sense of community for people" as well as a creative place to work and to express opinions about "what's going down." Nonetheless, the board of trustees ignored these criticisms and maintained its ban on the *Spectator*.[9]

Despite the university's ban, problems with printers, a constant money shortage, and several drug charges against staff members that were more hassles than serious threats, the *Spectator* continued to do its job as an underground newspaper. Writers took on the governor of Indiana, Edgar Whitcomb, conservative state legislators such as Dan Burton, and the new president of IU, Joseph Sutton, who had earlier led the attack on *Spectator* offices with a fire ax. Editors Jim Retherford and later Mike King criticized the university's involvement in the Vietnam war through research contracts with military and intelligence agencies. *Spectator* writers were among the first critics of the secrecy surrounding the Indiana University Foundation's accounts and budgets. Robert Johnson, a leader of African-American students on campus, wrote a series of articles exploring racial discrimination in beauty contests, athletics, and housing. Artist Wendel Field drew elaborate graphics for "Headitorials" and announcements of special dances or fundraising parties. Allen Gurevitz contributed

Spectator cover art.

poetry from time to time. Comic strips, including *Dr. Rex Organ* and the *Fabulous Furry Freak Brothers,* were regular features. And just to keep some members of the Bloomington community sufficiently outraged, staffers slipped in the odd nude photograph of John and Yoko or a particularly beautiful young flower child.

Since the *Spectator* could be sold only on the streets of Bloomington, street people were its vendors; together they often sold over a thousand

Spectator reader. *Arbutus,* 1970.

copies. Others were mailed to subscribers and to bookstores in cities as far away as Boston and San Francisco. At its peak, the *Spectator* had a circulation of about 1,700, publishing issues about fifty pages long twice a month. After reading a particularly insightful article on the writings of political theorist C. L. R. James, Paul Buhle, editor of *Radical America* in Madison, Wisconsin, sent a check for $10 as "a token of prospective disappointment if the Spectator should go under" along with compliments: "it's the most intellectually serious underground paper I've seen (no wonder you're broke). Hang on."[10]

J. Edgar Hoover, director of the FBI, believed that the New Left threatened national security, and his COINTELPRO campaign against it involved undermining the underground press. He instructed his agents around the country to disrupt New Left publications by preventing distribution, using obscenity laws to block production, using drug laws and conspiracy charges to arrest staff members, and practicing assorted dirty tricks to spread dissension and distrust among contributors. One of the FBI's favorite techniques was to raise suspicions among press staff that one of them was a FBI informer.[11]

If imitation is the highest form of flattery, then Hoover was the *Spectator's* biggest fan. He ordered his agents to produce their own versions of alternative newspapers to criticize and divide New Left journalists and their readers. Some, like the *Denver Arrow,* were completely imaginary operations, set up with a post office box so that the FBI could subscribe to the College Press Service. Others were real papers, including the *Rational Observer* in Washington, D.C., and Bloomington's *Armageddon News.*

Hoover took a real interest in the Bloomington paper. He ordered agents in the Indianapolis office to write articles that were antiwar in sentiment, but that urged readers to work within established political channels and vote pro-war politicians out of office instead of taking to the streets in protest. FBI agents were concerned about students who were attracted to SDS, but more especially those who joined the Committee to End the War in Vietnam.[12]

The FBI's first issue of *Armageddon News* showed the lack of experience the agents producing it had with the underground press:

> Don't be duped by the name of 'The Committee to End the War in Viet Nam.' Don't be taken in by it's [sic] alleged cause! We all want an end to this war, any war, all wars. These people are not really trying to end this war or any other war. . . .
>
> Ask yourself, then, what could be their true purpose? Could it perhaps be that they want the use of your name and your body for unwitting support of the Young Socialist Alliance and the Socialist Workers Party?
> TAKE A STAND FOR LAW AND ORDER!
> TAKE A STAND FOR A LOYAL, PATRIOTIC UNIVERSITY!
> DEDICATE YOURSELF TO EDUCATION, NOT DISLOYAL DISRUPTION!
> DON'T LET THE NEW LEFT WIN THE ARMAGEDDON AT IU.[13]

Hoover was critical of their efforts and wrote back to tell them that

> subsequent material must contain a more sophisticated approach. . . . Your leaflet should be prepared ostensibly by students who, while disagreeing with the Vietnam war policy and so forth, nevertheless deplore subversive elements on and off campus who are using these issues for their own purposes.

The agents tried again, with results that were more to the director's liking, but the effort was aborted after only a few issues. Producing *Armageddon News* was more trouble than it proved to be worth.[14]

All work and no play would have made the *Spectator* a dull job, and it was never that. Because people who worked on the paper usually lived together or near each other, opportunities to take a collective music break, throw a fund-raising party for someone's bail money or legal fees, or just kick back after a volunteer went barreling off in someone's car to take the latest issue to the printers were always available. *Spectator* gatherings were known for good music, lots of talking, the usual amount of dope, and a unique blend of free spirits. In the 1960s Bloomington counterculture, everyone knew each other. YSAers frowned on smoking pot as bourgeois corruption and an expensive drain on limited resources when it came to paying lawyers after the inevitable busts, but they enjoyed hanging out with others, even if the others were getting high.[15] Politicos drank beer with artists and musicians and listened to bands like Mrs. Seamon's Sound Band (later the Screaming Gypsy Bandits) or Roger Salloom and Robin Sinclair.

Mrs. Seamon's Sound Band was in many ways the essence of 1960s Bloomington rock and roll. Formed by IU School of Music students who were initially serious jazz players, the band evolved into a kind of fusion between jazz and rock and roll that was new to Bloomington. Its members wrote a lot of their own music, practiced in a garage next to the *Spectator* offices for a while, and played in Dunn Meadow, for dances in campus dormitories, and wherever anyone would pay a nominal fee for them to appear. They never made a lot of money, according to Chris Scanlon, their business manager, but they were, in the memories of many, "the very best band." It was music you could dance to, get high to, or just listen to, and it was Bloomington's own sound. "Mrs. Seamon" was the name of the nutritionist for Wilkie Quad, one of IU's large dormitory complexes.[16]

There was always a reason for a party and there were always people around to have one. Spontaneity was the name of the game. The important thing was to just be there when it was happening. *Spectator* artist Wendel Field recalled that he once left his house in the morning and did not return for three weeks, just going from one group of friends to another as events rolled along. When he finally got home, he found a strange couple in his front room who thought he was a cop. That kind of casual routine was a little extreme, but not wildly out of the ordinary. Graduate students tended to stick to academic timetables more closely than undergraduates because they needed to hang on to their teaching assistantships or research jobs. Still, campus lives in the 1960s were very different from the structured, organized, and often jam-packed schedules of today's students. Ruth Mahaney remembered that in the mid-1960s, IU's tuition was low and Bloomington was a relatively cheap place to live. She had a teaching assistantship in the English department, but she did not need other work to support herself while she was a graduate student at IU. And people made time for the things they wanted to do—whether it was organizing for political causes or exploring their inner consciousness on LSD or psilocybin. Mahaney was not interested in taking psychedelics, so in her group of friends she was the one who stayed straight and could take care of emergencies, drive the car, or answer the phone.[17]

Drugs were definitely part of the counterculture experience and Bloomington was no exception. Contemporary drugs like crack cocaine, methedrine, and heroin are mind-numbing, soul-destroying invitations to an early death. But that was not the way drug use among members of the counterculture began. No one started out on a suicide mission. The reasons for using drugs were quite the opposite. Drugs could help improve your life. Use of psychedelic drugs began as part of a series of psychological experiments in Swiss laboratories, Harvard classrooms, CIA hideouts, and hospital clinics. It soon took on a religious and cultural quality that made it part of a much larger revolution against political, social, economic, and military elites, or, in counterculture terms, "straight society." Jay Stevens argues in *Storming Heaven* that before Harvard psychologist Timothy Leary popularized the phrase "Turn on, tune in, drop out," drug users wanted to "Drop acid and change yourself, and then change the world." These phrases are succinct, but the psychedelic experience itself could not be summed up so neatly. As Stevens put it,

> Try describing the taste of ice cream to someone who has never had any, and multiply that difficulty by a thousand, and you will get some idea of how hard it was to describe what it felt like to be one with the universe, to know that you existed on a multitude of levels, and not just on the puny one called I. So many things happened in the psychedelic state that just couldn't be expressed in language.[18]

The idea that there was an intensely revealing way of looking at yourself and your relationships with others, at nature, at the world, and at the universe was being communicated from one person to the next. Using psychedelics was one way to strip away the superficial slickness of America's consumer culture and open up new angles of vision to old problems. There was a spiritual quality to the experience; it seemed that anyone could get out of old neurotic ways of thinking and find a higher plane of existence for about eight or ten hours (the usual length of the effects of LSD, psilocybin, or mescalin). Psychedelic drugs were a chemical way of de-conditioning layers of middle-class values, a means of unplugging egos, a mechanism for expanding minds. Of course all of these things were possible with other methods. Years of meditation or thousands of hours of psychoanalysis or a lifetime spent in thoughtful speculation might produce the same insights. The advantage of psychedelics was that if the chemicals were pure and the environment was right, anybody who wanted to could go on a trip of psychic exploration. Moreover, the experience could be a collective one as well. Doing psychedelics with a close friend or two created bonds that bridged age, sex, race, and class. It was both an extremely personal experience and the ultimate group action.

Sometimes the results could be a little disturbing. Letting go of ego made for some strange attitudes about power, ambition, and success. After a trip out to the edge of the universe, working as a sales manager from 9:00 to 5:00 and making monthly quotas lost its appeal. Like a lot of other counterculture centers, Bloomington experienced a small explosion of organic farmers, leather workers, potters, artists, and other craftspeople. By the end of the 1960s, a lot of kids from Indiana had gotten a taste of what it was like to be in "one of the highest states of grace a hippie could attain—to be perfectly attuned to the moment."[19]

As the community's source of truth from the streets, the *Spectator* reported what drugs were available, gave information on their prices and quality, and warned readers of potential rip-offs or adulterations. The *Spectator* also published reports of drug busts and noted the presence of undercover agents on Bloomington streets. Especially toward the end of the 1960s, using drugs involved a certain amount of justified paranoia. The FBI was often successful in its effort to throw political activists into disarray with drug-related arrests. After a series of arrests in December 1968, an FBI informer wrote,

> Tension ran very high for two weeks after the first bust. The Kirkwood Strip had very few, if any, hippies on it from Dec. 3 to Dec. 6. Across the street from The Other Side in an apartment above the Spudnut Shop was said to be a camera taking pictures of people on the Strip. Said window was totally covered with a tin or aluminum foil type substance. Some people said that they actually saw the camera behind 'a small lense [sic] hole' in the foil.

Tensions arose not only from the busts, but also from newspaper stories and false rumors, the fear that came from not knowing who to trust or whether one might be busted oneself at any moment. This informer heard rumors that from twelve to forty-two people would be busted in Bloomington.[20]

Paranoia, bad drugs, and bad trips created a need for a safe house in Bloomington. The *Spectator* informed its readers about Middle Way House, operated by volunteers, where people who needed it could find some peace and quiet. Aware that the house was under surveillance, *Spectator* staffers made it quite clear that no drugs were allowed on the premises.[21]

While marijuana was the most popular drug among IU students as a whole, taking psychedelics was considered part of the rites of passage into a new consciousness by some of Bloomington's leading adventurers on that journey. Bloomington was a perfect place to start the trip. There were serene forests nearby with trails that led to high cliffs and bluffs. From these heights, trippers had views of gently rolling farmland, dotted with small blue lakes. Nearby Brown County provided wonderful places for days of walking, contemplating, and talking it all over with a close companion or two, and for getting right out there on the edge and coming back again. Southern Indiana was free of the uptight city vibes that led to so many bad trips. The countryside was, for the most part, soft, mellow, and open to exploration. Bloomington had its share of experienced trippers, like Wendel Field, who could provide insightful advice on the quality and appropriate dosage of various chemicals and who, when needed, could soothe a troubled spirit. To many respectable citizens of the state of Indiana, Bloomington was the devil's own den where decent, ordinary young men and women went for a few years and "got weird."[22]

Sex was an important part of the counterculture's new lifestyle too. However, hippies were hardly the first Americans to advocate sexual liberation. During the 1920s, bohemians in Greenwich Village had adopted Freud's theories about the connections between sexual frustrations and neuroses, and openly expressed their determination to defy traditional conventions. The Beats rebelled against taboos on homosexuality and poet Allen Ginsberg publicly celebrated his male lovers. Still, during the 1960s, members of the counterculture declared that sex was fun, free, and essential to human health. When the government made birth control pills available to women in 1960, the sexual revolution became a reality for both sexes. Men and women experimented with sex in somewhat the same way that they experimented with drugs: as a way of better understanding themselves and each other. The old guilt trips were part of the past—sexual freedom was the way of the future.

From a 1990s perspective, much of what was said and written about sexual freedom in the 1960s is chauvinistic and oriented primarily toward male pleasure. Moreover, viewed from our own time and with today's knowledge of AIDS and other sexually transmitted diseases, hip attitudes about sex appear irresponsible. Yet, at the time, sexual liberation fit in with the overall hip philosophy—if it feels good and it doesn't hurt anyone, do it.

Some of the worst middle-class nightmares came true in Bloomington in the late 1960s. As university parietal rules were abandoned, students used their new freedom to explore their sexuality. Unmarried couples shared apartments, even though Bloomington apartment owners disapproved. One of the more bizarre examples of sexual exploration began when Robert Klawitter, a young English professor, converted his suburban home into an experiment in communal living. Sonja Klawitter went along with the project, although she was less enthusiastic than was her husband. The Klawitters invited several people, men and women, to move into their house, an ordinary yellow tract home in a Bloomington suburb. The house soon became known as "the yellow submarine." Everyone shared cooking duties and housework equally. In an effort to break down inhibitions, commune members regularly switched sexual partners, and women were often the initiators of sexual encounters. This communal experiment did not endure for long. Neither did the Klawitters' marriage. Bob Klawitter left Indiana University and moved to Brown County. Residents of the yellow submarine were part of a search for sexual equality and a different way of living that finally reached the limits of everyone's endurance.[23]

All of this might have been alarming enough on its own, but around 1968, yet another aspect of life in Bloomington began to raise eyebrows around the state. Even though Bloomington could hardly be called turbulent, there was a certain tension to it for those of the countercultural persuasion—hostile stares from store owners, angry reactions from landlords after parties of unusual intensity, and the perennial hassles from local police who followed decorated Volkswagen vans and other vehicles that had a hippie look about them. For some seekers of a new way of living, the next step was to leave town altogether, get some land out in the country, and learn to live with the earth. This move to surrounding rural counties took place on an individual basis. Connie Loftman and Guy Loftman moved into a friend's cabin in Brown County. Chris Scanlon lived on a farm in nearby Greene County for a while. Some people who bought farms around Bloomington in the late 1960s and early 1970s are still farming, still living a lifestyle of simplicity and naturalness. But the story of the Bloomington counterculture's fascination with rural living would not be complete without some mention of Needmore, a name that put southern Indiana on the national map of alternative lifestyles.

In 1967 Indianapolis native Kathy Noyes moved to Bloomington from Boston, where she had been enrolled in school. She was recently divorced from her husband, who had enlisted in the army after receiving his draft notice. She had an inheritance from her father, Evan Noyes, an executive with the pharmaceutical firm of Eli Lilly and nephew of the company's founder. In Bloomington Noyes met Larry Canada, a local boy, who in her own words "swept me off my feet." They got married in Beck Chapel on the IU campus. After the wedding, she followed her mother's advice about how to spend a little extra money—she bought some land in Brown County.[24]

Kathy Noyes Canada did more than just buy a farm and settle down to the joys of country living. Her husband had a vision of creating a new community in southern Indiana where people could come from all over the country and live freely off the land. The Canadas bought several farms around the little town of Needmore, amassing about a thousand acres. Word went out that anyone could come and live there for free. It did not take long for strangers from places as distant as Washington, D.C., and San Francisco to find their way to the Community Corner General Store that Larry Canada had opened to serve Needmore's growing population.[25]

Communal living is an ancient ideal. Early Christians lived together in religious communities. Native peoples in North America lived together in tribal groups. In the nineteenth century, radical political and religious communities such as Brook Farm and New Harmony experimented with utopian philosophies and lifestyles. Hip communes in the 1960s were rarely based on any central religious or political philosophy but rather on more general ideals of sharing, sexual liberation, and pure democracy.

Some of the earliest communes began on the West Coast: Tolstoy Farm in Washington (1963) and Morning Star Ranch outside Sebastopol, California (1966). Timothy Miller relates the growth of communes to rock festivals during the 1960s. The feeling of community that came with music created a need for a continuing experience. David Satterfield, a member of Bloomington's counterculture, compared communalism to bluegrass festivals like the ones that Bill Monroe put on in southern Indiana. Dancing together led to making music together, which inspired people to live together in a more permanent community based on joy and harmony.[26]

Communal living was a way of experiencing real human communication, away from the complications of urban complexities. In that sense, hippie communes reflected a basic American aversion to cities that emphasized love of nature, the purity of the land, and the value of agricultural labor. Rural communes represented a negation of city lifestyles—competition, greed, materialism, and intense individualism.

Unfortunately, many of the young people who flocked to communes in the 1960s had grown up in American cities and suburbs. While their enthusiasm for rural life was great, their expertise in rural living was minimal. Moreover, many hip women found that they did all the cooking and all the cleaning, while men discussed communal goals and philosophy. Not all women had that experience, but some who did left heterosexual communes and began to search for a better way to live together, without men.

Needmore was not a commune in the strict sense of the word. Individuals, couples, and families lived separately, not communally, in farmhouses and cabins built by previous owners, in shelters they built for themselves, and, sometimes, in tents and tepees. Also, there was no organized system of pooling and dividing labor, resources, and farm products, although the spirit of sharing and bartering dominated transactions. Larry Canada occasionally hired workers to put in fencing and do other odd jobs around the farms. There were weekly community meetings, usually held around a big campfire at a place called "the mound." People talked over problems, discussed various projects, and ended the day singing songs and playing music. For Kathy Canada these weekly gatherings of Needmore residents represented a family she felt that she had never had, and they remain some of her happiest memories of her days in the country.[27]

The FBI focused on Needmore because of Larry Canada's friendship with Rennie Davis, one of the original members of SDS and a leader in the national antiwar movement. When the Weathermen faction took over the leadership of SDS, Davis and Canada were suspected of being part of that group's plot to plant a bomb in the nation's capital. FBI agents came to Needmore looking for evidence that might be used against Canada. Local police arrested a few residents for possession of marijuana, but Kathy Canada suspected that they were more interested in finding out about her husband's political activities than they were in prosecuting people for pot. She also discovered that someone had planted a package of heroin under her car. After several months of surveillance, FBI agents arrested Larry Canada while he was sitting in Bloomington's People's Park, on land also owned by him and Kathy that had been the site of the Black Market until it was firebombed in 1968.[28]

As far as Kathy Canada was concerned, the situation at Needmore was going downhill quickly. She had a small daughter to take care of and she was beginning to get frightened. One night in June 1971, someone burned a cross in a field opposite her house. Her neighbors received Ku Klux Klan literature in the mail. Two hitchhikers from Minnesota were beaten when they stopped at the Needmore general store. People reported hearing sounds of gunshots and cars roaring through the night.

Finally Kathy divorced her husband and signed over the Brown County land to the newly organized Kneadmore Life Community Church. Early supporters like Guy Loftman and Connie Loftman moved out.[29]

Stories about the *Spectator,* psychedelic drug use, and Needmore illustrate different aspects of the counterculture in a place like Bloomington. In the 1960s a group of people lived in and around town who were connected in one way or another with the university or with people who were, and who formed a viable cultural alternative to the local academic and business community. They sought a way out of straight society, a money-based economy, and all the problems and contradictions that went with conventional lifestyles. It was not an easy search. Longtime residents were disturbed by newcomers who were drawn by Needmore's hospitality or Bloomington's attractiveness. Newspaper reporters wrote about these growing hostilities. What began as a peaceful cultural experiment turned into a battle between conflicting age groups and worldviews. Members of the counterculture took it all in as they continued to live their lives quietly on Bloomington's streets, in country houses, and on nearby farms.[30]

Today, Bloomington has its folksingers, blues bands, artists, organic farmers, potters, leather workers, and folks with long grey hair who drink coffee at various coffee houses close to campus. But there is a McDonald's on Kirkwood Avenue now and the shops around the downtown square have been rehabilitated from rundown artists' studios into boutiques, offices, and expensive art galleries. People's Park on Kirkwood Avenue has a limestone sculpture paid for by the city of Bloomington, a billboard with notices of concerts and political activities, and a fair sprinkling of local kids and university students hanging out, along with an infrequent street vendor selling jewelry or handmade leather goods. Few of the people in the park know the history of the place—the hippie head shops of the 1960s, the Black Market and the Klan firebombing in 1968, the connection with the Canadas and Needmore. Ask people today what Bloomington is like and you are more likely to hear about the town's links with the university, and especially with its nationally known basketball team. Yet for people who now live and work in downtown Indianapolis and around the state the memory lingers on. "Bloomington," they might say quietly with an odd knowing look in their eyes, "why, that's the town where all the hippies were in the 1960s," and then smile that strange little smile.

In the end, then, the hippie is both a symbol and a parody of the Sixties. Simplistically, hippies were long-haired, self-indulgent drug addicts and social parasites. They offended decent, hardworking Americans and created a backlash that reverberates to this day.

At the same time, cultural historian Thomas Frank has observed quite correctly that American consumer capitalists quickly coopted the counterculture's spirit of rebellion by incorporating hip symbols of liberation and freedom into advertising slogans and marketing strategies. Selling everything from Volkswagen to the Uncola, advertisers understood the psychological appeal of social deviancy to the average American. While conservatives continue to fight cultural wars against the spirit of the 1960s, they have been looking in the wrong places for the wrong enemies. The most popular promoters of Sixties insurrections are in the executive offices on Madison Avenue.[31]

On the highest level, however, the hip philosophy represents all that is best of that decade: love for each other, care for all creatures, a sense of joy in each day, and harmony with the earth. Hip people understood that capitalism brought out many of the worst features of human nature: greed, competition, envy, jealousy, and materialism. They tried, sometimes successfully, sometimes not, to promote a more humane society, where people could be more creative and more honest, and have more fun.

The hip creed was "Love yourself, love each other, love the earth." The counterculture, initially dominated by men, gave women an opportunity to discover their own voices. It also provided social space for gays and lesbians to find their own communities.

One of the most enduring legacies of the counterculture is the environmental movement, a direct descendant of the hip "back to the earth" communal living movement. Its advocates were inspired by Native American lifestyles and adopted the idea of being a part of a human tribe, the daughters and sons of Mother Earth. Earlier environmentalists like Aldo Leopold and Rachel Carson, along with Beat writers such as Gary Snyder, provided a written legacy for thousands of young hip enthusiasts in the 1960s who wanted to live in harmony with the land. From the first Earth Day in 1970 into the twenty-first century, more and more Americans have appreciated the fragility of our planet and the necessity to protect our air, our water, and our land. Today, most elementary and high school students have been raised in the ethics of recycling and with an appreciation for nature and its beauties.[32]

The popular mythology of hippies is that they turned into yuppies. Well, maybe some did, but not all of them. The hip ideal lives on wherever there are people who challenge conventional thinking, who are open to more creative ways of living, who strive to find spiritual fulfillment rather than settle for creature comforts, who see beyond the boundaries of conventional wisdom, and who still believe in love between their brothers and their sisters and peace on earth.

Epilogue: The End of an Era at Indiana University

The Sixties did not end precisely on December 31, 1969. The spirit of that decade lived on into the early 1970s. In one sense, the student antiwar movement ended with the massive demonstrations after the events at Kent State University in May 1970. Many young Americans admitted that they were tired of marching against a war that did not end and that continued to take the lives of their brothers and sisters.

At the same time, during the early 1970s, the campaign to end the war in Vietnam was a victim of its own domestic political success. As historian Terry Anderson concluded, "The call for peace, which a majority considered unpatriotic as late as 1968, now was patriotic. . . . [T]he idea of Peace Now had become in the national interest. The only question was, When? Across the nation the political center shifted. . . . The antiwar crusade became obsolete."[1]

This political shift at the national level inspired many students and former students to become more involved in local issues. Across the country, antiwar and civil rights activists began to focus their attention on matters closer to home. Paul Soglin, who protested the war as a student at the University of Wisconsin, was elected mayor of Madison, Wisconsin, in 1973. Julian Bond, one of the founders of SNCC, became a member of the state legislature in Georgia. Antiwar protestors who were concerned about the use of defoliants in Vietnam turned their attention to the use of pesticides in America. The environmental movement that began with the first Earth Day in 1970 had its origins in the peace movement of earlier years and it remains one of the most lasting contributions of Sixties activism.

Perhaps the most important social change to emerge from the 1960s, in Indiana and throughout the country, was the women's movement. During the 1970s, more and more women joined forces to promote gender equity in the workplace, in politics, and at home. Women whose organizing skills had been honed in the civil rights and antiwar movements began to apply themselves to improving their own lives and the lives of their daughters. "Sisterhood is powerful" was not just a feminist slogan but an enduring lesson at the end of the 1960s and for decades to come.

In Bloomington, activists in the early 1970s faced many of the same frustrations that challenged others across the country. People were getting tired. It was hard to go on, day after day, protesting against a war that most people agreed was unjustified but that continued to cost American lives, even though at less dramatic rates than before. However, an issue emerged in 1970 that galvanized the spirits of Bloomington citizens, young and old alike. Anyone who has ever lived in a university town knows that there are few problems that can provoke people more than . . . parking.

In July citizens and students formed the East Central Neighborhood Association to block a plan proposed by the Bloomington City Council to install three thousand parking meters on streets surrounding the campus. Council members wanted to use the ten-cent-per-hour parking charges to finance a high-rise building with a parking garage and apartments for senior citizens to be constructed on People's Park. Students and local residents were outraged at the inconvenience and expense that the meters would bring and they resented the way that the city government had approved the plan without voter participation. One reporter for the *Indiana Daily Student* wrote that if the meters were actually installed, students should fight them by putting epoxy glue in the coin slots. "The same friendly people who brought us the Vietnam War have awakened The Resistance to the value of guerrilla warfare." In response to the parking meter controversy, Alfred Towell, a graduate student in computer science and a computer consultant, organized the IU Voters Union to promote student issues in local elections.[2]

Opponents of the parking meter plan found out that Republican mayor John Hooker had used money from city funds to purchase People's Park, and they were able to prove that he had misappropriated the money and had failed to follow established accounting procedures. The mayor was indicted by a grand jury, found guilty of misapplication of municipal government property, and slapped on the hand with a two-dollar fine. Still, students and citizens had won their point. People's Park is still People's Park. The high-rise building was never built. There are no parking meters on residential streets around the campus.

That fall former *Spectator* editor Jim Retherford was fined $25 and sentenced to ninety days at the Indiana State Penal Farm by Monroe County Circuit Judge Nat Hill, who upheld Retherford's conviction by the Bloomington City Court for disorderly conduct during Clark Kerr's speech in March. In his defense, Retherford said that the youth revolution was a cultural revolution and that young people would succeed in liberating themselves from old values. He explained that throwing a pie at Clark Kerr was a warning to professors who talk down to their students and that "the pie in the sky may fall in their eye."[3]

Many people would have agreed with Retherford that a youthful cultural revolution was going on in Bloomington in the early 1970s. One way that students were liberating themselves was by smoking dope. Getting high became a popular pastime—not just for hard-core counterculture types but for fraternity and sorority members as well. The *Daily Student* featured a series on drug dealers on campus. During an interview over coffee at the Memorial Union, one dealer who sold to fraternity houses estimated that about 80% of the membership smoked marijuana. He liked selling to Greeks because "they're good kids, they don't haggle about price and they won't rat on you or burn you." Continuing, he picked up his coffee cup and asked, "You know what the universal measure for a lid of grass is in Bloomington? An Indiana Memorial Union coffee cup, filled level. Isn't that far out?"[4]

Arrests for possession of marijuana became so common that the local prosecuting attorney decided to try a new policy. Previously, possession had meant felony charges and a possible two-to-ten-year prison sentence. Under the new arrangement, simple possession was a misdemeanor, with a maximum one-year sentence.[5]

A quick look through the IU yearbook, the *Arbutus*, for 1970–71 and 1971–72 suggests that the dope dealer's estimate of drug use in Greek houses may have been right. There aren't many standard pictures of fraternity and sorority members in coats and ties or dresses arranged in orderly rows in front of their houses. Instead there are strange arrangements of people sitting up in trees or sprawled on floors, and inevitably someone is holding up fingers in the peace sign. Things had changed. Not everyone was pleased, however. One mother who had put several of her children through IU said,

> Their ideas change—you can't understand them. Six years ago it was easy. One of our kids graduated and settled down beautifully. Not the others though. If I had it to do over again I'd send them to school all right, but not away from home. There's too many bad influences—dope, violence, open

visitation. . . . We're deathly afraid of dope and riots. Our son let his hair grow long when he went away. . . . We know he's going to face problems.[6]

Normally IU students would learn about changes in possession charges, or Jim Retherford's conviction, on the pages of the *Spectator*. But the paper was late getting started in the fall of 1970. Over the summer the staff had met and almost disbanded. Some staff members felt that the May 1970 women's liberation issue had marked the beginning of the end. The feeling of community was gone and no one could see how it could be resurrected under the circumstances. Others argued that editorials had become "verbose doctrinaire bullshit." But mainly, the staff decided, "When only a few people are working on the paper, the exhaustion and compromises of overworked people are gonna show." They were having a difficult time getting advertisers and the operating budget, always tight, was nearly nonexistent. Contributing artists and writers sometimes did not get paid. "Even socialists," staff members argued, "need to be modestly reimbursed. People who work for free are being exploited." The *Spectator* was a nationally recognized underground paper and its reputation was among the highest in the country. However, after a late start in October, the staff was able to put out only a few more issues that fall. After over four years of nearly continuous production, the *Spectator* joined the ranks of other journals that had burned out in the war for free expression in the 1960s and ceased publication.[7]

By the next spring, several people who had worked on the *Spectator* had regrouped and put out a new paper called *Common Sense*. Organized as "a collective of common sense brothers who are each one part of a whole educational structure," this new alternative paper had no editor. In an effort to correct what they saw as errors made at the *Spectator,* all female staff members had absolute veto power over male members on any story or advertisement. "Women have traditionally been trampled and mistreated," staff member Steve Feebeck explained, "and they are more able to spot male chauvinism and what its effects on them will be."[8] *Common Sense* presented its version of a radical political perspective to Bloomington readers for two more years. In general, staff members were graduate students or Bloomington residents who were active in local politics. Thoughtful, clearly written, and carefully laid out, *Common Sense* was in some ways a more responsible paper than the *Spectator* had been, but it often lacked that fine edge of manic energy that the earlier paper had managed to exude.

During the fall of 1970, student government as it was practiced by student body president and Black Panther Party member Keith Parker and vice president Mike King was once again controversial. Parker and King had initiated a series of experimental programs supported by funds collected from student fees. They set up a student legal service to represent students who were charged with civil and criminal offenses and violations of university rules. Tom Ross, an IU law school graduate, was the first student legal defender and he set out an ambitious program to work on landlord-tenant relations, which he termed "outrageous." Not surprisingly, the board of trustees was suspicious of Ross's position, and soon after he took office they informed him that he could not sue the university, nor could he represent students in criminal cases. The board's restrictions made the office of student legal services less effective than the one envisioned in Parker and King's original proposal. Disgusted, Parker said it was about as helpful to students as "a lovelorn letters column." When asked if he was disillusioned with the university's lack of support in the fight with the trustees over legal services, Parker replied,

> I am not disillusioned with the University because I was never 'illusioned' in the first place. . . . We are continually told to work within the system . . . [but] the hypocrisy that we are having to deal with serves to politicize people who were apolitical. The contradictions are being exposed to the students, and you don't need long hair or radical politics to see them.

Ross worked hard that year on student legal problems, despite chronic case overloads, a shortage of help, and meager financing.[9]

Antiwar protests continued throughout the 1970–71 academic year, organized by a hard-core group of about 150 to 200 demonstrators, although the number of students who came to the demonstrations began to decline. Even though there was less interest in marches and protests, however, feeling against the war was much more widespread. A telling moment occurred that fall during the Indiana University–Michigan State football game, when IU's marching band formed the peace symbol during halftime ceremonies and the whole student section stood up and cheered.[10]

As part of his own contribution to the antiwar movement, Keith Parker announced that on November 22, 1970, he would leave for Hanoi, North Vietnam. Speaking after a performance of the San Francisco Mime Troupe that contained antiwar themes, Parker told the audience that he had been invited to travel with members of the National Student Association who hoped to sign a "people's peace treaty" with North Vietnamese students. The group left from New York for Moscow, where they stayed three days. Flying on to Hanoi, they met with student representatives from North Vietnamese universities. The trip concluded in Paris,

Keith Parker, student body president and member of the Black Panther Party. *Arbutus,* 1971.

where they met with peace negotiators. More than a few IU students criticized Parker for neglecting problems on campus. He replied that the trip was "a first step in bringing about an end to the war in Vietnam and a first step in beginning to forge alliances with students everywhere who feel the way we do, and long for a new society." He defended his decision to take part in the people's peace treaty: "I feel that I am representing my constituency by going to Vietnam and that what can be learned by talking to Vietnamese students will be of great value to us all as an alternative to media propaganda."[11]

Mike King supported Parker's trip as a demonstration of student solidarity and real internationalism. King criticized IU officials as being more concerned with "police training than serving human needs, in Indiana or Vietnam."[12]

Parker came back to Bloomington to report to students. Speaking to an audience of about a thousand in January 1971, Parker summarized the terms of the people's peace treaty. The signers called for total withdrawal of American troops, an immediate cease-fire, the release of all political prisoners, and independent, neutral governments in Laos and Cambodia.

Perhaps partially motivated by Parker's trip to Hanoi, state legislators slashed $51 million from the university's budget request. Angry about the student government's sponsorship of events like the San Francisco Mime Troupe's performance, the board of trustees voted to eliminate the fifty-cent student fee that was the basis of the student government operating budget. The relationship between student government and the university administration, as Parker described it, "was not one of love."[13]

The administration had gone through a few changes that year. President Sutton's wife died that fall and he resigned. Without conducting a national search, the trustees picked John Ryan to succeed Sutton. Ryan had been a vice president of the university and chancellor of the regional campuses.[14]

One of the experimental projects that student government had funded with student fees was the Hobbit House Day Care Center for children of students, staff, and faculty. Priscilla Allen, an English instructor, and Jean Romsted were early spokespersons for day care centers that were "small, autonomous, parent-controlled and parent-operated." They hoped that the university would provide "rent-free facilities, funds for equipment and supplies, and a work release program whereby full time staff parents would have a half-day off from their regular job to work with the children at their day care center each week." IU did not agree to those terms, but did allow them to rent a university-owned house close to campus on East 11th Street. The student government gave the center $1500 and agreed to pay its rent and utility bills. During the summer of 1970, parents cleaned, painted, furnished, and fenced Hobbit House.[15]

Hobbit House opened that fall. Volunteers cared for children aged from six months to four years. Parents met every few weeks to discuss organizational problems, and by the end of the first semester, Hobbit House was declared a success. Organizers prepared a survey in order to determine interest in opening other small centers on or near the campus. About one hundred families indicated that they wanted to participate in some kind of cooperative day care for their children. Parents met on November 22, 1970, and asked Chancellor Byram Carter to provide university houses for the centers.[16]

Carter and other administrators insisted that day care center organizers should pay rent on any houses that the university allowed them to use. They urged Hobbit House parents to collaborate with other groups—such as Women's Liberation—who also had children's centers and negotiate as a single organization with the university. The university would not rent houses to be used as day care centers unless parents agreed to meet state sanitation and health standards. Parents would have to pay for all repairs or renovations required to meet these standards and buy accident and fire insurance. Despite these challenges, parents from several groups were able to find, furnish, and open three new centers during the next semester.[17]

Not surprisingly, one of the groups involved in cooperative child care was Women's Liberation. The women's movement at Indiana University gained considerable momentum in the early 1970s. The Women's Studies Program had been approved and a few courses began to address women's issues in several departments.

IU's Women's Studies Program was one of the first in the country, even though many feminists thought that these programs existed only at well-known universities on the East or West Coasts. For example, Florence Howe told participants at a 1972 workshop, "Half of the programs are on the East Coast and half are on the West Coast. And so far none are in the middle of the country. The geography is much more important than you would imagine because the programs have tended to follow the movement. The programs exist where there is a strong women's movement."[18] This statement would have come as a surprise to feminists at Indiana University, who saw themselves as a part of the women's movement at both grass-roots and national levels.

Women faculty at IU joined with their professional sisters across the country in challenging university hiring and promotion policies. Collecting information as part of a case filed by the Women's Equity Action League (WEAL), a national organization based in Washington, D.C., with the Department of Health, Education, and Welfare in 1971, women faculty members were able to show that there was a pattern of sexual discrimination at Indiana University.[19]

By taking part in this action, IU's faculty women became part of a national movement that arose out of an executive order signed by President Johnson in 1967 that forbade sexual discrimination by all federal contractors. Since most large research universities received federal funds during the late 1960s and early 1970s, WEAL was able to file class-action suits that eventually involved over 360 institutions, including Indiana University.[20]

The effects of WEAL's legal action can be seen in the increase in the number of women faculty at IU. During the fall semester of 2000, 33% of the full-time faculty on all campuses were women: that is, 1,377 out of 4,136. On the Bloomington campus, there were 1,618 faculty members and 488 of them were women.[21]

Women at IU reflected other national trends as well. While women faculty came together to fight against discriminatory hiring and promotion policies, other feminists found themselves becoming increasingly polarized over the issue of sexual preference. At Indiana University, students gathered at the Women's Liberation Center, located in a house close to campus. The center provided a supportive atmosphere for consciousness-raising groups and those working to repeal restrictive abortion laws, as well as living space for several women. Early in the 1970s it became apparent that the first flush of cohesive unity was beginning to fade. Women began to declare their sexual preferences openly during their group meetings and the groups often split into heterosexual and homosexual camps. These divisions could be quite painful, especially since an atmosphere of emotional intimacy and trust had been established during the early years of the movement. Ruth Mahaney remembered an evening meeting where one woman declared her love for another woman in the group. The problem was that the feeling of love was reciprocal, but not identical. As the other woman tried to explain years later, "I loved her like a sister, but not that way." Feelings got hurt and bonds that had seemed strong began to fray. In this, Bloomington's women's movement was typical of other feminist groups across the nation. As Alice Echols observed in *Daring to be Bad,* in the early 1970s the "'gay-straight split' . . . crippled the movement, ending long-term friendships, partnerships, and groups."[22]

Women's liberation was the beginning of gay liberation, for both women and men. Gay students at IU felt the ripple effects of the Stonewall Inn riot that occurred in June 1969 in New York City. In that incident, police raided a bar known for its gay clientele, and instead of submitting to this kind of routine harassment, hundreds of gay men and women joined ranks and fought back. From that time forward, gays found a new sense of solidarity and pride. They formed the Gay Liberation Front and began picketing and protesting against companies and groups that discriminated against them. One year after Stonewall, ten thousand gay Americans marched on the streets of New York, celebrating gay pride.

Reflecting this national trend, during the fall of 1970, about a hundred members of the Bloomington Gay Alliance sponsored *The Boys in the Band,* a film about gay men. On October 31, 1970, the Bloomington Gay Liberation Front sponsored an All Campus Liberated Multi-Everything Halloween Party. The party's theme was "We *Will* Learn to Live and Love without Fear or Shame."[23]

While the women's movement was divided over the issue of sexual preference, the student movement was splintered into a myriad of interests and concerns. Spring elections in 1971 illustrated just how divergent student politics had become. Thirteen candidates ran for student body president. Their parties included Vietnam Veterans against the War, the Alliance for Student Advancement, the Independent Party, the French Commune Party, the Socialist Campaign, Anti-Women's Liberation, Think About It, and College Should Be a Good Time. Keith Parker's

United Student Movement was conspicuously absent from the fray. Parker admitted that he and his vice president Mike King had spent more time arguing with administrators than talking with students. "This was our major political failure," he said, and it contributed to the party's demise.[24]

Students elected Mary Scifres president and Jeff Richardson vice president. They promised students that they would give priority to campus issues—an obvious reaction to Parker's trip to Hanoi. Voter turnout was light and Scifres and Richardson did not win a majority. The election had been plagued by the malicious destruction of campaign posters, littering, charges of fraud, excessive spending, and disputed returns. All in all, it had been a disappointing spring campaign. The mood on the campus, according to an *Indiana Daily Student* reporter, was "subdued."[25]

Shortly after the election, Prof. Orlando Taylor came back to Bloomington from Washington, D.C., where he was teaching at Federal City College. Taylor returned to raise money to pay lawyers defending the Bloomington 7: himself and the six students who had been indicted by a grand jury following the Ballantine lock-in in May 1969. The trial was to be held in July. The two attorneys, John Moss and John Preston Ward, needed $11,000 for the defense. Taylor had raised almost $4,000 at parties in New York City and Boston. He told his friends, "I am guilty of nothing." In Bloomington, the faculty donated $2,500. Taylor's replacement as director of the African-American studies program, Dr. Herman Hudson, told him, "We want you to know that you do have the support of the black faculty and staff and the students." Rollo Turner joined Taylor for a weekend of speeches and marches. Addressing a crowd in Dunn Meadow, Turner told his audience of two hundred, "You're black, brothers and sisters, and it's time to come home. Peace on the inside, power on the outside. Roll on."[26]

The trial began on July 26, 1971, with prosecuting attorney Thomas Berry requesting that the felony charges of rout be dismissed and that the defendants be tried on charges of misdemeanor rout. The request was granted. The trial lasted until August 23. During the proceedings, vice president David Derge testified for the prosecution. He told the jury that the black students would not let him leave Ballantine Hall during the lock-in. But on cross-examination, none of the witnesses could say that they had seen any of the defendants actually keep anyone from leaving. Under further questioning, Derge admitted that it had been Orlando Taylor who had helped him get out of Ballantine.

Defense witnesses included Robert Klawitter from the English department and Richard Gray, chairman of the Department of Journalism. Defense attorney John Moss, who was blind, did an impressive job of engaging jury members' sympathies. His partner, John Ward, made an impassioned plea for a verdict of not guilty. He told the jury, "If they are found guilty for exercising good sound leadership, it would write a tragic chapter in the story of justice in these United States." The jury was out for fifty minutes and found the Bloomington 7 not guilty. Both Taylor and Turner expressed relief and praised their attorneys. Turner said he hoped that the trial had been an enlightening experience for jury members, who had listened to testimony from African Americans at Indiana University and in the process gained some insights into the lives of black students on that campus.[27]

As 1971's summer turned to fall, IU students came back to Bloomington and took up their regular academic lives. It was surprising, then, when reporters from the *Wall Street Journal* and the *New York Times* appeared in town, drawn by the mayoral election coming in November. Rumor had it that one of the candidates, Democrat Frank McCloskey, a recent graduate of Indiana University Law School, was seeking to beat incumbent mayor John Hooker with the power of student votes. The Twenty-Sixth Amendment (the Voting Rights Amendment) had been ratified in July, and for the first time virtually all college and university students could vote.[28]

On the front page of the *Wall Street Journal* on Oct. 28, 1971, readers saw the following headline: "A Lackluster Election in Indiana May Show Student Voting Power." With 33,000 residents and 31,000 students enrolled at the university, some Bloomington citizens were concerned that student power could affect the mayoral race and might even wreck the town. The reporter quoted a middle-aged businessman's remarks to an IU student campaigning for McCloskey: "I've lived here for 35 years and I'd like to know what gives you the right to try to make this an ideal town. Why you kids could put things over on us that we'll be paying for years after you've graduated and pulled out." The reporter also cited recent polls that gave McCloskey a four-to-one lead over Hooker among student voters. In addition, Mary Scifres, student body president, endorsed McCloskey for mayor.

Frank McCloskey did win that election, by 2,500 votes. It was the largest voter turnout in city history. The percentage of students eligible to vote who actually did so was also the largest in city history. Out of 9,636 registered student voters, 4,825 cast their ballots. McCloskey won 3,313 of those student votes. However, he would have won the election without a single student vote. The Democratic Party in Bloomington had used computerized voters' lists for the first time, and party workers had begun organizing and polling early in the fall. McCloskey won every precinct by a healthy margin. Democrats were able to take control of the city council as well. Several of the new council members were connected to IU: James Ackerman, a professor of religion; Professor Sherwin Mizell; Alfred Towell, a Ph.D. candidate and founder of the IU Voters Union; and Brian de St. Croix, a graduate student. Thirty-one-year-old Frank McCloskey may have looked like the students' choice and the harbinger of a new age of youth participation in the political process, but his victory was the result of old-style political polling and hard work.[29]

The same could be said of Paul Soglin's victory in his campaign to become mayor of Madison, Wisconsin. Soglin had been part of the antiwar movement while he was a student at the University of Wisconsin, and much was made of his popularity among students and the hip community that lived along Mifflin Street, that meeting ground of Madison's counterculture. But Soglin worked with Democratic Party regulars who ran his campaign using traditional tactics, and his victory was the result of their hard work as well as his own brand of protest politics.[30]

At the national level, the Democratic Party reflected many of the changes caused by the student movement of the Sixties. The party's 1972 convention in Miami attracted many delegates who had never been to one before. The hall was filled with more women, African Americans, and young people than had ever been seen in convention history. Gone were the days when a group of white men from unions, universities, and urban machines made party policy in smoke-filled back rooms. These delegates elected George McGovern, a senator from South Dakota, who opposed the war, favored amnesty for protestors, proposed decriminalization of marijuana, and supported women's liberation. While McGovern's overwhelming defeat by incumbent president Richard M. Nixon is usually cited as evidence of the failure of protest politics, his very nomination marks a distinct victory for those reformers who began their campaigns against the war and for gender and racial equity back in the 1960s in cities and towns across the country, from large to small, from East to West and in the heartland, including in Bloomington, Indiana.

The early 1970s were a turning point for activists of the previous decade, nationally and in Bloomington as well. Antiwar protestors felt a sense of both satisfaction and defeat. National polls proved that they had made their point and won. The majority of Americans wanted out of Vietnam. Yet President Nixon and his secretary of state, Henry Kissinger, continued to engage in prolonged peace talks in Paris that dragged on until January 1973.

Locally, Bloomington peace activists could feel pleased that students cheered the marching band's peace symbol. At the same time, they spent more and more time challenging local authority on issues like parking meters or cooperative day care for children. Environmental issues became more important, and People's Park was a symbol of popular support for green space along Kirkwood Avenue.

The end of the Sixties came home to Hoosiers and most Americans during the first half of the Seventies, when the economy began to slow and prices began to spiral upward. The effects of President Johnson's decisions to build the social programs of his Great Society and to fund the war in Vietnam by not raising taxes and balancing the budget became clear, especially in 1973 when leaders in the Middle East imposed an oil embargo. As prices for gasoline, oil, and food increased while more and more factories shut down, the buoyant confidence of the Sixties was gradually replaced with a national mood of hesitation, apprehension, and concern about the future.[31]

In the face of growing disparities between rich and poor and the continuing presence of racial inequities, many question the significance of the Sixties in American history. In Bloomington at the end of the period, students reflected a national trend away from trying to create social change and toward a tighter focus on personal goals. And yet the end of the decade was also the beginning of new challenges and new opportunities. The student movement's opposition to the war in Vietnam dissipated, but the movement shifted to take up issues of environmental protection and sexual preference, as well as continuing to work to improve racial and gender equity within the university community. Sixties activism did not dry up, either in Bloomington or across the country. It did, however, expand into many different channels. In doing so, it lost the dramatic force of earlier years, but it also became more deeply embedded in our culture and our daily lives.

Epilogue to the New Edition

In August 2013, I attended a reunion of Indiana University activists from the 1960s and 1970s. Organized by two IU alumni, Cathy Rountree and David Martin, along with assistance from the IU Archives and the Office of the President, activists from around the country gathered in Bloomington to reminisce, get reacquainted, and renew old bonds that lasted over time and distance.

It was a strangely rewarding event for me because while I was not technically an alumna and had only read or heard about the experience in newspaper accounts, archival records, or in conversations with participants, I often felt like I had been on campus during those times. It was wonderful to see people I had interviewed years ago and equally interesting to meet others whom I corresponded with or read about. I was finally able to put faces with names.

In addition to opportunities for telling stories, eating, drinking, singing along with activist/musician Roger Saloom with his ever-present guitar, and laughing (sometimes all at the same time), there was one day of panel discussions about the issues of the times that provoked spontaneous contributions from panelists and listeners alike. One of the highlights for me was to meet two of the Bloomington 3 whom I discuss in an early chapter about the Fair Play for Cuba march and who gained national fame through their prolonged legal battle with Monroe County's Prosecuting Attorney. There were also panels devoted to political activism and Bloomington events.

Surrounded by posters, buttons, photographs, and newspaper articles from the decade, there was a real sense of the past as well as its significance for the present. In addition, archivist Dina Kellams recorded a series of interviews with participants.

The theme of the reunion, which resonated with me, was how many had maintained their youthful ideals and translated them into meaningful lives after they left the university. One of my first interviews was with Guy Loftman, former president of the student body, one of the founders of Students for a Democratic Society (SDS), and antiwar activist, and Connie, his wife, fellow activist, and office manager, at their office on the corner of East 10th Street and North Walnut. They answered my barrage of questions and suggested names of others who might be able to help with my research. Guy and Connie completed their undergraduate degrees, and Guy continued on to graduate from IU's Maurer School of Law. He practiced law for thirty years and, along with his conventional legal work, handled pro bono cases for civil rights and other community causes. He and Connie have been and continue to be active in the Democratic Party, the Unitarian Universalist Church, and the Monroe County branch of the NAACP. In 2013, he was awarded the City of Bloomington's Human Rights Commission Award for his "commitment to racial and gender equality, to peace efforts and to voting rights, among others." The couple retired in 2015 but remain actively involved with family, friends, and community causes.

I conducted another interview over the telephone with Ruth Mahaney to ask about her part in both the antiwar movement and the early days of the women's movement. That conversation was very insightful. While in Bloomington for the reunion, she and Nancy Brand, another activist and Bloomington resident, recorded their memories of beginning the first abortion counseling service for students and women in surrounding communities. Listening to their accounts of the dangers they faced in those years before *Roe v. Wade* when Ruth's telephone number was pasted on bathroom walls all over southern Indiana, making her vulnerable to arrest and incarceration, I wished I had included this material in the first edition. But it also made me more aware of how precarious women's rights to control their own bodies are today during this era of increasing restraints on access to women's clinics. Commenting on the dangers they faced, Ruth said, "We were lucky to do what we did." After graduating from IU, Ruth went to Chicago to work with the Jane Collective, an abortion counseling service, and the New University Conference, a political organization founded after the demise of SDS. She then moved to San Francisco where she has taught women's studies at San Francisco State University, Sonoma State University, and the City College of San Francisco. Nancy helped found the first daycare cooperative in Bloomington and, after abortion became legal, worked at Planned Parenthood. She also has her own catering service.

During a reunion panel on activism, James Retherford recounted his experiences protesting the Vietnam War and his subsequent indictment on charges of violating the Selective Service Act. Despite the fact that he had not in fact violated the law, he was found guilty and sentenced to six years in prison. He served three months and was ultimately freed of charges after New York lawyer Leonard Boudin took his case. In his recorded interview with Dina, he also discussed his involvement with the production of antiwar protestor and Yippie Jerry Rubin's book *Do It!: Scenarios of the Revolution*. Working with designer Quentin Fiore, he was instrumental in creating the unique layout that characterized the book's revolutionary message. Jim ultimately moved to Austin, Texas, where he began working in graphic design at the University of Texas and is the graphic designer for a popular progressive online news magazine known as the Rag Blog, named after *The Rag*, one of the original underground newspapers of the 1960s.

Dan Kaplan, a former president of SDS and member of the Young Socialist Alliance, moved to the Bay area and taught courses in political science and comparative government in several community colleges, the City College of San Francisco, and San Francisco State University. He became executive director of the San Mateo Federation of Teachers, part of the California Federation of Teachers working for the rights of part-time and adjunct teachers.

Paulann (Groninger) Hosler Sheets who, along with Polly Smith led the march during the 1962 Fair Play for Cuba demonstration, graduated from IU in 1965 and went on to Columbia Law School. Her legal work has included cases involving issues of social, racial, and economic justice. Her current practice in Groton, Connecticut, focuses on property owners facing foreclosures.

Bloomington residents Patricia Cole and Charlotte Zietlow have both been active in city politics. Once a member of SDS, Pat is an artist with her own studio who expresses her concerns for social justice and peace through paintings and is active in community projects. Charlotte, an early participant in the women's movement at IU, was elected to the city council in 1971 and was part of a grassroots movement that radically changed Bloomington politics in the 1970s. In addition, she has served on Bloomington's Human Rights Commission.

Other reunion participants included Tom Morgan, one of the Bloomington 3 who is a family therapist and raises horses on a farm outside of Terre Haute; Nell Levin, musician and former antiwar activist, who has been a part of the Tennessee Alliance for Progress, mixing music and politics for the cause of social justice; Tom Balonoff, who was a leader in the protest against the tuition hike in 1968 and is now a leader in the Service Employees Union, working with the Justice for Janitors movement; and Ike Nahem, a member of the Student Mobilization Committee to End the War in Vietnam who is now a locomotive engineer and an active member of the Teamsters Union as well as an advocate for improved relationships with Cuba.

Two years after this reunion, another group of IU activist alumni met on campus. In April 2015, five members of the IU 10—African American football players who boycotted the team in 1969 for unequal treatment based on race—met with current administrators to talk about the reasons for the boycott and to bring about a reconciliation. During frank and open discussions, these former players were able to tell about the discrimination they faced and the effects that the boycott and subsequent dismissal from the team had on their lives. Acknowledging the importance of their role in improving race relations at IU, the president and other administrators officially reinstated them to the team and established an undergraduate class focused on the history of their boycott and its lessons on racial issues for current students. Those attending were Mike Adams (who organized the reunion), Clarence Price, Benny Norman, Charlie Murphy, and Don Silas. Two of the IU 10 are deceased—Greg Thornton and Bobby Pernell—and two did not attend—Greg Harvey and Larry Highbaugh.

Student activists at Indiana University in the 1960s agree that their experiences then represented significant turning points in their lives. Bloomington in the sixties was a special time and place, representing a unique confluence of events, personalities, and culture. Students at other campuses will undoubtedly express similar reactions to their own activities during those turbulent years. Yet I think Indiana's role is especially powerful because of its location in America's heartland and because that generation of students continues to contribute to the conversations that make up the history of our times. I'm glad I was able to capture at least a portion of this story so that others can know something of what happened at Indiana University in the 1960s as part of a larger understanding of America during an era when visions of a more hopeful future were part of growing up—and moving on.

Conclusion

What can we conclude about the significance of the 1960s in American culture as revealed in this history of Indiana University? Did the events of the 1960s make a difference? Absolutely. Changes that took place in the Sixties made American society and IU very different in almost every aspect from earlier years.

The student movement eliminated the role of the university *in loco parentis*. After the 1960s, university officials no longer assumed that students were part of a university "family" headed by themselves. Undoubtedly, the sheer size of the baby-boom generation entering colleges and universities in the Sixties guaranteed that these institutions would have to loosen their hold on campus life. Still, students' insistence on the right to control their own lives made a difference in the pace and manner of that institutional change. Because of the movement of the Sixties, students at IU today can choose to live in same-sex dormitories, coeducational dormitories, fraternity and sorority houses, residences for students with specific studies or interests, or off-campus apartments with roommates of their choice. They have no concept of women's hours or dress codes. Women and men have more freedom to live where they want, with whom they want, and how they want today than they did before the 1960s.

The antiwar movement not only protested against a war that many saw as unjust and unfair, but also questioned the morality and necessity of the military draft that sent young men off to it. This movement has become the subject of many myths, one of which is that most university students in the Sixties were antiwar protestors. Certainly the history of the movement at Indiana University contradicts that myth. In fact, the majority of students during the Sixties were either unaware of what was going on in Vietnam or supported the war. As several recent historians of the Sixties have made clear, this decade should be studied as the beginning not only of the New Left, but—just as significant—of the New Right as well. It took real courage to come out against the war. Antiwar protestors faced the loss of scholarships, future employment, and family affections. The success of the antiwar movement can be measured in the fact that by the early 1970s it was able to convince a majority of Americans that the war was wrong and that we as citizens had the right to oppose it.

More to the point, because of antiwar protestors during the 1960s, students at IU and across the country no longer face the same threat of the draft or the danger that the United States will again become involved in the kind of war that took the lives of so many young Americans—including IU students—during the 1960s. One of the most profound breakthroughs of that decade may be, in fact, that young people questioned the highest authorities in the land about why they should give their lives for their country. They changed the definition of patriotism from unquestioning acceptance of government to the demand for rational justifications.

The civil rights movement has made a significant difference in America and in Indiana University. The fight for racial equity has influenced the way we live our lives. It has changed the composition of classrooms and workplaces, of government agencies and corporate boardrooms. Activists believed that politics, and especially the judicial system, mattered, and they used their legislative and legal powers to reconstruct the way that Americans work, learn, and live. They committed themselves to a path that offered few material rewards but was rich in spiritual sustenance. And their efforts have not been in vain. Despite recent attempts to roll back affirmative action, civil rights activists have succeeded in creating a society that accepts—for the most part—the reality of an America made up of people of all colors and all creeds.

Once an almost completely white institution, IU has opened its doors to more students, staff, and faculty of color. It has also acknowledged the importance of studying the histories, literatures, languages, and arts of peoples who have added to the richness of American and world cultures. Student demands that the university hire minority faculty resulted in their increase from 2% of all faculty in the 1960s to almost 13% in 2000. Admittedly, IU (like institutions of higher education in general) has not succeeded in making itself accessible to all students and faculty who are qualified and want to become part of its community.

Still, it has made considerable progress toward achieving that goal. Without question, students in the Sixties built on the tradition of former chancellor Herman B Wells in welcoming and developing tolerance for all of the people who are part of Indiana University. Their resolute insistence that the university should reflect the people of the state and the nation is also a part of the Sixties legacy.

Emerging from the civil rights movement, the women's and gay liberation movements have also changed American culture. Many historians argue that the women's movement was the most influential social change to originate during the 1960s. By forcing men and women to examine their attitudes toward gender differences at very basic, personal levels, feminists substantially changed family and work relationships. Making the personal political and the political personal, activists focused national attention on the fact that all citizens are equal and have equal rights, regardless of gender or sexual preferences. At Indiana University, women have substantially increased their presence on the faculty (from 10% to 33%) and among undergraduate and graduate students. Women's studies, which were pioneered at IU, and courses that address issues of sexual orientation are part of IU's curriculum—issues that were either unheard of or largely ignored before the 1960s.

The influence of the Sixties counterculture persists into the twenty-first century, in everything from radio stations that play Sixties rock and roll to environmental protestors dressed up like sea turtles. The hip philosophy that we should love each other, love the earth, and love life has influenced Americans from Madison Avenue to rural communes. As descendents of the Beat generation of the 1950s, members of the counterculture carried on a tradition of challenging traditional conventions through art, literature, dance, music, theater, and lifestyle. Bloomington was called a "hippie town" during the 1960s, and subtle reminders of that past remain in its cultural climate today.

To list these influences from the 1960s is not to say that the visions of Sixties activists have been realized, nor that they originated in that decade. Nearly all of the elements of Sixties activism have their roots in the beginning of American history. American revolutionaries challenged traditional British authorities. Many early patriots—especially members of the Quaker faith—agonized over the existence of slavery in this country. Black freedom fighters from Denmark Vesey to Nat Turner fought for their people's liberty. Abigail Adams reminded her husband John to "remember the ladies" as he helped to form a new government. Henry David Thoreau protested against a war he considered unjust and praised the natural beauty that he found at Walden Pond. Sixties activists carried on those struggles in order that the foundations for a more open and equitable society might be put more solidly in place. There will probably never be another decade in which so many movements—civil rights, peace, and feminism—coalesce to produce such synergy. However, each generation contributes to these causes and others in its own way and in its own time. The important role that history plays is to acknowledge the efforts of those who worked in the past and show how others can build on them in the future.

The thesis of this book is precisely that the social, political, and cultural movements of the 1960s were not just products of East and West Coast elites. Many Midwesterners would like to cast the history of that decade as the story of "outside agitators" who unpleasantly influenced their basically good but naïve and impressionable youngsters. The antithesis of that assertion—and the underlying theme of this history—is that understanding the 1960s in the heartland is essential if we are to understand the decade's roots and significance in American history in general. In many ways, the history of Indiana University during the 1960s is an indicator of just how important and deeply embedded the movements of that decade were in shaping the history of the last decades of this century . . . not only on the Bloomington campus but across the country as well.

During the 1960s, some American historians affirmed the values of "grass-roots history" or "history from the bottom up." They believed that learning about the everyday lives of citizens was just as important, if not more so, as studying the lives of presidents and generals. This account of the people who made up Indiana University and the Bloomington community is my own contribution to that way of looking at the history of the 1960s, a decade that changed people's lives, the university, the community, the nation, and the world.

Notes

PROLOGUE

1. Charles Blanchard, ed., *Counties of Morgan, Monroe, and Brown, Indiana* (Chicago: F. A. Battey, 1884), 457.

2. James Albert Woodburn, *History of Indiana University,* vol. 1, *1820–1902* (Bloomington: Indiana University, 1940), 3.

3. James H. Madison, *The Indiana Way: A State History* (Bloomington: Indiana University Press, 1986), 107.

4. Emma Lou Thornbrough, *Indiana in the Civil War Era, 1850–1880* (Indianapolis: Indiana Historical Bureau, 1965), 508.

5. Ibid., 381; Blanchard, *Counties of Morgan, Monroe, and Brown, Indiana,* 459.

6. Thomas D. Clark, *Indiana University, Midwestern Pioneer,* vol. 3, *Years of Fulfillment* (Bloomington: Indiana University Press, 1977), 291.

7. Ibid., 235.

8. *Indiana Daily Student,* May 19, 1961, p. 1.

9. Herman B Wells, *Being Lucky: Reminiscences and Reflections* (Bloomington: Indiana University Press, 1980).

1. THE DAWN OF DISSENT

1. Interview with Elvis Stahr, April 12, 1990; Thomas D. Clark, *Indiana University, Midwestern Pioneer,* vol. 3, *Years of Fulfillment* (Bloomington: Indiana University Press, 1977), 537.

2. The Student Nonviolent Coordinating Committee is the subject of Clayborne Carson's *In Struggle: SNCC and the Black Awakening of the 1960s* (Cambridge, Mass.: Harvard University Press, 1981) and James Forman, *The Making of Black Revolutionaries* (New York: Macmillan, 1972), among many other works.

3. For extensive discussions of the founding of Students for a Democratic Society, see Kirkpatrick Sale, *SDS* (New York: Random House, 1973); James Miller, *"Democracy is in the Streets": From Port Huron to the Siege of Chicago* (New York: Simon and Schuster, 1987); and Tom Hayden, *Reunion: A Memoir* (New York: Random House, 1988).

4. This was how the president of the University of Delaware described IU to the parents of one prospective student, Guy Loftman. Interview with Guy Loftman, April 15, 1987.

5. For Hoosiers' distrust of government and unwillingness to support public education, see James H. Madison, *The Indiana Way: A State History* (Bloomington: Indiana University Press, 1986), 115, 131.

6. Gregory L. Schneider, *Cadres for Conservatism: Young Americans for Freedom and the Rise of the Contemporary Right* (New York: New York University Press, 1999) 76–77.

7. *Indiana Daily Student,* April 29, 1961, p. 1; Oct. 25, 1962, p. 1; Nov. 13, 1962, p. 1; *Bloomington Daily Herald-Telephone,* Oct. 25, 1962, p. 1; Clark, *Indiana University,* vol. 3, 553–54.

8. *Indianapolis Times,* May 5, 1965, p. 1.

9. *Indiana Daily Student,* March 26, 1963, p. 1.

10. *Indiana Daily Student,* Dec. 2, 1962, p. 1; Feb. 19, 1963, p. 1; *Bloomington Daily Herald-Telephone,* March 15, 1963, p. 4; David Cahill, *A History of Student Affairs at Indiana University* (1967 pamphlet in reference file, Indiana University Archives, Bryan Hall, Bloomington [hereafter cited as IU Archives]), 22–24; Clark, *Indiana University,* vol. 3, 555–57.

11. *Bloomington Daily Herald-Telephone,* May 21, 1963, p. 5.

12. *Bloomington Star Courier,* May 16, 1963, p. 1.

13. Ibid., p. 4.

14. The Committee to Aid the Bloomington Students, Records, 1960–1968, Social Action Collection, Archives Division, State Historical Society of Wisconsin, Madison. This collection contains extensive newspaper clippings of speeches made by the Bloomington 3 during 1963 from the *New York Times,* May 3, 4, 1963; *Chicago Tribune,* May 2, 1963; *Cleveland Press,* May 3, 1963; *UCLA Daily Bruin,* May 2, 1963; *Minnesota Daily,* May 8, 1963; *Indianapolis Times,* May 5, 1963.

15. *Indianapolis Times,* May 5, 1963.

16. *Indiana Daily Student,* Sept. 18, 1965, p. 4; Sept. 23, 1965, p. 7; interview with Mike Kelsey, March 6, 1990; interview with Guy Loftman, March 15, 1987.

17. Unsigned letter to Rick Ross, Students for a Democratic Society, Records, 1958–1970, microfilm series 2A, reel 75, State Historical Society of Wisconsin, Madison.

18. Letter from Robert Pardun to John Grove, Aug. 11, 1965, ibid.

2. The Awakening of Activism

1. *Indiana Daily Student,* Nov. 6, 1965, p. 4; Oct. 18, 1966, p. 1; Jan. 13, 1967, p. 14.

2. Terry H. Anderson, *The Movement and the Sixties: Protest in America from Greensboro to Wounded Knee* (New York: Oxford University Press, 1995), 39.

3. Interview with Guy Loftman, March 15, 1987.

4. *Indiana Daily Student,* Dec. 15, 1965, p. 1.

5. Anderson, *The Movement and the Sixties,* 97.

6. Anderson, *The Movement and the Sixties,* 98–99.

7. David Cahill, *A History of Student Affairs at Indiana University* (1967 pamphlet in reference file, IU Archives), 39; *Indiana Daily Student,* Dec. 15, 1965, pp. 1, 4; Jan. 11, 1966, p. 4.

8. *Indiana Daily Student,* Jan. 1, 1966, p. 4.

9. *Indiana Daily Student,* Dec. 10, 1965, p. 1; Feb. 17, 1966, p. 4.

10. *Indiana Daily Student,* Feb. 18, 1966, p. 1; Feb. 24, 1966, p. 4.

11. *Indiana Daily Student,* Sept. 15, 1966, p. 4.

12. Cahill, *History of Student Affairs at Indiana University,* 73.

13. Student forum file, April 26, 1967, IU Archives.

14. *Indiana Daily Student,* April 8, 1967, p. 1; Cahill, *History of Student Affairs at Indiana University,* 72–73.

15. *Indiana Daily Student,* March 18, 1967, p. 4; Cahill, *History of Student Affairs at Indiana University,* 76.

16. *Indiana Daily Student,* April 15, 1967, p. 3, 5; Cahill, *History of Student Affairs at Indiana University,* 76; interview with Connie Loftman, March 15, 1989; interview with Ted Najam, May 24, 1989.

17. *Indiana Daily Student,* April 27, 1967, p. 1; *Bloomington Tribune,* April 21, 1967, p. 1; student forum file, IU Archives.

18. "Berkeley in the '60s," California Newsreel, 1991.

19. *Indiana Daily Student,* April 9, 1966, p. 1.

20. Ibid.

21. Cahill, *History of Student Affairs at Indiana University,* 54–55.

22. Interview with Allen Gurevitz, July 22, 1992.

23. *Indiana Daily Student,* Sept. 15, 1966, p. 1; Cahill, *History of Student Affairs at Indiana University,* 56; Robert H. Shaffer, "Statement of Fact Regarding Arrest of Bruce Klein and Allen D. Gurevitz," unpublished paper in my possession.

24. *Indiana Daily Student,* Sept. 16, 1966, p. 1; Cahill, *History of Student Affairs at Indiana University,* 57; Shaffer, "Statement of Fact Regarding Arrest of Bruce Klein and Allen D. Gurevitz."

25. *Bloomington Daily Herald-Telephone,* Sept. 17, 1966, p. 3; *Bloomington Tribune,* Oct. 30, 1966, sec. 3, p. 2.

26. *Indiana Daily Student,* Sept. 17, 1966, p. 1; Sept. 20, 1966, p. 1; Cahill, *History of Student Affairs at Indiana University,* 53–60.

27. *Indiana Daily Student,* Sept. 23, 1966, p. 1; Oct. 1, 1966, p. 1; Oct. 15, 1966, p. 1; Oct. 22, 1966, p. 5.

28. Student Liberation Front, "Songs of Subversion and Satire Dedicated to Indiana University," 1966, protest file, IU Archives.

29. Interview with Allen Gurevitz.

30. *Indiana Daily Student,* Jan. 12, 1967, p. 4; Feb. 15, 1967, pp. 4–5; Jan. 18, 1967, p. 4; Cahill, *History of Student Affairs at Indiana University,* 66–68.

31. *Indiana Daily Student,* March 11, 1967, p. 1.

32. *Indiana Daily Student,* Jan. 13, 1966, p. 4.

33. To be considered conscientious objectors, young men had to prove to their draft boards that they were members of a religious group that forbade them to take up arms (e.g., that they were Jehovah's Witnesses or Quakers) or that they had a consistent history of pacifist beliefs backed up by letters, testimonials, and records of past actions. The latter required a sophisticated understanding of the law and strong community connections.

34. Lawrence M. Baskir and William A. Strauss, *Chance and Circumstance: The Draft, the War, and the Vietnam Generation* (New York: Knopf, 1978), 14–61. For a realistic although fictional account of a young man grappling with the choice between being drafted and fleeing to Canada, see Tim O'Brien, *The Things They Carried: A Work of Fiction* (New York: Penguin, 1990), 41–63.

35. Tom Wells, *The War Within: America's Battle over Vietnam* (Berkeley: University of California Press, 1996), 24.

36. Interview with Leonard Lundin, Feb. 17, 1989.

37. *Indiana Daily Student,* Oct. 15, 1965, p. 4; "The March on Washington," SDS *Newsletter,* Nov. 27, 1965, Students for a Democratic Society, Records, 1958–1970, microfilm series 3, reel 22, State Historical Society of Wisconsin, Madison.

38. *Indiana Daily Student,* Oct. 5, 1965, p. 1; Oct. 6, 1965, p. 1; Nov. 17, 1965, p. 1; Nov. 18, 1965, p. 4.

39. *Indiana Daily Student,* March 16, 1966, p. 13; Karl North, "SDS Identity and Strategy and the Campus Community," SDS *Newsletter,* Nov. 24, 1965, SDS Records, series 3, reel 23.

40. "Face-to-Face Organizing," SDS *Newsletter,* Nov. 17, 1965, SDS Records, series 3, reel 22.

41. Bernella Satterfield, "On Proposed SDS (National Office) Draft Program," SDS *Newsletter,* Nov. 17, 1965, SDS Records, series 3, reel 22.

42. James Madison, *The Indiana Way: A State History* (Bloomington: Indiana University Press, 1986), 303. Jenner's son, William Jenner, Jr., attended Indiana University and was an active leader of those students who opposed the protestors.

43. "Picket Line Decorum for Support Vance Hartke Demonstration" (leaflet), no. 100-14831-1A1, IP 100-14837, section 1, IU-CEWV file, FBI, J. Edgar Hoover FBI Building, Washington, D.C.

44. Wells, *The War Within*, 80–82.

45. "Minutes of General Meeting, March 9, 1966," SDS *Newsletter*, March 17, 1966, SDS Records, series 3, reel 22.

46. Interview with James Dinsmoor, Sept. 25, 1989.

47. Flyers no. 100–14837–1A5, IU-CEWV file, FBI.

48. *Bloomington Daily Herald-Telephone*, May 3, 1966, p. 1; interview with James Wallihan, June 5, 1989.

49. Memo, Communist Party, United States of America, Public Appearances of Party Leaders, May 12, 1966, no. 100–14262, Indiana University, W. E. B. Du Bois Club of America file, FBI.

50. *Indiana Daily Student*, March 4, 1966, p. 1; May 6, 1966, p. 1; May 7, 1966, p. 4.

51. Memo from SA to SAC (100–14837) (P), Aug. 8, 1966, no. 100–14837–44, IU-CEWV file, FBI.

52. "What Happened in Indianapolis, July 23, 1966?" flyer no. 100–14837–1A9, IU-CEWV file, FBI.

53. *Indianapolis Star*, Aug. 6, 1966, p. 7.

54. *Indiana Daily Student*, Feb. 9, 1967, p. 4; Cahill, *History of Student Affairs at Indiana University*, 70–72.

55. *Indiana Daily Student*, Feb. 14, 1967, p. 4; March 1, 1967, p. 4; March 10, 1967, p. 8; March 17, 1967, p. 1; March 18, 1967, p. 1; March 24, 1967, p. 4; Cahill, *History of Student Affairs at Indiana University*, 72.

56. Interview with James Wallihan, May 15, 1989.

57. Interview with Guy Loftman, March 15, 1987.

3. THE ANTIWAR MOVEMENT

1. George C. Herring, *America's Longest War: The United States and Vietnam, 1950–1975* (Philadelphia: Temple University Press, 1986), 191.

2. *Indiana Daily Student*, June 23, 1967, pp. 1, 5.

3. *Indiana Daily Student*, July 13, 1967, p. 3.

4. *Indiana Daily Student*, Aug. 5, 1967, p. 1; Aug. 8, 1967, p. 1.

5. *Indiana Daily Student*, Sept. 11, 1967, p. 1.

6. *Bloomington Tribune*, Sept. 15, 1967, p. 2.

7. *Spectator*, Sept. 25, 1967, p. 7.

8. Memo from SA to SAC, Chicago, Illinois, Oct. 19, 1967, no. 100-14837173, IU-CEWV file, FBI, J. Edgar Hoover FBI Building, Washington, D.C.

9. *Indiana Daily Student*, Nov. 11, 1967, Saturday supplement; interview with Mark Ritchey, Dec. 15, 1989; interview with Connie Loftman and Guy Loftman, April 15, 1987.

10. "Day of Obstruction," *Wisconsin Alumnus*, Nov. 1967, student demonstration file, IU Archives.

11. Julian Foster and Durward Long, eds., *Protest! Student Activism in America* (New York: Morrow, 1970), 229–45.

12. *Spectator*, Oct. 30, 1967, p. 1.

13. Interview with Mark Ritchey; interview with Guy Loftman, April 15, 1987.

14. Interview with Mark Ritchey.

15. This account of the Dow demonstration relies on the *Indiana Daily Student*, Nov. 1, 1967, p. 1; Student-faculty Viet-Nam controversy file, IU Archives; interview with Mark Ritchey; interview with Guy Loftman, April 15, 1987; interview with George Walker, Dec. 1, 1989; Foster and Long, eds., *Protest!*, 229–45.

16. *Indiana Daily Student*, Nov. 1, 1967, p. 1; *Bloomington Tribune*, Oct. 31, 1967, p. 4.

17. *Indiana Daily Student*, Nov. 16, 1967, p. 4.

18. Student-faculty Viet-Nam controversy file, IU Archives; Foster and Long, eds.,

Protest! 229–45; *Indiana Daily Student,* Nov. 1, 1967, p. 1; Dec. 9, 1967, p. 3; Dec. 11, 1967, p. l.

19. "The Rites of the Left," *A CEWV Newsletter,* Dec. 13, 1967, no. 100–14837–186, IU-CEWV file, FBI; Fritz Ringer, unpublished manuscript in my possession.

20. *Indiana Daily Student,* Dec. 2, 1967, p. 1; Dec. 9, 1967, p. 5; Carl Davidson, "Toward Student Syndicalism," *New Left Notes,* Sept. 9, 1966, p. 11; interview with Robert Shaffer, May 8, 1989.

21. IU-CEWV Newsletter, Jan. 5, 1968, no. 100–14837–192, IU-CEWV file, FBI; SA to SAC, Chicago, Illinois, Jan. 13, 1968, no. 100-12158-716, Young Socialists Alliance/Indiana file, FBI.

22. *Indiana Daily Student,* Jan. 30, 1968, p. 1; Feb. 3, 1968, p. 1; *Spectator,* March 11, 1968, p. 9; interview with George Walker.

23. *Indiana Daily Student,* March 2, 1968, p. 1; March 23, 1968, p. 1.

24. Interview with Connie Loftman and Guy Loftman, April 15, 1987.

25. Interview with Robert Shaffer.

26. *Indiana Daily Student,* March 22, 1968, p. 4; *Spectator,* April 15–21, 1968, p. 6.

27. Gregory L. Schneider, *Cadres for Conservatism: Young Americans for Freedom and the Rise of the Contemporary Right* (New York: New York University Press, 1999), 114–16. After Ronald Reagan's election, Tyrell moved from Bloomington to Washington, D.C., where he continues to publish *The American Spectator,* a conservative journal. Tyrell, by the way, never served in the military, because he had a graduate student deferment.

28. *Indiana Daily Student,* April 3, 1968, p. 1; April 27, 1968, p. 1; *Spectator,* March 18, 1968, p. 8.

29. Robert F. Kennedy, *RFK: Collected Speeches,* edited and introduced by Edwin O. Guthman and C. Richard Allen (New York: Viking, 1993), 157.

30. David Halberstam, *The Unfinished Odyssey of Robert Kennedy* (New York: Random House, 1968), 68–123.

31. *Indiana Daily Student,* June 9, 1968, p. 1; interview with Elvis Stahr, April 12, 1990.

32. Interview with Ted Najam, May 24, 1989.

33. Ted Najam, "A Look at the Student Conscience," typewritten manuscript in my possession.

34. *Indiana Daily Student,* Sept. 21, 1968, p. 1.

35. *Indiana Daily Student,* Oct. 11, 1968, p. 1.

36. *Indiana Daily Student,* Sept. 24, 1968, p. 4; Oct. 4, 1968, p. 5.

37. *Indiana Daily Student,* Sept. 24, 1968, p. 4.

38. *Indiana Daily Student,* Oct. 2, 1968, p. 1; Oct. 11, 1968, p. 1.

39. *Indiana Daily Student,* Oct. 11, 1968, p. 1.

40. Terry H. Anderson, *The Movement and the Sixties: Protest in America from Greensboro to Wounded Knee* (New York: Oxford University Press, 1995), 107–10; Bil Gilbert, "The Great World and Millersburg," *Saturday Evening Post,* April 20, 1968, pp. 36–45.

41. Minutes of the board of trustees meeting, May 24, 1968, IU Archives.

42. *Indiana Daily Student,* Oct. 17, 1968, p. 1; *Spectator,* Oct. 22, 1968, pp. 4–5.

43. *Spectator,* Oct. 22, 1968, p. 2; interview with Herman B Wells, May 23, 1989.

44. *Indiana Daily Student,* Oct. 29, 1968, p. 1; Nov. 1, 1968, p. 4; *Bloomington Daily Herald-Telephone,* Nov. 1, 1968, p. 1; interview with Herman B Wells.

45. Kenneth O'Reilly, *Racial Matters: The FBI's Secret File on Black America, 1960–1972* (New York: Free Press, 1989), 292.

46. Charles DeBenedetti, with Charles Chatfield, *An American Ordeal: The Antiwar Movement of the Vietnam Era* (Syracuse, N.Y.: Syracuse University Press, 1990), 231.

47. SAC, Indianapolis, to J. Edgar Hoover, June 3, 1968, no. 100-449698-21-1, COINTELPRO–Disruption of New Left file, FBI, J. Edgar Hoover FBI Building, Washington, D.C.; untitled report, June 25, 1968, ibid.; Hoover to SAC Indianapolis, June 17,

1968, no. 100-449698-2-1, ibid.; interview with Elvis Stahr, March 26, 1990; interview with Dan Kaplan, May 6, 1989.

48. Interview with Elvis Stahr, March 26, 1990.

49. *Spectator,* Nov 5, 1968, p. 14; *Bloomington Courier-Journal,* Sept. 25, 1966, Topix sec., pp. 4–5; ibid., Oct. 2, 1966, p. 10; SAC, Indianapolis, Dec. 17, 1968, no. 100-449698-21-21, COINTELPRO–NEW LEFT file, FBI; interview with Joseph Fuhrman, Jan. 2, 1990; interview with James Wallihan, May 15, 1989.

50. SAC, Indianapolis, to Hoover, Nov. 14, 1968, no. 100-16858, YSA File, FBI.

51. Interview with Mike Kelsey, March 6, 1989.

52. *Spectator,* Nov. 5, 1968, pp. 4–5; *Indiana Daily Student,* Dec. 3, 1968, p. 4.

53. *Spectator,* Nov. 5, 1968, p. 7; *Indiana Daily Student,* Nov. 20, 1968, p. 4.

54. *Spectator,* Nov. 5, 1968, p. 9.

55. *Indiana Daily Student,* Dec. 11, 1968, p. 1; Dec. 13, 1968, p. 1; Dec. 14, 1968, p. 1.

56. *Indiana Daily Student,* Jan. 27, 1969, p. 1; Feb. 7, 1969, p. 1; Feb. 8, 1969, p. 1; Feb. 13, 1969, p. 1.

57. *Indiana Daily Student,* Jan. 16, 1969, p. 1; Feb. 20, 1969, p. 4.

58. *Indiana Daily Student,* March 8, 1969, p. 1; March 13, 1969, p. 4; March 22, 1969, p. 4; April 12, 1969, p. 4.

59. *Spectator,* March 18, 1967, p. 3.

60. SAC, Indianapolis, April 18, 1969, no. 105–5821–1a2, COINTELPRO–NEW LEFT file, FBI.

61. *Spectator,* March 18, 1967, p. 3; *Indiana Daily Student,* April 14, 1969, p. 4; April 19, 1969, p. 1.

62. *Indiana Daily Student,* April 26, 1969, p. 4.

63. *Indiana Daily Student,* April 29, 1969, pp. 1, 4.

64. SAC, Indianapolis, to Hoover, April 28, 1969, no. 100–12158, YSA file, FBI.

65. *Indiana Daily Student,* May 3, 1969, p. 1; *Bloomington Daily Herald-Telephone,* May 2, 1969, p. 5.

66. *Indiana Daily Student,* May 8, 1969, p. 1; *Spectator,* May 13, 1969, p. 9; *Bloomington Daily Herald-Telephone,* May 8, 1969, p. 1.

67. *Indiana Daily Student,* May 8, 1969, p. 1; *Bloomington Daily Herald-Telephone,* May 7, 1969, p. l.

68. *Indiana Daily Student,* May 9, 1969, p. 1; May 10, 1969, p. 1; *Spectator,* May 13, 1969, pp. 6–7; *Bloomington Daily Herald-Telephone,* May 9, 1969, p. 1; interview with Rollo Turner, April 17, 1989; interview with Orlando Taylor, Aug. 10, 1989.

69. SAC, Indianapolis, to Hoover, April 28, 1969, "Student Agitation against Fee Increases at Indiana University, Bloomington, Indiana," no. 100-12188-904, YSA file, FBI.

70. *Indiana Daily Student,* May 13, 1969, p. 1; *Spectator,* May 13, 1969, pp. 3–4.

71. *Bloomington Daily Herald-Telephone,* May 10, 1969, p. 1; *Spectator,* June 17, 1969, p. 1.

72. *Indiana Daily Student,* June 20, 1969, p. 4; *Spectator,* June 17, 1969, p. 3.

4. A PRECARIOUS PEACE

1. Peter B. Levy, *The New Left and Labor in the 1960s* (Urbana: University of Illinois Press, 1994), 7–25, 147–66.

2. *Indiana Daily Student,* Sept. 8, 1969, p. 1; *Spectator,* Sept. 10, 1969, p. 2.

3. Kenneth J. Heineman, *Campus Wars: The Peace Movement at American State Universities in the Vietnam Era* (New York: New York University Press, 1993), 202.

4. Minutes of the board of trustees meeting, June 6–9, 1969, IU Archives; *Indiana Daily Student,* Sept. 8, 1969, p. 1; Sept. 27, 1969, p. 1.

5. *Indiana Daily Student,* Sept. 9, 1969, p. 4; Sept. 8, 1969, p. 4; Sept. 10, 1969, p. 4.

6. *Spectator,* Oct. 14, 1969, p. 3.

7. *Spectator,* Oct. 14, 1969, p. 3; Sept. 10, 1969, p. 4; Oct. 7, 1969, pp. 12–13.

8. *Spectator,* Oct. 7, 1969, pp. 3–5; Sept. 30, 1969, p. 3; *Indiana Daily Student,* Sept. 30, 1969, p. 1; Oct. 2, 1969, p. 4.

9. *Indiana Daily Student,* Oct. 10, 1969, p. 1; Oct. 15, 1969, p. 1; *Spectator,* Oct. 14, 1969, p. 24.

10. *Bloomington Daily Herald-Telephone,* Oct. 16, 1969, p. 1; *Indiana Daily Student,* Oct. 15, 1969, p. 1.

11. *Bloomington Daily Herald-Telephone,* Oct. 16, 1969, p. 1.

12. *Spectator,* Oct. 21, 1969, pp. 6–7, 9; *Bloomington Daily Herald-Telephone,* Oct. 16, 1969, p. 14; Oct. 17, 1969, p. 1.

13. *Bloomington Daily Herald-Telephone,* Oct. 16, 1969, p. 2; *Indiana Daily Student,* Oct. 16, 1969, p. 1.

14. SAC, Indianapolis, to Hoover, no. 100-14837-476, CEWV file, FBI, J. Edgar Hoover FBI Building, Washington, D.C.15. *Indiana Daily Student,* Nov. 12, 1969, p. 1; *Spectator,* Feb. 4, 1970, p. 19.

16. *Spectator,* Nov. 19, 1969, pp. 3–5.

17. *Bloomington Daily Herald-Telephone,* Nov. 13, 1969, p. 1; *Indiana Daily Student,* Nov. 18, 1969, p. 8; *Spectator,* Nov. 19, 1969, pp. 3–5.

18. *Indiana Daily Student,* Nov. 15, 1969, p. 1.

19. SAC, Indianapolis, "Student Mobilization Committee, Indiana University, Bloomington, Indiana," Dec. 17, 1969, no. 100-14837-466, CEWV file, FBI.

20. *Indiana Daily Student,* Dec. 4, 1969, p. 1; Dec. 11, 1969, p. 1; *Spectator,* Dec. 8, 1969, pp. 6, 10, 23; Jan. 8, 1970, pp. 4–5.

21. *Spectator,* Nov. 19, 1969, p. 15; Dec. 8, 1969, p. 4; Dec. 15, 1969, p. 9.

22. SAC, Indianapolis, to Hoover, Nov. 16, 1970, no 100-12158-1130, YSA/Indiana file, FBI.

23. *Bloomington Courier-Tribune,* Feb. 17, 1970, p. 1; Feb. 18, 1970, sec. B, p. 1; *Bloomington Daily Herald-Telephone,* Feb. 5, 1970, p. 1; Feb. 20, 1970, p. 14; *Indiana Daily Student,* Feb. 20, 1970, p. 4; *Spectator,* Feb. 18, 1970, p. 4.

24. *Indiana Daily Student,* Feb. 24, 1970, p. 1; March 10, 1970, p. 1; *Spectator,* April 22, 1970, p. 3; *Bloomington Daily Herald-Telephone,* May 11, 1970, p. 14.

25. *Spectator,* March 11, 1970, p. 2; *Indiana Daily Student,* March 20, 1970, p. 1; March 24, 1970, p. 1.

26. SA to Hoover, Feb. 18, 1970, no. 100–12158, YSA file, FBI; Tom Wells, *The War Within: America's Battle over Vietnam* (Berkeley: University of California Press, 1994), 297.

27. *Indiana Daily Student,* March 12, 1970, p. 5.

28. *Indiana Daily Student,* April 14, 1970, p. 1; April 16, 1970, p. 1; April 20, 1970, p. 5; *Spectator,* April 15, 1970, p. 3.

29. Rachel Carson, *Silent Spring* (Boston: Houghton Mifflin, 1962).

30. Terry H. Anderson, *The Movement and the Sixties: Protest in America from Greensboro to Wounded Knee* (New York: Oxford University Press, 1995), 348; Benjamin Kline, *First along the River: A Brief History of the U.S. Environmental Movement* (San Francisco: Acada Books, 1997), 84.

31. *Indiana Daily Student,* April 23, 1970, p. 1; April 27, 1970, p. 1; May 1, 1970, p. 8.

32. *Bloomington Daily Herald-Telephone,* May 1, 1970, p. 1; *Indiana Daily Student,* May 2, 1970, pp. 1, 6.

33. *Indiana Daily Student,* May 2, 1970, p. 1; Robin Hunter, unpublished diary in my possession.

34. *Bloomington Courier-Tribune,* May 1, 1970, pp. 1–2; *Indiana Daily Student,* May 2, 1970, p. 1; Hunter diary.

35. *Bloomington Daily Herald-Telephone,* May 6, 1970, p. 1; *Indiana Daily Student,* May 5, 1970, p. 1; Hunter diary.

36. *Bloomington Daily Herald-Telephone,* May 7, 1970, sec. 4, p. 35; *Indiana Daily Student,* May 6, 1970, p. 1; May 7, 1970, p. 1; Hunter diary.

37. *Indiana Daily Student,* May 6, 1970, pp. 1, 4.

38. *Bloomington Courier-Tribune,* May 11, 1970, p. 1; *Indiana Daily Student,* May 6, 1970, p. 9.

39. SAC, Indianapolis, to Hoover, May 14, 1970, no. 100-14837-517, CEWV file, FBI.

40. *Bloomington Courier-Tribune,* May 12, 1970, p. 1; *Indiana Daily Student,* May 12, 1970, p. 1.

41. Anderson, *The Movement and the Sixties,* 352.

42. Heineman, *Campus Wars,* 250–53.

43. *Indiana Daily Student,* May 13, 1970, p. 1; Hunter diary.

44. SAC, Indianapolis, to Hoover, May 22, 1970, no 100-14837-522, CEWV file, FBI.

45. *Indiana Daily Student,* May 14, 1970, p. 1; Hunter diary.

46. *Bloomington Courier-Tribune,* May 14, 1970, p. 1; *Indiana Daily Student,* May 14, 1970, p. 1; Hunter diary.

47. *Indiana Daily Student,* May 16, 1970, p. 1; May 18, 1970, p. 1; Hunter diary.

48. SAC, Indianapolis, to Hoover, May 22, 1970, no. 100-14837-522, CEWV file, FBI.

49. *Bloomington Daily Herald-Telephone,* May 7, 1970, sec. 4, p. 35; *1971 Arbutus.*

50. Tom Bates, *Rads: The 1970 Bombing of the Army Math Research Center at the University of Wisconsin and Its Aftermath* (New York: HarperCollins, 1992), 290–304.

5. Student Rights, Civil Rights

1. For further discussion of the Cornell protest and black student activism in general, see Terry H. Anderson, *The Movement and the Sixties: Protest in America from Greensboro to Wounded Knee* (New York: Oxford University Press, 1995), 199–200; Harry Edwards, *Black Students* (London: Free Press, 1970), 158–83; Julian Foster and Durward Long, eds., *Protest! Student Activism in America* (New York: Morrow, 1970), 459–82.

2. James H. Madison, *The Indiana Way: A State History* (Bloomington: Indiana University Press, 1986), 171, 289–95.

3. Ernest D. Butler, Oral History Series, Monroe County Public Library, Bloomington, Indiana; Elizabeth Bridgwaters, ibid.

4. Interview with Herman B Wells, May 23, 1989; Herman B Wells, *Being Lucky: Reminiscences and Reflections* (Bloomington: Indiana University Press, 1980), 289–91.

5. *Statistical Abstract of the United States* (Washington, D.C.: U.S. Bureau of the Census, 1972), 28.

6. *Indiana Daily Student,* March 6, 1966, p. 16.

7. Edwards, *Black Students,* 10.

8. Mary Logan Rothschild, "White Women Volunteers in the Freedom Summers: Their Life and Work in a Movement for Social Change," *Feminist Studies* 5 (fall 1979), 466–95.

9. Delia Crutchfield Cook, "Black Student Activism in a Border State: An Historical Analysis of Black Student Government, 1968–1994" (unpublished paper in my possession); Mike Fisher, "The Turbulent Years: The University of Kansas, 1960–1975, A History," Ph.D. diss., University of Kansas, 1979; Rusty L. Monhollon, "'Away from the Dream': The Roots of Black Power in Lawrence, Kansas, 1960–1970" (unpublished paper in my possession).

10. *Atumpan* (newsletter of the Department of Afro-American Studies, Indiana University), winter 1991, p. 5; interview with Rollo Turner, April 17, 1989.

11. SA to SAC, Indianapolis, "Counterintelligence Program, Black Nationalist-Hate Groups, Racial Intelligence," March 22, 1968, no. 157-965-10, COINTELPRO-CPUSA file, FBI.

12. *"The Rites of the Left," A CEWV Newsletter,* Dec. 13, 1967, no. 100-14837-192, IU-CEWV file, FBI, J. Edgar Hoover FBI Building, Washington, D.C.

13. *Indiana Daily Student,* March 28, 1968, p. 1; March 30, 1968, p. 1.

14. *Indiana Daily Student,* April 4, 1968, p. 5.

15. *Indiana Daily Student,* March 30, 1968, p. 5.

16. Interview with Rollo Turner.

17. *Indiana Daily Student,* April 2, 1968, p. 1.

18. Robert F. Kennedy, *RFK: Collected Speeches,* edited and introduced by Edwin O. Guthman and C. Richard Allen (New York: Viking, 1993), 355–57.

19. *Indiana Daily Student,* April 5, 1968, p. 1; May 17, 1968, p. 1; *Spectator,* April 15–21, 1968, p. 3.

20. The movie *Breaking Away,* which put Bloomington on the movie map in the 1970s, provides an entertaining explanation of the Little 500.

21. *Indiana Daily Student,* May 11, 1969, pp. 1, 4; interview with Rollo Turner; interview with Orlando Taylor, Aug. 10, 1989.

22. SAC, Indianapolis, to Hoover, May 14, 1968, no. 157-965-16, COINTELPRO, AAASA file, FBI.

23. *Indiana Daily Student,* May 16, 1968, p. 1.

24. *Indiana Daily Student,* Sept. 28, 1969, p. 4; *Bloomington Daily Herald-Telephone,* Sept. 17, 1969, p. 1; *Spectator,* Oct. 8, 1968, p. 5.

25. Patrick D. Kennedy, "Reactions against the Vietnam War and Military-Related Targets on Campus: The University of Illinois as a Case Study, 1965–1972," *Illinois Historical Journal* 84 (summer 1991), 108.

26. Anderson, *The Movement and the Sixties,* 228.

27. *Indiana Daily Student,* Oct. 12, 1968, p. 1; Oct. 15, 1968, p. 1; *Spectator,* Oct. 15, 1968, pp. 3–4.

28. Interview with Herman B Wells.

29. *Indiana Daily Student,* Nov. 13, 1968, p. 1; Nov. 20, 1968, p. 1.30. Interview with Rollo Turner.

31. SAC, Indianapolis, Nov. 13, 1968, no. 157-965-48C, COINTELPRO, AAASA file, FBI.

32. *Indiana Daily Student,* Nov. 12, 1968, p. 1; *Spectator,* Nov. 19, 1968, p. 7.

33. *Indiana Daily Student,* Nov. 16, 1968, pp. 1–2; Dec. 6, 1968, p. 5.

34. *Bloomington Sunday Tribune,* Nov. 3, 1968, p. 1; *Bloomington Courier-Tribune,* Nov. 15, 1968, p. 1; *Spectator,* Nov. 19, 1968, p. 9.

35. *Bloomington Courier-Tribune,* Dec. 26, 1968, p. 1; *Indiana Daily Student,* Jan. 7, 1969, pp. 1–4; Jan. 8, 1969, p. 1; Jan. 11, 1969, p. 1; *Spectator,* Jan. 7, 1969, pp. 4–5.

36. Interview with Rollo Turner.

37. *Indiana Daily Student,* Jan. 8, 1969, p. 1; Jan. 11, 1969, p. 1; Feb. 21, 1969, p. 3; Sept. 16, 1969, p. 3; Sept. 27, 1969, p. l.

38. Edwards, *Black Students,* 144–55.

39. *Indiana Daily Student,* Nov. 6, 1969, p. 1; Nov. 8, 1969, p. 1; Nov. 11, 1969, p. 1; Nov. 12, 1969, p. 4; *Spectator,* Nov. 10, 1969, p. 6.

40. *Bloomington Daily Herald-Telephone,* Nov. 7, 1969, p. 1; Nov. 9, 1969, p. 1; Nov. 16, 1969, p. 1.

41. *Spectator,* April 8, 1970, p. 3; interview with Rollo Turner.

6. THE WOMEN'S MOVEMENT

1. Interview with Robert Shaffer, May 8, 1989; interview with Herman B Wells, May 23, 1989; *Indiana Daily Student,* Sept. 15, 1965, p. 4; Oct. 22, 1965, p. 3; Nov. 23, 1965, pp. 9–14.

2. *Indiana Daily Student,* April 5, 1966, p. 1.

3. Thomas D. Clark, *Indiana University, Midwestern Pioneer,* vol. 3, *Years of Fulfillment* (Bloomington: Indiana University Press, 1977), 208, 267; Herman B Wells, *Being Lucky: Reminiscences and Reflections* (Bloomington: Indiana University Press, 1980), 214; interview with Robert Shaffer.

4. Wells, *Being Lucky,* 223.

5. *Indiana Daily Student,* Feb. 18, 1966, p. 1; Feb. 22, 1966, p. 8.

6. Minutes of the board of trustees meeting, July 8–10, 1955, IU Archives.

7. *Indiana Daily Student,* April 12, 1966, p. 1; May 17, 1966, p. 4; May 18, 1966, pp. 1, 6.

8. *Indiana Daily Student,* May 25, 1966, p. 4; May 27, 1966, p. 1.

9. "B-1: A Bill Submitted to the Student Body," dean of students' copy, in minutes of the board of trustees meeting, July 8–10, 1966, IU Archives.

10. Beth Bailey, *Sex in the Heartland* (Cambridge, Mass.: Harvard University Press, 1999), 89.

11. *Indiana Daily Student,* April 15, 1967, p. 3; interview with Guy Loftman and Connie Loftman, April 15, 1987.

12. *Indiana Daily Student,* April 13, 1967, p. 4; April 27, 1967, p. 1.

13. *Indiana Daily Student,* April 29, 1967, p. 1; May 2, 1967, p. 9.

14. *Indiana Daily Student,* May 12, 1967, p. 1.

15. Ted Najam, "Student Unrest in Higher Education," Aug. 1968, unpublished paper in my possession; *Indiana Daily Student,* Sept. 21, 1968, p. 1; interview with Connie Loftman and Guy Loftman, March 15, 1987.

16. Sara Evans, *Personal Politics: The Roots of Women's Liberation in the Civil Rights Movement and the New Left* (New York: Vintage Books, 1980), 189.

17. *Spectator,* Feb. 18, 1969, p. 21; Feb. 25, 1969, p. 21; New University Conference newsletter, March 1969, p. 1, Local New University Conference, spring 1969 file, IU Archives; interview with Martha Vicinus, Oct. 10, 1990; interview with Allyne Rosenthal, Oct. 12, 1990; interview with Sonja Johnson, Oct. 22, 1990; interview with Ruth Mahaney, Nov. 3, 1990.

18. "Bloomington Women's Liberation Position Paper," Local New University Conference, spring 1969 file, IU Archives; interview with Ruth Mahaney; interview with Allyne Rosenthal; interview with Martha Vicinus; interview with Sonja Johnson.

19. "Bloomington Women's Liberation Position Paper"; interview with Martha Vicinus; interview with Allyne Rosenthal; interview with Sonja Johnson; interview with Ruth Mahaney.

20. *Spectator,* April 8, 1970, pp. 8–9.

21. *Spectator,* April 22, 1969, p. 7; May 20, 1969, p. 7; July 1, 1969, pp. 6–8; July 29, 1969, p. 12; Dec. 15, 1969, p. 16; interview with Ruth Mahaney.

22. *Spectator,* May 20, 1970, p. 23; interview with Nancy Brand, Aug. 22, 1990; interview with Sonja Johnson.

23. *Indiana Daily Student,* April 12, 1969, p. 1; *Spectator,* April 22, 1969, p. 7.

24. Interview with Martha Vicinus; interview with Allyne Rosenthal; interview with Ruth Mahaney; "Preamble to NUC Constitution passed June 14, 1969," NUC National Convention, Position Papers on NUC's Theoretical Position file, IU Archives.

25. *Spectator,* July 29, 1969, p. 10; interview with Charles Kleinhans, Oct. 12, 1990.

26. "Study of the Status of Women Faculty at Indiana University, Bloomington Campus," American Association of University Professors Committee on the Status of Women, January 1971, accession number 0556, Women's Status, Dean of Faculties file, President Joseph Lee Sutton papers, IU Archives; memo from Martha Vicinus, Feb. 18, 1970, Martha Jeanette Vicinus papers, Hatcher Library, University of Michigan, Ann Arbor.

27. "Proposal on Women's Studies," women's studies file, Dean of Faculties, general office files, 1968–76, President Joseph Lee Sutton papers, IU Archives.

28. *Spectator,* March 11, 1970, p. 3; interview with Ruth Mahaney.

29. *Spectator,* Feb. 11, 1970, p. 21; Feb. 26, 1970, p. 7; March 11, 1970, pp. 8–9; May 20, 1970, pp. 14–15, 6–7, 18.

7. BLOOMINGTON AND THE COUNTERCULTURE IN SOUTHERN INDIANA

1. See Morris Dickstein, *Gates of Eden: American Culture in the Sixties* (New York: Penguin, 1989); Andrew Jamison and Ron Eyerman, *Seeds of the Sixties* (Berkeley: University of California Press, 1994); and Timothy Miller, *The Hippies and American Values* (Knoxville: University of Tennessee Press, 1991).

2. Bil Gilbert, "The Great World and Millersburg," *Saturday Evening Post,* April 20, 1968, pp. 36–52; David Ohle, Roger Martin, and Susan Brosseau, *Cows Are Freaky When They Look at You: An Oral History of the Kaw Valley Hemp Pickers* (Wichita, Kans.: Watermark, 1991).

3. Interview with Wendel Field, April 3, 1991; interview with Dan Kaplan, May 1, 1988.

4. Abe Peck, *Uncovering the Sixties: the Life and Times of the Underground Press* (New York: Pantheon, 1985), 292.

5. Raymond Mungo, *Famous Long Ago: My Life and Hard Times with Liberation News Service* (Boston: Beacon, 1970), 76.

6. Interview with Chris Scanlon, June 8, 1991; interview with Allen Gurevitz, April 30, 1991.

7. Jay Stevens, *Storming Heaven: LSD and the American Dream* (New York: Harper and Row, 1987), 246, 331.

8. *Indiana Daily Student,* Dec. 13, 1969, p. 4.

9. *Indiana Daily Student,* Dec. 13, 1969, p. 4; *Spectator,* Dec. 30, 1967, p. 1; March 4, 1968, p. 1; March 13, 1969, p. 4; *Bloomington Daily Herald-Telephone,* Feb. 27, 1970, sec. 6, p. 5.

10. *The Spectator,* Jan. 8, 1970, p. 4.

11. Geoffrey Rips, *The Campaign against the Underground Press* (San Francisco: City Lights Books, 1981).

12. SAC, Indianapolis, to Hoover, Sept. 3, 1968, no. 100-14837-278, IU-CEWV file, FBI, J. Edgar Hoover FBI Building, Washington, D.C.

13. SAC, Indianapolis, to Hoover, August 27, 1968, no. 105-5821-41, New Left–Indiana folder, COINTELPRO file, FBI.

14. David Armstrong, *A Trumpet to Arms: Alternative Media in America* (Los Angeles: Houghton Mifflin, 1981), 145; Hoover to SAC, Indianapolis, Oct. 11, 1968, no. 100-449698-21-18, New Left–Indiana folder, COINTELPRO file, FBI.

15. The YSA was well aware that the FBI used drug busts to break up antiwar protest organizations and informed members that "the use of narcotics will not be allowed." SA to SAC, Chicago, Aug. 23, 1970, no. 100-12158-1095, YSA/Indiana file, FBI.

16. Interview with Chris Scanlon; interview with Allen Gurevitz.

17. Interview with Ruth Mahaney, Nov. 3, 1990.

18. Stevens, *Storming Heaven,* xv, xvi. See also Dickstein, *Gates of Eden;* Nicholas Von Hoffman, *We Are the People Our Parents Warned Us Against* (Chicago: Ivan R. Dee, 1968); and Tom Wolfe, *The Electric Kool-Aid Acid Test* (New York: Bantam Books, 1981) among hundreds of works devoted to descriptions of the psychedelic experience.

19. Stevens, *Storming Heaven,* 303.

20. "Effects of Narcotics Arrests in December, 1968 on New Left," no. 100-14837-36, IU-CEWV file, FBI.

21. Armstrong, *A Trumpet to Arms,* 257; *Spectator,* Oct. 12, 1970, p. 16.

22. Interview with Wendel Field, April 25, 1991; interview with Betty Sander, June 3, 1991.

23. Interview with Sonja Johnson, Oct. 22, 1990; interview with Allyne Rosenthal, Oct. 12, 1990.

24. Interview with Kathy Canada, May 17, 1991.

25. Interview with Kathy Canada; *Bloomington Courier-Tribune*, Aug. 13, 1971, p. 14.

26. Miller, *The Hippies and American Values,* 142; *Spectator,* Dec. 2, 1969, p. 4.

27. Interview with Kathy Canada.

28. Interview with Kathy Canada; *Bloomington Courier-Tribune*, Aug. 13, 1971, p. 14.

29. Interview with Kathy Canada; *Bloomington Daily Herald-Telephone,* June 15, 1971, p. 1.

30. *South Central Times,* June 29, 1971, p. 1.

31. Thomas Frank, *The Conquest of Cool: Business Culture, Counterculture, and the Rise of Hip Consumerism* (Chicago: University of Chicago Press, 1997).

32. Aldo Leopold, *A Sand County Almanac, and Sketches Here and There* (New York: Oxford University Press, 1949); Rachel Carson, *Silent Spring* (Boston: Houghton Mifflin, 1962); Gary Snyder, *The Back Country* (New York: New Directions, 1968).

EPILOGUE

1. Terry H. Anderson, *The Movement and the Sixties: Protest in America from Greensboro to Wounded Knee* (New York: Oxford University Press, 1995), 380–81.

2. *Indiana Daily Student,* July 23, 1970, p. 4; July 30, 1970, p. 3.

3. *Indiana Daily Student,* Sept. 14, 1970, p. 11.

4. *Indiana Daily Student,* Dec. 15, 1970, p. 1.

5. *Indiana Daily Student,* Oct. 31, 1970, p. 1.

6. *Indiana Daily Student,* Sept. 30, 1970, p. 1.

7. *Spectator,* Oct. 26, 1970, p. 2.

8. *Common Sense,* May 15, 1971, p. 3.

9. *Indiana Daily Student,* Sept. 15, 1970, p. 4; Feb. 19, 1970, p. 1; July 2, 1972, p. 4.

10. *Indiana Daily Student,* Nov. 2, 1970, p. 1.

11. *Indiana Daily Student,* Nov. 17, 1970, p. 1; Dec. 1, 1970, p. 1.

12. *Indiana Daily Student,* Dec. 8, 1970, p. 4.

13. *Indiana Daily Student,* Feb. 1, 1971, p. 4.

14. *Indiana Daily Student,* Dec. 18, 1970, p. 1; Feb. 1, 1971, p. 1; Feb. 3, 1971, p. 4; Feb. 9, 1971, p. 1.

15. Priscilla Allen and Jean Romsted, "Cooperative Day Care Centers," Martha Vicinus Papers, Department of Rare Books and Special Collections, Hatcher Library, University of Michigan, Ann Arbor.

16. Ibid.

17. Ibid.

18. Florence Howe, "Women's Studies: An Overview," in Jean Ramage Leppaluoto, ed., *Women on the Move: A Feminist Perspective* (Eugene: University of Oregon, 1973), 58.

19. *Indiana Daily Student,* Oct. 23, 1971, p. 1.

20. Winifred D. Wandersee, *On the Move: American Women in the 1970s* (Boston: Twayne Publishers, 1988), 106.

21. Indiana University Budget Office, *I.U. Fact Book* (2000), 61.

22. Interview with Ruth Mahaney, Nov. 3, 1990; Alice Echols, *Daring to Be Bad: Radical Feminism in America, 1967–1975* (Minneapolis: University of Minnesota Press, 1989), 204.

23. *Spectator,* Oct. 12, 1970, p. 18; interview with Ruth Mahaney.

24. *Indiana Daily Student,* April 20, 1971, pp. 1, 4.

25. *Indiana Daily Student,* May 1, 1971, p. 1; May 5, 1971, p. 4; May 6, 1971, p. 7.

26. *Indiana Daily Student,* April 30, 1971, p. 5; May 17, 1971, p. 11.

27. *Indiana Daily Student,* July 26, 1971, p. 8; Aug. 23, 1971, p. 1; Aug. 30, 1971, p. 1; interview with Orlando Taylor, Aug. 10, 1989; interview with Rollo Turner, April 17, 1989.

28. *Indiana Daily Student,* Oct. 28, 1971.

29. *Indiana Daily Student,* Nov. 3, 1971, pp. 1, 16; Nov. 4, 1971, p. 1.

30. Tom Bates, *Rads: The 1970 Bombing of the Army Math Research Center at the University of Wisconsin and Its Aftermath* (New York: HarperCollins, 1992), 405, 443.

31. William H. Chafe, *The Unfinished Journey: America since World War II* (New York: Oxford University Press, 1986), 445–50.

Select Bibliography

The explosion of articles and books on the 1960s has produced more sources than I could reasonably list here. The following materials are those that I found most useful.

MANUSCRIPT AND DOCUMENT COLLECTIONS

COINTELPRO–New Left, especially files on Indiana University–CEWV, YSA/Indiana, AAASA, and CPUSA. FBI. J. Edgar Hoover FBI Building, Washington, D.C.

Oral History Series. Monroe County Public Library. Bloomington, Indiana.

Social Action Collection. State Historical Society of Wisconsin. Madison, Wisconsin.

Students for a Democratic Society, 1958–1970 (microfilm). State Historical Society of Wisconsin. Madison, Wisconsin.

President Joseph Lee Sutton Papers and reference files, Indiana University Archives, Bryan Hall. Indiana University. Bloomington, Indiana.

Martha Vicinus Papers. Hatcher Library. University of Michigan–Ann Arbor.

INTERVIEWS (CONDUCTED BY THE AUTHOR)

Block, Russell. April 2, 1988.
Brand, Nancy. Aug. 22, 1990.
Canada, Kathy. May 17, 1991.
Dinsmoor, James. Sept. 25, 1989.
Field, Wendel. April 3, 1991; April 25, 1991.
Fuhrman, Joseph. Jan. 2, 1990.
Gurevitz, Allen. April 30, 1991; July 22, 1992.
Johnson, Sonja. Oct. 22, 1990.
Kaplan, Dan. May 1, 1988; May 6, 1989.
Kelsey, Mike. March 6, 1990.
Kleinhans, Charles. Oct. 12, 1990.
Loftman, Connie. March 15, 1987; April 15, 1987.
Loftman, Guy. March 15, 1987; April 15, 1987.
Lundin, Leonard. Feb. 17, 1989.
Mahaney, Ruth. Nov. 3, 1990.
Najam, Ted. May 24, 1989.
Ritchey, Mark. Dec. 15, 1989.
Rosenthal, Allyne. Oct. 12, 1990.
Sander, Betty. June 3, 1991.
Scanlon, Chris. June 8, 1991.
Shaffer, Robert. May 8, 1989.
Stahr, Elvis. March 26, 1990; April 12, 1990.
Taylor, Orlando. Aug. 10, 1989.
Turner, Rollo (Clarence). April 17, 1989.

Vicinus, Martha. Oct. 10, 1990.
Walker, George. Dec. 1, 1989.
Wallihan, Jim. May 15, 1989; June 5, 1989.
Wells, Herman B. May 23, 1989.

NEWSPAPERS

Bloomington Daily Herald-Telephone
Bloomington Star Courier
Bloomington Tribune (later *Bloomington Courier-Tribune*)
Indiana Daily Student
Indianapolis Star
Indianapolis Times
The Spectator

PUBLISHED SOURCES

Anderson, Terry H. *The Movement and the Sixties: Protest in America from Greensboro to Wounded Knee.* New York: Oxford University Press, 1995.
Armstrong, David. *A Trumpet to Arms: Alternative Media in America.* Los Angeles: Houghton Mifflin, 1981.
Bailey, Beth. *Sex in the Heartland.* Cambridge, Mass.: Harvard University Press, 1999.
Baskir, Lawrence M., and William A. Strauss. *Chance and Circumstance: The Draft, The War, and the Vietnam Generation.* New York: Knopf, 1978.
Bates, Tom. *Rads: The 1970 Bombing of the Army Math Research Center at the University of Wisconsin and Its Aftermath.* New York: HarperCollins, 1992.
Blanchard, Charles, ed. *Counties of Morgan, Monroe, and Brown, Indiana.* Chicago: F. A. Battey, 1884.
Carson, Clayborne. *In Struggle: SNCC and the Black Awakening of the 1960s.* Cambridge, Mass.: Harvard University Press, 1981.
Carson, Rachel. *Silent Spring.* Boston: Houghton Mifflin, 1962.
Chafe, William H. *The Unfinished Journey: America since World War II.* New York: Oxford University Press, 1986.
Clark, Thomas D. *Indiana University, Midwestern Pioneer.* Vol. 3, *Years of Fulfillment.* Bloomington: Indiana University Press, 1977.
Cobbs Hoffman, Elizabeth. *All You Need Is Love: The Peace Corps and the Spirit of the 1960s.* Cambridge, Mass.: Harvard University Press, 1998.
DeBenedetti, Charles, with Charles Chatfield, assisting author. *An American Ordeal: The Antiwar Movement of the Vietnam Era.* Syracuse, N.Y.: Syracuse University Press, 1990.
Dickstein, Morris. *Gates of Eden: American Culture in the Sixties.* New York: Penguin, 1989.
Echols, Alice. *Daring to Be Bad: Radical Feminism in America, 1967–1975.* Minneapolis: University of Minnesota Press, 1989.
Edwards, Harry. *Black Students.* London: Free Press, 1970.
Engelhardt, Tom. *The End of Victory Culture: Cold War America and the Disillusioning of a Generation.* Amherst: University of Massachusetts Press, 1995.
Evans, Sara. *Personal Politics: The Roots of Women's Liberation in the Civil Rights Movement and the New Left.* New York: Vintage Books, 1980.
Farrell, James J. *The Spirit of the Sixties: Making Postwar Radicalism.* New York: Routledge, 1997.
Forman, James. *The Making of Black Revolutionaries.* New York: Macmillan, 1972.

Foster, Julian, and Durward Long, eds. *Protest! Student Activism in America.* New York: Morrow, 1970.

Frank, Thomas. *The Conquest of Cool: Business Culture, Counterculture, and the Rise of Hip Consumerism.* Chicago: University of Chicago Press, 1997.

Friedan, Betty. *The Feminine Mystique.* New York: Norton, 1963.

Gilbert, Bil. "The Great World and Millersburg." *Saturday Evening Post,* April 20, 1968.

Halberstam, David. *The Unfinished Odyssey of Robert Kennedy.* New York: Random House, 1968.

Hayden, Tom. *Reunion: A Memoir.* New York: Random House, 1988.

Heineman, Kenneth J. *Campus Wars: The Peace Movement at American State Universities in the Vietnam Era.* New York: New York University Press, 1993.

Herring, George C. *America's Longest War: The United States and Vietnam, 1950–1975.* Philadelphia: Temple University Press, 1986.

Howe, Florence. "Women's Studies: An Overview." In *Women on the Move: A Feminist Perspective,* ed. Jean Ramage Leppaluoto. Eugene: University of Oregon, 1973.

Jamison, Andrew, and Ron Eyerman. *Seeds of the Sixties.* Berkeley: University of California Press, 1994.

Kennedy, Patrick D. "Reactions against the Vietnam War and Military-Related Targets on Campus: The University of Illinois as a Case Study, 1965–1972." *Illinois Historical Journal* 84 (summer 1991).

Kennedy, Robert F. *RFK: Collected Speeches.* Edited and introduced by Edwin O. Guthman and C. Richard Allen. New York: Viking, 1993.

Kline, Benjamin. *First along the River: A Brief History of the U.S. Environmental Movement.* San Francisco: Acada Books, 1997.

Leopold, Aldo. *A Sand County Almanac, and Sketches Here and There.* New York: Oxford University Press, 1949.

Levy, Peter B. *The New Left and Labor in the 1960s.* Urbana: University of Illinois Press, 1994.

Madison, James H. *The Indiana Way: A State History.* Bloomington: Indiana University Press, 1986.

Miller, James. *Democracy Is in the Streets: From Port Huron to the Siege of Chicago.* New York: Simon and Schuster, 1987.

Miller, Timothy. *The Hippies and American Values.* Knoxville: University of Tennessee Press, 1991.

Mungo, Raymond. *Famous Long Ago: My Life and Hard Times with Liberation News Service.* Boston: Beacon, 1970.

O'Brien, Tim. *The Things They Carried: A Work of Fiction.* New York: Penguin, 1990.

Ohle, David, Roger Martin, and Susan Brosseau. *Cows Are Freaky When They Look at You: An Oral History of the Kaw Valley Hemp Pickers.* Wichita, Kans.: Watermark, 1991.

O'Reilly, Kenneth. *Racial Matters: The FBI's Secret File on Black America, 1960–1972.* New York: Free Press, 1989.

Peck, Abe. *Uncovering the Sixties: The Life and Times of the Underground Press.* New York: Pantheon, 1985.

Rips, Geoffrey. *The Campaign against the Underground Press.* San Francisco: City Lights Books, 1981.

Rossinow, Doug. *The Politics of Authenticity: Liberalism, Christianity, and the New Left in America.* New York: Columbia University Press, 1998.

Rothschild, Mary Aickin. *A Case of Black and White: Northern Volunteers and the Southern Freedom Summers, 1964–1965.* Westport, Conn.: Greenwood, 1982.

Schneider, Gregory L. *Cadres for Conservatism: Young Americans for Freedom and the Rise of the Contemporary Right.* New York: New York University Press, 1999.

Snyder, Gary. *The Back Country.* New York: New Directions, 1968.

Steigerwald, David. *The Sixties and the End of Modern America.* New York: St. Martin's Press, 1995.

Stevens, Jay. *Storming Heaven: LSD and the American Dream.* New York: Harper and Row, 1987.

Thornbrough, Emma Lou. *Indiana in the Civil War Era, 1850–1880.* Indianapolis: Indiana Historical Bureau, 1965.

Tischler, Barbara L., ed. *Sights on the Sixties.* New Brunswick: Rutgers University Press, 1992.

Von Hoffman, Nicholas. *We Are the People Our Parents Warned Us Against.* Chicago: Ivan R. Dee, 1968.

Wandersee, Winifred D. *On the Move: American Women in the 1970s.* Boston: Twayne Publishers, 1988.

Wells, Herman B. *Being Lucky: Reminiscences and Reflections.* Bloomington: Indiana University Press, 1980.

Wells, Tom. *The War Within: America's Battle over Vietnam.* Berkeley: University of California Press, 1994.

Wolfe, Tom. *The Electric Kool-Aid Acid Test.* New York: Bantam Books, 1981.

Woodburn, James Albert. *History of Indiana University.* Bloomington: Indiana University, 1940.

UNPUBLISHED SOURCES

Cahill, David. *A History of Student Affairs at Indiana University.* 1967 pamphlet in reference file, Indiana University Archives, Bryan Hall. Indiana University. Bloomington, Indiana. Copy also in my possession.

Cook, Delia Crutchfield. "Black Student Activism in a Border State: An Historical Analysis of Black Student Government, 1968–1994." In my possession.

Fisher, Mike. "The Turbulent Years: The University of Kansas, 1960–1975, A History." Ph.D. diss., University of Kansas, 1979.

Hunter, Robin. Personal diary. In my possession.

Monhollon, Rusty L. "'Away from the Dream': The Roots of Black Power in Lawrence, Kansas, 1960–1970." In my possession.

Index

Page numbers in *italic type* indicate illustrations.

Abraham, Ken, 31
Aceves, Peter, 52
Ad Hoc Committee against Racism, 124
Ad Hoc Committee to Oppose U.S. Aggression
  in Cuba, 13–14, *15*
Adams, Abigail, 192
Adams, John, 192
Afro-Afro-American Students Association
  (AAASA), 67, 121–124
Allen, Joel, 95
Allen, Priscilla, 178
The Alternative: An American Spectator, 62
American Civil Liberties Union (ACLU), 131
American Council of Education, 23
American Federation of State, County and Mu-
  nicipal Employees (AFSCME), 29, 67
Air Force Language Institute, 74
Alcott, Bronson, 3
Allen, Joel, 86
American Association of University Professors
  (AAUP), 6, 34–35, 59
American Civil Liberties Union (ACLU), 35, 60
American Legion, 6, 43
Americans for Democratic Action (ADA), 38
Anderson, Terry, 67, 172
Ann Arbor, Michigan, 155
Anthony, Susan B., 3
Aptheker, Herbert, 43–45
Arbutus, 127–128, 174
Armageddon News, 162
Armstrong, James, 97
Association of Women Students (AWS), 29
  137, 139–141

Bains, Wilfred C., 4
Baker, Ella, 10, 115
Ball State University, 62, 72
Ballantine Hall "lock-in," 85–86
Baptist Youth Federation, 6
Bardagjy, Mimi, 159
Bayh, Birch, 136
Berkeley, California, 155
Berkeley Barb, 155

Berry, Thomas, 181
Bingham, James, 13–14, 16–17, 102
Bizarri, Larry, 98
Black Market, 77, 91, 106, 128, *129, 131;*
  bombing of, 130, 155, 175
Black Panther Party, 78, 102–103, 128–129,
  134, 155, 175
Black Studies Institute, 87, 130, 133
Block, Russell, 55–56, 61, 77, 80–81, 147, 169
"Bloomington 3," 16–17, 20, 185, 188
Bloomington City Council, 173
Bloomington Cooperative Day Care Center,
  146
Bloomington Courier Tribune, 80, 157
Bloomington Gay Alliance, 180
Bloomington Herald-Telephone, 16, 157
Bloomington Optimists Club, 129
Bloomington Star Courier, 17
Bloomington Tribune, 52
Bloomington Veterans Committee for Peace in
  Vietnam, 104
Bond, Julian, 172
Boston University, 90
Boudin, Leonard, 17
Bourne, Mike, 151
Boutelle, Paul, 76
Boys in the Band, 180
Braden, Samuel, 16
Brand, Nancy, 146, 186–187
Branigan, Roger D., 62–63
Bridgwaters, Elizabeth, 118
Briscoe, Carlisle, 131
Brook Farm, 168
Brooksville, Indiana, 156
Brown County, Indiana, 166–168
Bryan, William Lowe, 4, 118
Buhle, Paul, 161
Burton, Dan, 79, 159
Butler, Ernest D., 118
Byrnes, Robert F., 74

Cagan, Steve, 42
Cahill, David, 36, 81

Campbell, Finley, 106
Canada, Kathy Noyes, 128, 167–170
Canada, Larry, 57, 106, 128, 167–170
Carnegie Foundation Commission on the Future of Higher Education, 94
Carson, Rachel, 105, 171
Carter, Byram, 178
Central Intelligence Agency (CIA), 61, 74–75
Chaney, William, 131
Chicago, Illinois, 1, 155
Civil Rights Act (1964), 135, 149
Clergy and Laymen Concerned about Vietnam, 93, 99, 103–104
Cleveland, Ohio, 167
Coalition against the War, 104
COINTELPRO (Counter Intelligence Program), 80, 88, 161
Coleman, Les, 92–93
College Press Service, 162
Columbia University, 64, 75, 77–78, 92
Committee for a Sane Nuclear Policy (SANE), 39, 93
Committee to Aid the Bloomington Students, 16
Committee to End the War in Vietnam (CEWV), 35, 42, 44–45, 51–53, 55, 59, 66–67, 73, 93, 97–98, 100, 148
Common Sense, 175
Communist Party (CP), 6, 32, 44, 73
Community Corner General Store, 168
Concerned University Women, 150
Cottner, James, 17

Davidson, Carl, 60
Davis, Rennie, 169
"Days of Rage," 92
de St. Croix, Brian, 183
Dellinger, David, 53
Democratic Party, 113, 182–183
Dennis, Rev. William, 76
Denver Arrow, 162
DePauw University, 113
Derge, David, 83, 85, 108, 181
Diamond, James, 100
Dillencourt, Jane, 147
Dillon, Capt., 56
Dinsmoor, James, 42, 44–45
Dixon, Marlene, 142–143
Dixon, Spike, 113
Douglass, Frederick, 3
Dow Chemical Company, 37; demonstration against, 54–58, 60–61, 157
Dowdell, Rick "Tiger," 120
Dr. Rex Organ, 160
Du Bois Club. See W. E. B. Du Bois Club
Dunbar, Roxanne, 151
Dunn's Woods, 3

Eagleson, Preston Emmanuel, 118
Earlham College, 26, 53

Earth Day (1970), 105, 170, 171–172
East, James R., 44, 85
East Central Neighborhood Association, 173
East Village Other, 155
Eckert, Charles, 59
Economic Research Action Project (ERAP), 40, 136
Edwards, Harry, 119, 132
Ellis, Nancy, 141
Environmental Action, 105
Equal Employment Opportunity Commission (EEOC), 135, 149
Equal Rights Amendment (ERA), 136
Ernie Pyle School of Journalism, 156
Eschenbach, Jesse, 65
Evans, Sara, 142
Everroad, Lynn, 27, 138

Fabulous Furry Freak Brothers, 160
Faculty Committee on Race Relations, 133
Fair Play for Cuba Committee, 13, 102, 185
Federal Bureau of Investigation (FBI), 60; agents on campus, 71–73, 80, 88, 102, 121, 126, 145, 158, 161–162, 165, 169. See also COINTELPRO
Federal City College, 133, 181
Feebeck, Steve, 175
Feminine Mystique, 136
Field, Wendel, 158–159, 163, 166
Fifteenth Amendment (1868), 135
First Amendment, 17, 20
Fletcher National Bank, 90
Flynn, Elizabeth Gurley, 151
Forman, James, 115
Founders Day, 111
Franklin College, 121
Free Speech Movement (FSM), 12, 20, 31, 45, 94
Frick, Dave, 25
Friedan, Betty, 136
Fuhrman, Joseph, 19, 51

Gandhi, Mahatma, 10, 115
Gary, Indiana, 155
General Electric, 37; strike against, 100–102
George, Henry, 3
Gilbert, Bil, 68
Ginsberg, Allen, 53, 157, 166
Glavaty, Vaclav, 4
Gockley, Pam, 97, 109
Goldberg, Jackie, 31
Gonso, Harry, 132
Gray, Richard, 181
Greenbaggers, 18
Greene County, Indiana, 167
Greenwich Village, 166
Grove, Bob, 36, 72–73
Grove, John, 19–20, 24
Gruening, Ernest, 41

Guevara, Che, 78
Gulf of Tonkin Resolution (1964), 41
Gurevitz, Allen, 33–36, 51, 156, 159

Haden, Patricia, 152
Hammond, Indiana, 83, 102
Hanoi, North Vietnam, 176–177, 181
Hartke, Vance, 41–42, 113
Harvard University, 38, 90, 92
Harvey, William B., 85
Hayakawa, S. I., 78
Hayden, Casey, 135
Hayden, Tom, 11, 13
Helmke, Paul, 81–82
Hendricks, Charles D., 32
Hershey, Lt. Gen. Lewis B., 43
Highlander Folk School, 90
Hill, Nat U., 131, 174
Hillel Foundation, 100
Hiroshima Day, 45, 51
Hoadley, Thomas, 14–16
Hobbit House Day Care Center, 178
Hoffman, Abbie, 53
Holliday, Bill, 101
Hooker, John, 86, 173
Hoosiers for Peace in Vietnam, 53
Hoover, J. Edgar, 14, 71, 161
Horton, Myles, 89
House UnAmerican Activities Committee
    (HUAC), 11–12
Howard University, 133
Hudson, Herman, 181
Hunter, Robin, 19, 26–27, 30, 34, 45–47, 61,
    102, 108, 139
Huston, Tom Charles, 13, 25
"Huston Plan," 14

Indiana Anti-Subversive Act, 14–15
Indiana Central University, 62
Indiana Daily Student, 28, 30, 35, 40, 46, 57, 66,
    70, 77, 79, 81–82, 87, 100, 130, 138–139,
    156, 158, 173–174, 181
Indiana Seminary, 3
Indiana State University, 73
Indiana University Foundation, 80, 108, 111,
    124, 159
Indiana University Safety Division, 130
Indiana University Voters Union, 173, 183
Indianapolis, Indiana, 167
Indianapolis Star, 45, 158
in loco parentis, 23, 137
Institute for Defense Analysis (IDA), 7
Institute for Sex Research, 5
International Brotherhood of Electrical Work-
    ers (IBEW), 100, 102
International Voluntary Service, 59
International Women's Day, 151

Jackson State University, 113

James, C. L. R., 161
Jenkins, Carol, 126
Jenner, William E., 42
Johnson, Lyndon Baines, 44–46, 59, 87, 149,
    179, 184
Johnson, Robert, 51, 56, 60, 63, 67, 86, 92,
    121, 124, 129, 132, 159
Joint Committee on Discriminatory Practices,
    127
Jones, Mother, 151
Jones, Robert, 94
Jordan, David Starr, 4
Joyner, John, 125, 127

Kaplan, Allyne Rosenthal, 80, 147
Kaplan, Dan, 147, 155, 187
Kappa Alpha, 120
Kappa Alpha Psi, 119
Katzenbach, Nicholas, 32
Kelsey, Mike, 20, 74
Kennedy, John F., 7, 10, 13, 65
Kennedy, Robert F., 50, 63, 87, 123
Kent State University, 42, 90, *110,* 172; demon-
    strations after shootings at, 108–110, 113–
    114
Kerr, Clark, 12, 23, 45, 94, *95,* 96
King, Gaylord "Skip," 32
King, Dr. Martin Luther, Jr., 50, 63, 71, 87,
    109; assassination of, 115–116, 123, 125
King, Mary, 135
King, Mike, 93, 102–103, 106, 147, 159, 176–
    177, 181
Kinser, Jackie, 131
Kinsey, Alfred C., 5, 70
Kirk, Greyson, 78
Kissinger, Henry, 183
Klassen, Albert, 59
Klawitter, Robert, 167
Klawitter, Sonja, 146, 167
Klein, Bruce, 33–36
Kneadmore Life Community Church, 169
Ku Klux Klan, 77, 86, 91, 109, 116–117, 122,
    125–126, 130–131, 169–170
Kuntz, Linda, 66

Lafayette, Indiana, 121
Lanard, Jody, 111
Lawrence, Kansas, 154
Leary, Timothy, 154, 164
Leopold, Aldo, 171
Levitt, Ralph, 14, 16–17
Liberation News Service, 156–157
Lilly, Eli, 5, 167
Lilly Foundation, 62
Little 500 Bicycle Race, 79; protest against,
    124–126
Lloyd, Arthur, 35
Loftman, Connie Kiesling, 30, 61–62, 67, 141–
    142, 167, 169, 186

Loftman, Guy, 24–25, 27–28, 30, 35, 39, 46–
    48, 51–53, 55, 57, 61, 65, 67, 137, 139,
    141–142, 156, 167, 169, 186
LSD, 163–164
Lundin, Leonard, 38, 57
Lynd, Staughton, 76–77

McCarran Act (1950), 32
McCarthy, Eugene, 63
McCarthy, Joseph, 6, 11, 42
McCloskey, Frank, 182–183
McGovern, George, 183
McHenry, Robert, 102
McKinney, Frank, 44, 83, 90
McNamara, Robert, 10
McRae, Leroy, 15
Madison, James, 2
Madison, Wisconsin, 155, 161, 172, 183
Mahaney, Ruth, 145, 148, 163, 180, 186
Malcolm X, 60, 103
Mann, Wade, 158
"March for Life," 99
March on the Pentagon (1967), 53
March on Washington (1969), 98–99
Martinsville, Indiana, 126, 130
Masiello, Andrew, 69
Massachusetts Institute of Technology, 90
Mencke, Robert, 37
Meyers, Willie, 59
Michigan State University, 112
Middlesburg, Pennsylvania, 154
Middleton, Donna, 152
Minnick, Charles, 75
Miss America Pageant, 126
Miss Indiana University, 127
Mizell, Sherwin, 183
Monroe, Bill, 168
Monroe County, 2, 117, 130
Monroe County State Bank, 106
Montague, Peter, 19
Morgan, John, 16–17
Morgan, Robin, 151
Morgan, Thomas, 14, 188
Morning Star Ranch, 168
Morrill Act, 3
Morris, Bernard, 109
Morrison, Tim, 103
Morse, Wayne, 41
Moses, Bob, 115
Moss, John, 181
Mother Jones, 155
Mrs. Seamon's Sound Band, 163
Muller, Hermann J., 4
Mungo, Ray, 156

Najam, Ted, 61–62, 64–65, 67, 77, 142
Nash, Diane, 115
National Association for the Advancement of
    Colored People (NAACP), 51, 72

National Conference on Negroes in Higher Ed-
    ucation, 122
National Mobilization Committee to End the
    War in Vietnam ("the Mobe"), 53
National Organization for Women (NOW),
    136, 149
National Science Foundation, 32
National Student Association, 176
Needmore, 168–170
Nelson, Gaylord, 105
Neu, Irene, 57
New Harmony, Indiana, 4, 168
New Left, 24, 45, 62, 66, 80, 91–92, 121, 141–
    142, 147, 155, 161, 191
New Right, 13–14, 25, 62, 68
New University Conference (NUC), 76, 92–93,
    98, 104, 143, 147–148, 150–151
New York City, 155
New York Times, 17, 155, 182
Newsome, Kenneth, 86, 124, 131, 133
Niebuhr, Reinhold, 10
Nineteenth Amendment (1920), 135
Nixon, Richard M., 38, 50, 88–90, 108, 111,
    183
No More Fun and Games, 151
North, Karl, 19, 40
North Carolina A & T College, 101
Northwestern University, 133
Noyes, Evan, 161

Ochs, Phil, 53
Oglesby, Carl, 39
O'Reilly, Kenneth, 71
Organization for University Reform (OUR), 25–
    27
Oring, Mark, 52, 62, 66–67, 81
Ott, Chuck, 28
Owen, Richard, 3

Pardun, Robert, 20
Parker, Keith, 102–104, 106, 109, 112–113,
    134, 175–176, 177, 178, 181
Patten Lectures, 94
Peace Corps, 37
Peck, Abe, 155
Pennsylvania State University, 112
People's Park, 106, 169–170, 173, 184
Peterson, Margaret, 150
Phi Delta Theta, 126
Phi Gamma Delta, 126
Pic-A-Chic Ranch, 148
Planned Parenthood, 105
Pont, John, 132–133
Port Huron Statement, 11, 19, 24, 46
Price, Clarence, 132, 188
Progressive Reform Party (PRP), 27–29, 46–47,
    51, 55, 102; and women's hours, 137–141
Project Themis, 75
Pulliam, Eugene, 158

Purdue, John, 3
Purdue University, 62, 73, 81, 83, 133, 140
Purdy, Lisa, 141

Quaker Peace Committee, 131

Radical America, 161
Raff, Jeff, 126
Ramparts, 42
Rat, 151
Rational Observer, 162
Republican Party, 14
Reserve Officer Training Corps (ROTC), 18, 20, 66, 70, 73, 82, 108, 111, 113, 157
Retherford, Jim, 95, *96,* 101, 156–159, 173, 175, 187
Reuther, Walter, 89
Revolutionary Insurgency Training Corps (RITC), 73–74
Revolutionary Student Party, 80, 93, 147
Revolutionary Youth Movement 2 (RYM2), 92
Rice, Fred, 14
Richardson, Jeff, 181
Ringer, Fritz, 59
Ritchey, Mark, 53, 55–56, 61
Robinson, Patricia, 152
Robinson, Ruby Doris, 115
Rockefeller Foundation, 5
Roe v. Wade, 136, 186
Rogers, Virginia, 137
Rolling Stone, 155
Romsted, Jean, 178
Roosevelt, Theodore, 3
Rose Bowl, 132
Ross, Edward A., 4
Ross, Tom, 176
Rubin, Jerry, 94–95, 187
Rudd, Mark, 78, 92–93
Rusk, Dean, protest against, 54–55, 57, *58,* 59, 96, 157
Ryan, John, 178

Salloom, Roger, 52, 163
San Francisco, California, 168
San Francisco Mime Troup, 176–178
San Francisco State University, 77–78
San Jose State University, 77
SANE. *See* Committee for a Sane Nuclear Policy
Satterfield, Bernella, 19, 24, 32, 41, 46, 101, 141
Satterfield, David, 19, 24, 46, 101, 141, 168
Savio, Mario, 12
Scanlon, Chris, 156, 163, 167
Scheer, Robert, 42
Schlafly, Phyllis, 136
Schreck, Thomas C., 33
Scifres, Mary, 181–182
Scott County Journal, 158
Scottsburg, Indiana, 158

Screaming Gypsy Bandits, 163
Seale, Bobby, 108, 111
Sebeok, Thomas A., 74
Second Baptist Church, 117
Seed, 155
Seminary Township, 2–3
"Sex and Caste: A Kind of Memo," 135
Shaffer, Robert H., 28, 31, 33–34, 57, 61–62, 137, 139–140
Sharlet, Jeffrey, 36, 42–44, 46, 51
Sigma Chi, 120, 128
Sigma Nu, 120
Silent Spring, 105
Sinclair, Nancy, 163
Smith, Herbert, 56
Smith, Polly, 14, 187
Snider, J. Douglas, 54
Snyder, Gary, 171
Snyder, John, 77, 81–83, 85, 90
Socialist Workers Party, 71–72, 104
Soglin, Paul, 172, 183
Southern Christian Leadership Council (SCLC), 10, 115
Southern Illinois University, 53
Spannuth, William G., 34, 54
Spectator, 95, 100–103, 151, 155–163, *159, 160, 161,* 165, 169, 174–175
Spock, Benjamin, 53
Stahr, Dorothy, 10, 123
Stahr, Elvis J., 7, 10, 14, 31, 44–45, 52, 54, 63, 72, 120, 122, 125, 132
Stanford University, 4
Stare, Frederick, 59
Stillman College, 118
Stonewall Inn, 180
Stop the Draft Week (1967), 53
Stubbs, Ray, 119
Student Mobilization Committee (SMC), 100, 104
Student Non-Violent Coordinating Committee (SNCC), 10–11, 114–116, 119, 135, 172
Student strike (1968), 81–87, *84*
Student Strike Alliance, 100
Students for a Democratic Society (SDS), 11, 18–20, 24–25, 32, 38–39, 41, 46–48, 55, 59–60, 66–68, 70, 73–74, 92–94, 102, 114, 135–136, 140, 142, 147, 156, 186, 187
Subversive Activities Control Board, 32–33
Sutton, Joseph, 31, 72, 75–76, 83, 85, 108, 112–113, 125, 158–159, 178

Taylor, Maxwell, 42
Taylor, Orlando, 73, 85–87, 116, 125, 127, 129–130, 133, 181
Thirteenth Amendment (1865), 135
Thoreau, Henry David, 192
Thresher, Clifford, 86
Tolstoy Farm, 168
Towell, Alfred, 173, 178

Truth, Sojourner, 151
Turner, Bob, 35
Turner, Clarence "Rollo," 85–87, 123–125, *125,* 127–128, 131, 181
Turner, Nat, 192
Tuscaloosa, Alabama, 118
Twenty-sixth Amendment, 182
Tyrell, R. Emmett, Jr., 62

underground newspapers. *See Spectator*
Underground Press Service, 157
Unitarian Universalist Church, 146
United Anti-Racist Movement (UARM), 126
United Auto Workers, 89
United States Department of Health, Education, and Welfare, 179
United States Office of Education, 150
United Student Movement, 80, 93, 102–103, 112, 147
University Lutheran Church, 129
University of California, Berkeley, 11, 20, 31–32, 45, 94, 106, 113
University of Chicago, 76–77, 142–143
University of Illinois, 26, 53, 126, 140
University of Iowa, 133
University of Kansas, 120, 140
University of Michigan, 11, 38, 45
University of Minnesota, 26
University of Notre Dame, 53, 62, 73
University of Pittsburgh, 87
University of West Virginia, 7
University of Wisconsin–Madison, 4, 54, 105, 113–114, 148, 172
University Students for America, 43

Veller, Thomas, 106
Vesey, Denmark, 192
Veterans for Peace, 103–104
Vicinus, Martha, 148, *149,* 150
Vietnam, 39–41, 46, 52–54, 69, 155–156, 172, 177, 183
Voegelin, Charles F., 4
Voegelin, Ermine Wheeler, 4

Wabash College, 19
Walker, George, 56, 59, 60–61, 77
Wall Street Journal, 182
Wallihan, Jim, 19, 26, 32, 42, 46, 51
Ward, John, 181–182

Washington, D.C., 162, 168, 181
Washington Moratorium (1969), 104
W. E. B. Du Bois Club, 32–33, 35–36, 42, 47, 50–51, 67, 71, 73
Weathermen, 104
Webster, William R., 35
Wells, Herman B, 4–7, 10, 61, 63, 66, 70, 72, 76, 83, 116, 118, 120, 125, 127, 136, 138, 192
Wells, Tom, 38
West Lafayette, Indiana, 3
Westmoreland, William, 49
Wheeler, Barry, 28, 30, 51
Whitcomb, Edgar, 79, 81, 85, 112, 159
Wilbern, York, 110
Wiley, Bill, 104
WITCH. *See* Women's International Conspiracy from Hell
Women's Equity Action League (WEAL), 149, 179
Women's hours, campaign against, 137–141
Women's International Conspiracy from Hell (WITCH), 103, 105, *107,* 137, 148–149
Women's Liberation, 100, 178–179
Women's Studies Program, 179
Woodhull, Victoria, 151
Woodstock, 91
Worker, Dwight, 40, 57, 59
World War II, 135, 138, 146
Wylie, Andrew, 3

Yale University, 76
Yancey, Mel, 147
Yippies, 94
Young Americans for Freedom (YAF), 13, 25, 62, 68
Young Democrats, 28, 35, 93, 101
Young Men's Christian Association (YMCA), 93, 99
Young People's Socialist League (YPSL), 33, 38, 47–48
Young Socialist Alliance (YSA), 13–16, 18–19, 38, 47–48, 60, 66–67, 73, 93, 103–104, 163
Young Women's Christian Association (YWCA), 111
Youth for Christ, 68

Zinn, Howard, 59–60
Zirker, Priscilla, 59, 152

Mary Ann Wynkoop retired as Director of the American Studies Program at the University of Missouri-Kansas City. Since then, she has consulted on projects for Kansas City Public Television, the Henry W. Bloch Foundation, and the National Endowment for the Humanities.

Printed and bound by CPI Group (UK) Ltd, Croydon, CR0 4YY

09/06/2025

14685934-0001